Families of the Forest

Families of the Forest

The Matsigenka Indians
of the Peruvian Amazon

Allen Johnson

UNIVERSITY OF CALIFORNIA PRESS

Berkeley / Los Angeles / London

Cau

Unless otherwise indicated, all photographs and figures are by the author.

University of California Press
Berkeley and Los Angeles, California

University of California Press, Ltd.
London, England

© 2003 by
The Regents of the University of California

Library of Congress Cataloging-in-Publication Data

Johnson, Allen W.
    Families of the forest : the Matsigenka Indians of the Peruvian Amazon /
Allen Johnson.
        p.   cm.
    Includes bibliographical references and index.
    ISBN 0-520-23241-0 (cloth : alk. paper).—ISBN 0-520-23242-9 (paper :
alk. paper)
    1. Machiguenga Indians—Kinship.   2. Machiguenga cosmology.
3. Machiguenga Indians—Social life and customs.   4. Amazon River
Region—Social life and customs.   I. Title.
F3430.I.M3 J64   2003
305.898′39—dc21   2002018748

Manufactured in the United States of America
12   11   10   09   08   07   06   05   04   03
10 9 8 7 6 5 4 3 2 1

The paper used in this publication is both acid-free and totally chlorine-
free (TCF). It meets the minimum requirements of ANSI/NISO Z39.48-1992
(R 1997) *(Permanence of Paper).* ♾

For
Walter Goldschmidt
and
Johannes Wilbert,
who know about ethnography

I believe that if our philosophers had lived among the Machiguengas . . . they would have greatly doubted the concept of Man as a social animal.

Padre Andres Ferrero, *Los Machiguengas,* 1966

Tienen cosa linda, ellos. ("They have a beautiful thing, those folks.")

Peruvian living in a Matsigenka settlement near the Pongo de Mainique, 1972

Contents

Illustrations

Figures

Maps

Tables

Preface

I did the fieldwork that forms the basis of this ethnography between 1971 and 1980 in southeastern Peru. I had always intended to write it up as an ethnography and in fact had already drawn up an outline for a book by fall 1972, within a few months of beginning serious fieldwork in the Matsigenka community of Shimaa. But I felt I had rushed my previous ethnography (Johnson 1971) into print before I had taken the time to analyze all the data and to understand more fully what I had learned during fieldwork. Not wanting to make that mistake again, I set about writing a series of articles describing more limited issues in Matsigenka life and in methodology and theory that arose as I worked up my data. Those projects led me to new theoretical questions and also gradually made it clear that I had to reconfigure my data if I were to get the information I needed from them. Time passes more quickly than any sensible person would like, and so it is that I find myself, more than two decades after my last visit to the Matsigenka, finally having completed the ethnography I first conceived of thirty years ago.

From my perspective, the long lag time between first exploratory field trip and final manuscript preparation has had a particularly significant benefit: I have come to see the Matsigenka as an important case study in the way of life common to what Steward (1955) called "the family level of sociocultural integration." Familiar with his concept from reading *Theory of Culture Change*, I had nonetheless not made the connection to the Matsigenka as a family level society while I was in the field. But in writing about them and in discussing them with colleagues, I came to recognize that they were an excellent example of his controversial category. Although many anthropologists who have done research with such groups instantly recognize the similarity to the Matsigenka, I still find a certain degree of skepticism among anthropologists who have worked in larger-scale, more elaborate societies. Trying to convince them of the reality of a family level society has given me a specific purpose and organizing theme for this book.

Any undertaking of this scope depends on the generosity and the dedication to the accumulation of knowledge of many people. At Columbia University, my colleagues Kenneth Kensinger, Robert Murphy, and Charles Wagley gave me early advice that set my research direction. Roberta Campos and Thomas Moore helped make an exploratory field visit in 1971 a success. Gerhard Baer has been a conscientious professional correspondent who has enthusiastically shared his published Matsigenka research over the years.

Funding from National Science Foundation grant #GS-33012 made my first year of fieldwork possible, and several small grants from the UCLA Academic Senate kept it going. In Peru, Joe and Christine Weiss were most gracious hosts, as were the families of Alejandro Camino and Stefano Varese. Jorge Capriata, Alberto Chirif, Fritz du Bois, Ramón Ferreyra, Fernando Fuenzalida, Carlos Mora, General Luis Uzategui, and César Vivanco rendered crucial advice and support. Stefano Varese was an early and continuous supporter of the project, and Alejandro Camino served ably as a research assistant. Scholars and associates at the Summer Institute of Linguistics were unfailingly friendly and helpful throughout my research, especially Pat Davis, Larry and Lois Dodds, Jerry and Eunice Hammil, Don Lindholm, Dick Rutter, Wayne and Betty Snell, Jan and Al Townsend, Mary Ruth Wise, and Jaime Wroughton.

At various points in the research, valued colleagues helped to keep the research on track and to gather additional data, including Rita Erikson, Patricia Lyon, Edward Montgomery, John Rowe, Janet Siskind, Connie Weil, and James Weil. Joe Lopatin of Calculogic Corporation managed to process a set of observational data in mid-research quickly and efficiently. Michael Baksh followed up my brief research in the Matsigenka community of Camaná and gave me many new insights and wonderful comparative data. He also reviewed and commented on a draft manuscript of this book, as did David Dodds, Walter Goldschmidt, Thomas Gregor, Joseph Henrich, Carolina Izquierdo, Kenneth Kensinger, Glenn Shepard, and Johannes Wilbert.

In the community of Shimaa, our Matsigenka hosts were models of tolerance, good humor, and intelligence. In particular, without the support and dedication of Pedro Vicente ("Maestro") and Roberto Yokari, this book would not have been possible. None of this, however, not even the research itself, would have been possible without the love, wisdom, and strength of my life companion and colleague, Orna Johnson.

Among the Matsigenka

No somos muy unidos aquí, "We are not very united here," were nearly the first words Orna Johnson and I heard from "Maestro," as the people of Shimaa called Pedro Vicente, their Matsigenka schoolteacher. His words, spoken on our arrival in the community in July 1972, were meant to be discouraging, not from any opposition to our doing research there, but from embarrassment. He assumed that we, like other outsiders, respected only communities of some size, where individual households could pull together in building a political entity capable of taking its place in modern Peru. He had learned in teacher training that building such a community was one of his missions as an employee of the department of education.

His words were a lament, for himself and for the haphazard collection of families that had come to settle in the vicinity of the schoolhouse at Shimaa since 1968 but that had achieved only a scant and shaky political cohesion. Few could understand better than Maestro what a frustrating and contradictory task it was to try to persuade some 125 Matsigenka in five loose hamlets and several scattered homesteads that they were part of something bigger than themselves, to which they owed loyalty and for which they were being asked to make sacrifices.

A Family Level Society

The Matsigenka of Shimaa at the time of our research (1972–80) lived at what Steward (1955: 120) called "the family level of sociocultural integration." The idea of a family level society has been discussed and disputed by anthropologists for nearly half a century, and it continues to raise doubts (Johnson and Earle 2000: 41–52). My central purpose in this book is to provide a well-rounded ethnography of the Matsigenka in order to demonstrate that the family level of sociocultural integration is for them a lived reality and that they cannot be understood or appreciated except as a family level society. I intend to show how it is economically and politically feasible to live at the family level, why it is advantageous under their circumstances to do so, and what the implications are for them personally, economically, socially, and politically.

As a family level society, the Matsigenka of Shimaa do not fit any standard notion of what "tropical-forest villagers" or "tribal peoples" are like: they are not engaged in suprafamily activities like calendrical or initiation rituals, raiding and warfare, feasting and group gift exchange, descent-group exogamy, or spouse exchange. In a phrase, the Matsigenka have not been subordinated much to the constraints of the "social cage" (Maryanski and Turner 1992). It is extremely difficult to motivate them to participate in group activities: they listen to exhortative speeches attentively with mild expressions and then generally walk away and refuse to join in, whether the project is to maintain the central clearing of the community or to attend Maestro's Columbus Day celebration. They are most reluctant to be led. Maestro had to use strong words of persuasion backed up by his considerable access to steel tools, manufactured clothing, and medicines to overcome this reluctance even among families that had lived in the vicinity of Shimaa for four years.

Steward (1938) originally proposed the family level as a construct to account for the Great Basin Shoshone. In his account, the Shoshone spent most of the year as dispersed family foragers who lived in a "competitive" mode (Steward 1955: 105–7). Here, competitive does not imply that the people were forever competing with one another (although that element was always present) but rather that they found little economic benefit in cooperating in the food quest with other families, so they scattered to stay out of each other's way. By dispersing much of the year, they avoided conflict and did not have to experience the frustration of trying to forage in areas recently exploited by another family. Seasonally, they tended to aggregate in somewhat greater numbers around pine-nut groves, where they could harvest and store nuts to help tide them over the harsh winter. This pattern of seasonal aggregation and dispersion is common in family level groups.

Steward was criticized, however, for implying that the family level was a normal possibility for human social organization. Service (1962:

64–66) denied that any human community organized below the level of the "band" of sixty or more members would exist unless it had been disrupted by modern contact. A similar criticism has been leveled at Lee's (1979) description of !Kung camps, which are a form of family level organization (Johnson and Earle 2000: 65–82); there again it was argued that the small-scale fragmentation evident in their group organization was the result of long-term contact with powerful outsiders who had marginalized them and somehow inhibited them from displaying the more complex social order to which they could otherwise aspire.

This is a difficult criticism to counter because all contemporary social groups, no matter how isolated they may appear, have had centuries of exposure to powerful and intrusive expansionist societies seeking their labor and the resources of their land. For both the Shoshone and the !Kung, however, it was possible to test archaeologically whether a family level model accounted for their prehistoric record, before outside political developments profoundly disrupted their landscape. The archaeology does solidly support Steward's and Lee's versions over their critics' (Johnson and Earle 2000: 64–66; Sadr 1997; Thomas 1983). Although comparable archaeology has not been done on the Matsigenka, other evidence suggests that the family level has characterized their society for as far into the past as we can even sketchily project.

The anthropological discovery in the early twentieth century of kin-based societies, and particularly those with unilineal descent groups and their tribal elaborations in ceremony, sodality, and war, may have overshadowed the real occurrence of family level societies. Anthropologists like Steward who studied them were often put on the defensive. Steward (1955: 120) even appeared to accept Service's critique of his concept when he called his Shoshone case "typologically unique." And Gulliver (1955: v), on introducing his ethnography of the almost family level Turkana herders of Kenya, sought to defend himself to anthropologists who might "search for a more truly anthropological description"—by which he apparently meant a more typically structural elaboration of African society. Anthropologists who work with such groups are often reduced to describing them in terms of what is missing: for example, no lineages, no group ceremonies, "chiefs" with no power (Holmberg 1969: 128, 140, 144–45). The Matsigenka have been described in similar negatives (see chapter 4). Yet there is a positive side. Living at the family level of sociocultural integration suits the Matsigenka: it really is the best way for them to meet their "family's customary requirements" (Sahlins 1972: 77; cf. Descola 1994: 4–9).

Fieldwork in an Amazon Community

Judging from contemporary popular culture, there is still a good bit of romance about the Amazon basin and its native peoples, much as there was in the 1970s, when I worked in Shimaa. The Amazon River and its surrounding forest, or selva, have been part of the consciousness of the literate world since the first reports of European explorers were written. The name evokes vivid and powerful images, idealizations both positive (Green Mansion) and negative (Green Hell). Whichever idealization colors the presentation, it generally includes images of fecundity, wildness, painted natives, and unplumbed mysterious depths.

In the past and today, explorers have undertaken "extravagant adventures of exploration" of the Peruvian Amazon in search of El Gran Paititi (Haskins 1943: 93), which in some versions is the ancient wealthy land from which the great Inka empire sprang (Ferrero 1966: 26–30). Such legends and adventures are part of the larger history of Europeans seeking El Dorado and thus reflect the deeply ingrained European mythic motif of finding buried treasure. Following the conquest of Peru, the Spanish gathered all the gold they could find for shipment home and then pursued all available means to find and develop gold mines (Goodspeed 1961: 103–4). By no means all searchers were motivated by gold; many would have been fulfilled by being recognized as the discoverers of a wonderful ancient city (Savoy 1970). But whether the treasure they sought was fortune or fame, the motivation was seldom to understand, let alone to respect, the people whose ancestors had lived there for millennia before gold became more than a bright decoration.

For the fieldworker preparing to do research in a native community in the Peruvian Amazon, the Green Hell image is constantly brought forward by a host of friends and colleagues who wonder why anyone would voluntarily go there. They raise the subjects of deadly snakes, diseases, and hostile tribes, and reflect the general sense that this is a dangerous place, far from hospitals and police. The Green Mansion idealization is less prominent, but one's cohort may mention peacefulness, innocence, forest vastness, and the curative powers of herbs. All these images have a certain probabilistic reality.

That such images have a depth of cultural history behind them struck me when I was reading Paul Marcoy's (1872: 1:181) account of his trip down the Urubamba gorge in the 1860s; his guide warned him of being shot full of arrows ("like St. Sebastian") by the Matsigenkas of the area (then known as Antis). Orna Johnson and I had the same experience in 1972, when our waiter at a restaurant in Quillabamba, on learning of our intention to live among the Matsigenka, asked whether we weren't afraid of being shot full of arrows. The Matsigenka, being unusually peaceful, have only occasionally turned violent and then under extreme provocation, and yet Peruvians who live right on the edge of their territory still project onto them images of wild savagery with virtually no basis in fact.

In April 1960 Peter Matthiessen (1961) traveled down the Río Urubamba, passing the mouth of the Río Kompiroshiato but not venturing upstream (where Shimaa is). Earlier, in the Brazilian Amazon, he had remarked, "There is something strange in these jungle airs, no doubt about it, something of foreboding. Man seems ill at ease here" (Matthiessen 1961: 28). From the moment of his departure from Quillabamba he and his companions found the going along the Río Urubamba increasingly rough in every respect, from the dangerous means of transportation to the unfriendly reception from people met along the way. Required to abandon a large share of their equipment and provisions and forced to eat unfamiliar foods, they felt "left by ourselves . . . [to contemplate] the insects and the mud" (1961: 174).

The most potent consequence of Green Hell imagery is the antagonism toward the natural forest. In this view, the forest must be tamed and transformed into a landscape dominated by human purpose. Its marketable trees should be removed to lumber or paper mills, its useless ones eliminated and replaced. Its game are for eating, its pests for exterminating. In discussing this view, Marcoy (1872: 1:338) referred to "an inexpressible sentiment of terror and admiration—the *sacred horror of the woods,* as ancient writers have called it." At best, this Amazon is a region that challenges heroic men and nations to unparalleled new accomplishments of mastery (Haskins 1943: 102). Here is Amazonia as a mighty dragon to be slain or at the very least defanged and taught to do tricks.

A convenient fiction that supports this attitude is the pervasive description of the selva as "uninhabited." People like the Matsigenka who live there and who may well have lived there in reasonable ecological balance for thousands of years are dismissed in a word. This characterization may have permitted many to neglect careful study of the region and its inhabitants, as in the case of the historian who, as late as 1971, had almost nothing to say about the selva except to mention a tribe "that had an extremely simple language, that only consisted of the words *inje-inje,* with which they explicated everything according to the modulations and gestures with which they accompanied them" (Alarco 1971: 142). What must he have thought of the humanity of such a people that he could ascribe to them a language even less elaborate than that of baboons?

As a young anthropologist, I too carried my own burden of images into Shimaa. I was excited by the ideas of the Amazon and the "tribal." I hoped to find a world fundamentally different from my own. I expect that part of the excitement was a sense that this fieldwork was a dangerous, and perhaps heroic, undertaking. I felt a certain mystery about the Matsigenka. What was it like to subsist with a nonindustrial technology? To live with the most elementary of what Claude Lévi-Strauss had called the "elementary structures of kinship" (Hornborg 1988: 122)? To believe intrinsically and without clerical challenge in an animistic, shamanic world-view?

I did not articulate it at the time, but I think I hoped to discover something essentially human that had been lost, or suppressed, along the road to our proud civilization. In retrospect I felt something missing in my own life to that point and was convinced that there had to be more, although I could not define what that "more" was. In this sense, you could say that I too was looking for buried treasure in the Peruvian Amazon. Add the expectable career anxieties of a nontenured professor, with a corresponding need for his research to be found "interesting," and my images of Amazonia become as complex and worthy of scrutiny as any others.

I do not, however, intend to place myself at the center of this narrative. I still believe in objectivity as a goal, however unattainable in the purest sense. Much of what I report in this book is an effort at responsible and detached description, based on explicit methodology, which has the advantage that the assumptions guiding the research are fairly evident. But the matter is undeniably complex, as anthropologists have amply acknowledged in recent decades. I want to be fair and truthful in describing the Matsigenka, but I also feel close to them and want other people in my own culture to understand them and to feel as far as possible the same affection and respect that I feel. In appropriate places in this book I have included my own thoughts and feelings because I am convinced that others from my cultural background would have reacted similarly much of the time. If not, then at least my reactions may serve as clues to my own state of mind while I was doing my study.

For now, however, I will close with a few general observations about Shimaa, a setting of astonishing natural beauty. The selva at Shimaa, classified as montane rain forest, is rather open under a canopy perhaps twenty-five meters high. For the most part it is also extraordinarily quiet. Once, as I sat alone awaiting a companion several kilometers up a mountain trail west of Shimaa, I noted complete silence. Although a stiff breeze had been blowing upstream along the Río Kompiroshiato, the air here was still. After I sat quietly for perhaps a quarter of an hour, my attention was drawn by a distinct crackling sound, and I turned to look. A leaf had detached from a branch some fifteen meters away and was drifting to earth; I clearly heard it rustle as it landed.

This daytime silence was a complete contrast to the levels of noise reached at night, especially at the edge of the forest near the river. Here, as dusk settled in, a great wall of sound rose, made up of the quavering tones, rattles, gongs, croaks, buzzes, hoots, and whistles of frogs, insects, and birds. Each sound had its own unique rhythm, so that the roar rose and fell with the degree of synchronicity among the various voices, phasing into symphony, out to cacophony, and back into symphony again. On different evenings, depending on temperature and humidity, different voices dominated. Matsigenkas sitting outside on mats after dark would listen to the chorus and could, if asked, imitate the sounds of the animals and name those responsible for each separate contribution. Some animals make sounds so distinctive the Matsigenka have given them onomatopoetic names, like *papapani,* the frog that cries *papapapapapapapapapa* . . . in the night, and the bird *kavari (kavavavava . . .).*

Viewed from a boulder near the mouth of the Río Shimaa, the forest rises massively in every direction, shimmering with the reflected light of countless leaves turning in the breeze, a panorama energized by the rasping of birds and insects and the constant white noise of the river. Or, the whole place is transformed by an early-morning mist, dominated by the strange powerful roars of the howler monkeys. Matsigenkas crossing the clearing, their bare feet hidden from view by the low weeds, seem to float like shadows before suddenly disappearing into a house whose presence was apparent only from its column of faint blue smoke rising into the surrounding fog.

My strongest memory is of sunny days in clear mountain air, with occasional white clouds, fresh breezes blowing upstream, exuberant vegetation, and a warm aroma tinged with decay rising from the damp earth. I loved to ride down the Río Kompiroshiato on a balsa raft, shooting the rapids as if on the world's greatest roller coaster—alert to the genuine danger yet emboldened by the enthusiasm of my fellow raftsmen—surrounded by sheer cliffs or spreading forest, spectacularly untamed.

That I had the privilege of enjoying these surroundings owed most to the Matsigenka themselves, generous and tolerant hosts whose unselfconscious exuberance and skill made them the best of companions. An anecdote of Marcoy's (1872: 1:469–70) captures a characteristic moment:

[At a point] remarkable for a succession of frightful rapids whose waves mingled together, rolled over each other, and whirled about as if they had been made to boil by a blazing furnace beneath, the Antis [Matsigenka] Simuco, who had attached his canoe to a raft manned by his brother, and was standing up holding on by its side to assist if necessary, executed before our eyes a veritable *tour de force*. At the moment when the raft, towing the canoe with the two women seated in it, passed between the rocks, the sharp eye of the savage discovered in the midst of the tumultuous waves a *sabalo* or shad *(Salmo andensis),* which was mounting the current. Stooping down he seized his bow, placed an arrow in it, aimed at the fish, and pierced it through and through, and all this with such rapidity that had it been night the whole action would have been visible in the gleam of a single flash of lightning. If the danger that surrounded us had not counseled prudence, I could have sprung to my feet, clapped my hands, and cried "Encore," so superb was the Indian in artistic *verve* and activity of movement, with his hair streaming in the wind, his sac inflated by the rapidity of the course down the rapid, and flapping in the air behind him.

Verve is a good word for the Matsigenka, part of what makes them such fine collaborators and mentors.

Plan of the Book

I have always enjoyed reading ethnographies. The old-fashioned ones I first read as a student tended to be highly descriptive and quite comprehensive, such that a reader could browse across a range of subjects from economics to social organization to politics and religion. More recent generations have moved away from preparing such compendia toward writing more theoretically focused monographs, unfolding arguments bolstered by extensive evidence (Johnson 1987). Although the old model still holds many attractions, the new one has guided me here. For the most part I have tried to discipline my descriptions to the flow of argument analyzing the Matsigenka as a family level society. At times, I have felt it necessary to include descriptions that force this rule somewhat: for example, I have gone into considerable detail about the shamanic spiritual beliefs of the Matsigenka, although these may hardly be said to characterize a family level society more so than many other kinds of society. But understanding this spiritual system is part and parcel of understanding the Matsigenka way of life, and the comparativist may even find features of the system, like the low emphasis on witchcraft, that might distinguish small isolated societies from more densely settled shamanic communities where witchcraft is pervasive.

Chapter 1 provides an overview of the history and geography of the Matsigenka and establishes the likelihood that their current settlement and adaptation pattern continues a most ancient heritage. Chapter 2 offers a description of the economy, making the case for the material self-sufficiency of the Matsigenka in the household and extended-family hamlet. Chapter 3 then explores the development of Matsigenka character and interpersonal relations in household-centered families. Chapter 4 expands the discussion to the larger social world of the Matsigenka, showing the remarkable extent to which their everyday lives and interactions focus on the hearth and homestead of the nuclear-family household, even in cases of hamlet living and polygynous marriage. Chapter 5 provides an account of Matsigenka cosmology that reveals the concern with impulse control and harmonious living that the Matsigenka recognize as central to their family-centered way of life. The Conclusion briefly summarizes the findings and restates the case for the Matsigenka as a family level society.

A Note on Naming

A most unusual feature of Matsigenka culture is the near absence of personal names (Snell 1964: 17–25). Because personal names are widely regarded by anthropologists as a human universal (e.g., Murdock 1960: 132), this startling assertion is likely to be received with skepticism. When I first read Snell's discussion of the phenomenon, before I had gone into the field myself, I suspected that he had missed something (perhaps the existence of secret ceremonial names) despite his compelling presentation of evidence and his conclusion:

I have said that the names of individual Machiguenga, when forthcoming, are either of Spanish origin and given to them by the white man, or nicknames. We have known Machiguenga Indians who reached adulthood and died without ever having received a name or any other designation outside of the kinship system. Smith, in dealing with this subject, says, "It is indeed a primitive group that does not name its individuals. Very few tribes have been discovered that exist without some sort of personal appellation, although certain aborigines in Australia have been found to be without personal names. . . . When you consider it, you will see that men without names can be little higher than animals when they can live together without feeling the imperative need to designate each other in some exact way by the spoken word" (Smith 1950: 178). Smith in my opinion is entirely wrong. Living in small isolated groups there is no imperative need for them to designate each other in any other way than by kinship terminology. Although there may be only a "few tribes" who do not employ names, I conclude that the Machiguenga is one of those few. (Snell 1964: 25)

Experience has taught me that Snell was right. Although the Matsigenka of Shimaa did learn the Spanish names given them and used them when it was necessary to refer to someone outside their family group, they rarely used them otherwise and frequently forgot or changed them. When they did use them, they made their pronunciation conform to Matsigenka patterns: Florinda became Pororinta; Carlos, Karoroshi; Domingo, Omenko; and so on. When Matsigenka words were used to name individuals, these were often nicknames (like Nigankinirira, "middle one," referring to the second of three sons). Some names, like Yokari or Shoshovi, cannot be traced to such nicknaming, however, and we should qualify Snell's conclusion to say that some individuals (more often men than women) do have personal names, while most do not. No ethnographer working with the Matsigenka, however, has encountered anything like special, secret, or ceremonial names, and it is obvious to anyone working with them for any length of time that personal names are of little significance.

I have vacillated in determining the most meaningful way of naming the Matsigenka in this book. To use kin terms is out of the question because I must describe members of many family groups. The Matsigenka handle the problem of having to refer to more than one sister, for example, by adding information such as: "Sister, the one who slipped in the river. . . ." This solution would not work here. I considered assigning nicknames to those who had them and borrowing nicknames for the others from Matsigenkas not included in this study. But in doing so I would risk giving the people I am describing ridiculous or insulting names. Finally, I settled on using in most cases the Spanish names that had been assigned to them by Maestro and the Summer Institute of Linguistics fieldworkers (using the Lima telephone directory) prior to my arrival in 1972, keeping for some their distinctive Matsigenka pronunciations. Throughout the text I have also used Matsigenka terms for some key concepts, and for these I have provided a glossary.

CHAPTER I

Setting and History

It is a fact of which European botanists are perhaps not aware, that a tropical forest which has once suffered by the hand of man never recovers its original splendour, even were it left to itself for a century. Some will say that this indelible mark is the seal with which man, as king of creation, impresses his conquest; others will be inclined to think that this miserable biped has, like the fabled harpies, the sad faculty of soiling and withering whatever he touches.

Marcoy 1872: 2:480

Although the Matsigenka have, perhaps for millennia, occupied a historically important crossroads, their practice appears to have been to minimize contact with the larger world rather than to confront and try to control it. They have done so by remaining off the beaten path, in a marginal environment where their most favored foods, game animals and fish, are scarce. Good land for horticulture is ample, however, and the low population density and widely scattered small settlements have meant only minimal competition among family groups for what seasonal wild foods there are.

The Montaña of the Upper Amazon

In the beginning, say the Matsigenka of Shimaa, all of existence (*timatsi,* "what exists") was covered with water *(oani)*. Then a being came and said, "Why are there no gardens here, why no soil?" He mounded up the earth *(kipatsi)*. He told the people who lived there to wait. After many weeks, the earth was ready—no hills yet, only pure flat earth, without plants. He told them, "Now, I will go home. This earth is for you to live better."

FORMATION

In a curious parallel to the Matsigenka legend, our scientific knowledge of the origin of Amazonia also begins with a tale of a flat earth being formed in a vast waterscape. Before the rise of the Andes Mountains some fifteen to twenty million years ago, the Amazon River flowed from the eastern Guiana and Brazilian highlands into a western sea. But the rise of the Andes blocked the old river's path, forming a vast brackish lake (Webb 1995). Before a new outlet to the east was carved, sedimentation had made the basin so flat that today the Río Amazonas loses only one meter elevation for every twenty-five kilometers it flows from Pucallpa in Peru to its mouth at the Atlantic Ocean; for this reason early Portuguese explorers called it O Rio Mar, "the River Sea" (McIntyre 1972: 456).

However, west from Pucallpa, toward the Andes, lies the *montaña*. The terrain shifts first to rolling foothills and then, at an altitude of six hundred to nine hundred meters, to abrupt rises and massive escarpments split by cascading rivers. In contrast to the broad winding rivers of the *selva baja* (low forest or lower floodplain [Moran 1995]), the rivers of the montaña plummet through *selva alta* (high, or montane, forest), with its "steep slopes, near vertical cliffs, V-shaped valleys, deep gorges and . . . angular landscape" (Drewes and Drewes 1957: 6). The Matsigenka of Shimaa live in such an angular landscape, along river valleys surrounded by forested mountains (map 1).

Rivers in the selva alta tend to be small and swift. Only the larger ones, like the Río Kompiroshiato, permit travel by balsa raft or, rarely, canoe. The banks of small streams are good sites for homesteads, even though they yield few fish and may even dry up for part of the year. From the standpoint of Matsigenka raftsmen, navigating a river alternates between carefree gliding along smooth water and strenuous paddling to fight rapids. In the dry season, beaches appear, still pools form where the river flow is cut off, and islands stand in tufts high above the water line. In the wet season, streams and rivers grow to swirling brown torrents that obliterate these features and are nearly impossible to navigate. Great rivers like the lower Río Urubamba (map 1) are not found

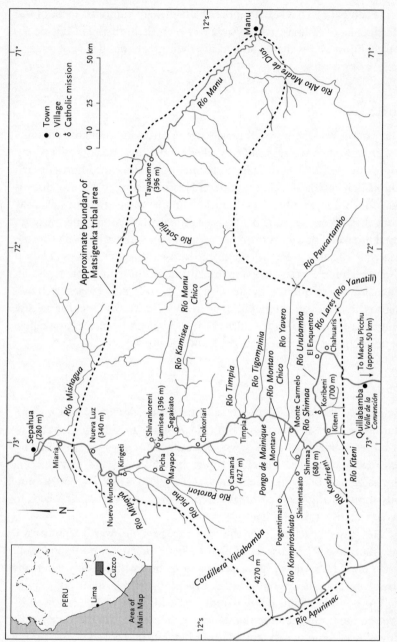

MAP 1. Approximate extent of Matsigenka territory (adapted from Baksh 1984: 25).

in the selva alta. They are no more than a distant rumor to most of the Matsigenka of Shimaa, who have never seen them firsthand but nonetheless know about them—especially their great abundance of aquatic life—from stories.

SOILS

Many of the most remote tributaries of the Amazon originate in the Andes, in mountain streams and tiny lakes. The Andes, geologically young and composed largely of marine sediments, weather into nutrient-rich runoff that regularly delivers mineral-laden deposits to the floodplains that line the major tributaries (Junk and Furch 1985: 9–11). But soils away from these floodplains, as a rule, sustain a verdant forest only through rapid uptake of nutrients from decaying organic matter in a thin topsoil. Clearing the forest for horticulture exposes the soils to degradation (Richards 1952; Roosevelt 1980: 79). Although this condition applies in a general way to Shimaa, in the selva alta, its soils are relatively rich owing to their Andean parentage. Nonetheless, as we shall see, the soils of Shimaa still degrade under cultivation and benefit from the long fallow periods characteristic of Matsigenka horticulture.

CLIMATE

Being near the border between selva baja and selva alta, Shimaa is hot during the day (25°C to 30°C) but cool at night (16°C to 19°C; figure 1). It is often chilly enough at dawn, especially on foggy mornings in winter, that Matsigenkas complain about the cold and stand over the fire, the rising heat billowing their *cushma*s (cotton gowns). They are fastidious about lifting their cushmas when walking through dewy weeds to avoid the discomfort of damp skirts.

The general pattern is for the day *(kutagiteri)* to warm rapidly until late morning, when breezes begin to blow upriver. The temperature peaks in mid-afternoon, approaching 30°C, but, with a steady wind, any shady place is usually comfortable. Except for extensive periods of rainfall in the wet season, heavy clouds and rain pass quickly, followed by the prevalent intense blue skies and drifting white clouds. Breezes die down by evening, when temperatures range from cool to warm but the air is rarely muggy or stifling. Such days are described as "good days," *kametiri kutagiteri* (or, in contraction, *kametigite*).

Because the sun *(poreatsiri)* is usually visible, people use its trajectory

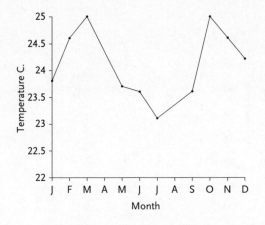

FIGURE I. Daily average temperatures
at Shimaa, 1972–73.

as a kind of sundial. To set an appointment, they simply point to the
place in the sky where the sun will be at the time proposed. When I co-
ordinated this system with my habit of using a wristwatch, the Matsigenka and I were rarely off by more than fifteen minutes in keeping ap-
pointments. Although the moon *(kashiri)* changes position each night,
the same system can be used for some nighttime references, as when a
man reported having seen a snake the previous night at *kaatinka kashiri,*
"straight-up moon."

The weather in Amazonia moves generally from east to west. As the
humid air moves against the Andes and starts to rise, the orographic
cooling increases the likelihood of rain. Thus, whereas Pucallpa in the
selva baja receives about 1,500 millimeters of rainfall per year, communities in the selva alta receive from 2,500 to 5,000 millimeters, the amounts
declining at higher altitudes after peaking between 400 to 700 meters
(Drewes and Drewes 1957: 7). Variability from year to year and across
short distances can be quite large. For example, in Shimaa (altitude
680 meters) in the fieldwork year of 1972–73, 2,700 millimeters of rain
fell; in Camaná (altitude 427 meters), less than fifty kilometers away, the
annual total in 1979–80 was 5,800 millimeters (Baksh 1984: 27).

The typical pattern in Amazonia south of the equator is for rainfall
to be heavy in the summer months of November through February and
light to moderate during the winter months of May through August
(figure 2). In Shimaa, the wet season runs from October through February. During the January peak it rains nearly every day and fifty to sev-

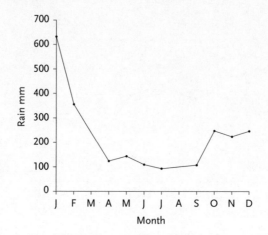

FIGURE 2. Monthly rainfall totals for
Shimaa, 1972–73.

enty-five millimeters of rain may drop in a few hours. Big storms are often accompanied by strong winds that topple trees and drive people into
the secure cover of their houses. In this season of high water (*kimoari-
niku*, "grown water time") muddy trails and sudden downpours make
the traveler's progress difficult. Many planned hunting trips are can-
celed because of rain, and fishing is limited to the use of nets by the
opaque turbulence of the water—hence the other name for this season,
oshintsiatanaira, "rushing water."

In low-water time *(shiriagariniku)* the river retreats to its central
channel, exposing a large beach of rocks and driftwood, and the water
turns clear. It still rains over one hundred millimeters per month in low
water, however, and the forest floor is seldom dry. I saw it dry only for
a period of a few days one August and appreciated how much easier it
was to get around when my feet were not constantly slipping out from
under me on muddy mountain trails. But in low-water season the streams
that supply household needs during high water can dry up, forcing
people to lug river water in heavy, sloshing gourds up steep trails to their
houses. And dry spells occur of long enough duration that crops in
well-drained fields begin to wilt under the intense sun and Matsigenkas
anxiously watch the skies for welcome signs of rain.

Also during low water Shimaa is subject to the *fríos* (cold spells) that
afflict the whole of Amazonia in winter, as frigid air masses sweep north
from Antarctica. During fríos the temperature drops to 14°C at night
and does not rise above 22°C or 23°C during the day. It is difficult to

stay warm, with the sun obscured by clouds and stiff breezes blowing through well-ventilated houses and cotton garments, and people complain of the cold. Cold drizzles add to the misery. People get up several times during the night to add wood to the fire and warm themselves. On such occasions it is easy to understand why the Matsigenka of Shimaa devote such a major part of their time and energy to the production of cotton cloth while their fellows at lower altitudes do without. A frío, however, will usually last no more than a week or two, and fríos generally end by mid-August.

Most of these variations in weather are not regarded by the Matsigenka as having spiritual significance, although the heavens themselves are of spiritual interest. In their cosmology, the sky is a superior level (actually, several levels) of the universe; the *terira ineenkani* ("unseen ones") reside there free of suffering. (In contrast, the level beneath us, underground, is an inferior place peopled by demons.) Some believe that the stars are the campfires of the unseen beings, as thunder is the sound of their shotguns. But the Matsigenka of Shimaa do not assign names to the stars and seem rather incurious about them. Some of the men knew what satellites were, however, and pointed them out to me matter-of-factly as they passed overhead.

GEOGRAPHY

The rivers and the mountain slopes of the area are the central features of Matsigenka folk geography. Although the Matsigenka do draw a distinction between east (*ikontetira poreatsiri*, "his-arrival sun") and west (*iatira poreatsiri*, "his-departure sun"), they rarely speak in these terms. Rather, they use the four cardinal points of *katonko*, "upstream"; *kamatikya*, "downstream"; *oaku*, "at the river"; and *inkenishiku*, "in the forest." These define the practical, everyday Matsigenka compass (figure 3). Implicit is the knowledge that moving away from the river and into the forest entails steep ascents on slippery trails through dense rainforest. *Intaati*, "across the river," is also an important direction, and good places to ford the river are well known. Major trails run parallel to the river (upstream and downstream, either at the river's edge or along the crests of the watershed) and perpendicular to it (from river to forest). The resulting network of trails constitutes the basic grid along which the Matsigenka trek in search of food and raw materials.

Although some Matsigenka in the Shimaa vicinity know how to make and use canoes, and all can make and use balsa rafts, their preferred

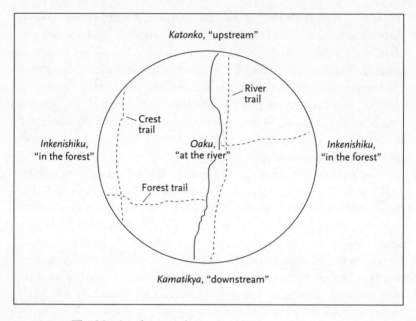

FIGURE 3. The Matsigenka everyday compass.

means of travel is by trail. Waters are often too rough and rocky for a canoe, or even a balsa raft, to pass. Furthermore, although traveling downstream on a balsa raft is speedy and thrilling, it is dangerous and occasionally fatal. And then, the raft must be hauled back upstream on the return trip.

The main trails—along the rivers and the mountain crests that separate them—are generally well maintained. Even main trails may have hazardous stretches, but they have undergone a long selection process and are well-groomed through frequent use. As people walk along, they make improvements: breaking away eye-level branches, removing fallen logs, fashioning footholds in muddy slopes. The great (and probably ancient) trail running up the watershed between the Shimaa and Kompiroshiato rivers is one to two meters broad and clear overhead to more than two meters. It is the local equivalent of a highway with full public access, in contrast to the small feeder trails leading to households and gardens; these narrow and overgrown pathways are considered private.

FLORA AND FAUNA

Among the most fundamental distinctions the Matsigenka make regarding *timatsi* is that between living things (*aityorira iraniane* or *aityorira*

TABLE I. Basic Categories of Existence (*timatsi,* "what exists/is")

	Has Breath (Living)	No Breath (Nonliving)
Inanimate	*Aityorira aniane* Plants	*Terira ontime aniane* Rocks, water, etc.
Animate	*Aityorira iraniane* Animals, spirits	*Terira ontime iraniane* Stars

aniane, "there-is its-breath") and the nonliving (*terira ontime aniane* or *terira ontime iraniane,* "not exist its-breath"). In these constructions, the two terms for "its-breath" differ grammatically between animate (*iraniane*) and inanimate (*aniane*). Rocks and soils, water, air, and stars are nonliving. Although they are sometimes inhabited by spirit beings, they are themselves breathless, mere inert matter. The living (breathing) world includes biological life forms as well as all kinds of spirit beings.

The grammatical animate-versus-inanimate distinction creates a de facto separation of plants and animals. In general usage, animals (and spirit beings) "have breath [animate]" (*aityorira iraniane*), whereas plants "have breath [inanimate]" (*aityorira aniane*). Most nonliving things are grammatically referred to as inanimate, but, interestingly, stars are animate. Table 1 summarizes the two basic dimensions: living versus nonliving and animate versus inanimate.

In the Forest (Inkenishiku).   The Amazon rainforest is known for its great diversity of species (Gentry 1988; Chesser and Hackett 1992), but I was most impressed with the stillness. The daytime silence is in part a reflection of the scarcity of birds and mammals in the selva alta. The main work of the forest is bound up in plant life. Animals are a small proportion of the biomass, and most of them are insects. Because insects are for the most part herbivores and no freezing winters slow their activities, they are a constant threat to the vegetation, which has evolved various defenses that affect human use of the environment. Many palms, for example, have developed extremely hard, dense outer woods against burrowing insects (Pires and Prance 1985: 118). These woods, when shaped and polished, make sharp, durable tools. Many other plants have developed biochemical defenses against predators (Janzen 1985); these supply humans with a pharmacopoeia of poisons, medicines, and hallucinogens (Peru 1987: 68–70). As a result, gathering honey is something of an adventure for the Matsigenka because whatever pollen the bees are

FIGURE 4. Maestro with a shotgun and a bearer with a peccary.

using imparts its properties to the honey. Many men have stories about how, while foraging, they became disoriented after eating honey and had to be guided home by relatives or had to make their own way home a day or two later, after recovering their senses.

Although the Matsigenka can name hundreds of trees and seemingly enjoy nothing better than naming all the trees in sight faster than an anthropologist can write, they consider most of them to be of little use. It is the fauna of the forest that are most eagerly sought. Reflecting the basic compass, the Matsigenkas' main distinction among animals is between *inkenishikunirira,* "forest dwellers," and *oakunirira,* "water dwellers."

Among *inkenishikunirira,* the most abundant and important in the Matsigenka diet are not game animals but insect larvae, year-round sources of dietary fats and protein. Larger animals—game birds, monkeys, peccary, and tapir—are favorite foods but are scarce and difficult to obtain in the selva alta. In the montaña the abundance of game declines with a rise in elevation (Denevan 1980: 18–21). Only one tapir and a handful of peccaries were killed by the Matsigenka during my fieldwork in Shimaa (see figure 4). When they were encountered, peccaries were in groups of four or five, in contrast to reports from the selva baja of great bands of peccaries running together. Spider monkeys, howler monkeys, guans, tinamous, toucans, parrots, and curassows are often bagged, with occasional catches of Andean cock-of-the-rock, kingfisher, heron, and dove rounding out the supply.

A number of other species are present in the forest but are rarely encountered. These include deer, spectacled bear, anteater, sloth, and armadillo. Most of the men I talked with had never sighted these animals, although they had encountered their spoor in the forest. Other animals are slightly more common but are rarely taken for food either because they are considered inedible or because they are nocturnal and difficult to hunt: tayra, *añuje,* paca, squirrel, rat, and bat are prominent among these.

There are no mosquitoes in Shimaa, a blessed absence confirmed by Marcoy (1872: 1:540) in the 1860s. The small, bloodsucking pium flies *(tsigito),* however, leave everyone covered with tiny red spots that itch. As the old bites fade away after a few days, new ones appear. A characteristic scene with the Matsigenka is for people suddenly to interrupt whatever they are doing to slap at an exposed part of their body—arm, lower leg, neck—and then examine their palm and fingers for traces of *tsigito.* It is a genuine relief that these pests disappear each evening at sunset. Head lice *(mamperiki)* are common and a major preoccupation of grooming; the groomer slaps the subject's head sharply, then immediately roots around in the hair, picking lice out between the nails of the thumb and first finger and cracking them. Cockroaches and termites are ubiquitous, in every container, but termites at least are edible.

The selva hosts several deadly snakes *(maranke),* including rattler *(Crotalus durissus),* bushmaster *(Lachesis muta),* and *loro machaco (Bothrops bilineatus).* The *loro machaco* may be the feared *terori*—blamed for the death of Oscar's father (all inhabitants of Shimaa are listed in table 25 [chapter 4] with birth years and other identifying information). The *terori* hides on branches and strikes from above, inducing almost immediate hemorrhaging and death. In Matsigenka belief, snakes are the arrows of an unseen hunter who views humans as his peccaries (Shepard 1999: 141). The Matsigenka respond by reasonably considering all snakes to be poisonous and killing them whenever possible. Ideally, the dead snake should be buried deep in the ground or, better, thrown in the river to be carried so far away it will be unable to inform its kin of the whereabouts of the human who killed it (see figure 27 in chapter 5).

A subject of concern for the Matsigenka, although ultimately less a source of anxiety than snakes are, is *matsontsori,* a category that includes jaguar *(Felis onca),* puma *(Felis concolor),* and ocelot *(Felis pardalis).* Although several people were bitten by snakes during our fieldwork (none died), none were attacked by jaguar. Indeed, when Oscar came across a puma killing a deer, he calmly killed it with bow and arrow, then finished off the deer as well, bringing both back home, where I came across the meat smoking and elicited the story. The main complaint against the big cats was that they broke into the pens where fowl were kept at night. Jaguar, snake, deer, and certain other creatures are of special importance in Matsigenka religious beliefs because their spirit rulers have power to kill humans, in some cases by metamorphosing into demons with human shape.

At the River (Oaku).   The rivers of Amazonia often contain a diverse fauna that ultimately play a larger role in the native diet than do wild forest foods (Carneiro 1995: 63; cf. Roosevelt 1980: 118–159). But the large species found in the selva baja simply disappear in the selva alta. The Matsigenka of Shimaa in 1972–73 were harvesting fish at a rate comparable to that of other native fishermen in the Amazon (Jordan 1989: 39), but their yields declined rapidly as they remained in Shimaa for several years instead of moving elsewhere as they would have done in the past.

River dwellers *(oakunirira),* like forest fauna, can be further distinguished by their specific habitats. For example, creatures that live in deep pools are contrasted with those that live under rocks and those who live in still waters or along shale outcrops. Such a typology can be expanded according to the many microenvironments the Matsigenka identify in rivers and streams.

The river itself is a source of real danger. Surprisingly, many Matsigenka say they do not know how to swim. Life histories often include tales of relatives who died in the river, generally when a raft overturned and its occupants were dashed against boulders or drowned in powerful currents before they could reach shore.

The Cloud Forest.   The range of forest the Matsigenka normally exploit does not rise much above 2,500 meters. The families at Shimaa do not plant gardens above 1,000 meters, although families who live far up the headwaters of the Kompiroshiato and other tributaries of the Urubamba do plant up to 1,800 meters. Observers who have flown over the area say Matsigenka gardens are never found above 2,000 meters.

The reason for this limited range of cultivation is the cloud forest, a cold, wet region between 2,000 and 3,000 meters, where dense cloud cover prevents much sunlight from penetrating. Climbing the ridge trails out of Shimaa, one notices that the trees become progressively smaller and more heavily draped in lichens.

[In general,] the cloud forest presents a distinctly weird appearance with twisted, crooked, deformed trees and shrubs, the branches of which are festooned with Bromeliads, epiphytes, bryophytes and lichens. The trees are generally less than 50 feet tall. . . .

It is almost impossible for a man to penetrate this vegetation because the trees and shrubs grow very much intertangled, and the ground is a mass of wet, spongy, decaying vegetation into which a person's foot sinks. Water drips from the leaves even when it is not raining. In addition, the cloud forest is usually associated with exceedingly steep slopes. Visibility through the vegetation is never more than 10 to 15 feet. There is practically no human occupance in the zone. (Drewes and Drewes 1957: 14–15)

Thus, rather than competing with hostile neighbors for land, the Matsigenka border a no-man's-land at the higher elevations. Doubting this description, a group of explorers from the National Geographic Society in 1963 parachuted into the Cordillera de Vilcabamba (the watershed between the Urubamba and Apurimac drainages), not far from the headwaters of the Río Kompiroshiato (Baekeland 1964). From the air they spotted vast grasslands they assumed would be fertile for agriculture (presumably overlooked by native populations), but instead they found tall grass on top of a deep layer of moss covering a substratum of soft black mud into which they sank up to their thighs. Icy rain and clouds enveloped them, and they saw neither fish nor game. They planned fifteen days for their descent of the Apurimac to areas known to be inhabited by Campa Indians but instead required sixty-one. They recorded with joy their emergence into warm sunshine at about fourteen hundred meters, when they began to notice signs of game of all kinds.

SHIMAA

The settlement at Shimaa is centered on a cluster of eight households near the schoolhouse at the confluence of the Río Shimaa and the Río Kompiroshiato (map 2); a narrow flat in the bend of the river has been cleared as a landing strip for single-engine planes, primarily those flown by Summer Institute of Linguistics (SIL) pilots. A few houses are built on the slight rise just at the edge of the flood channel, while the others

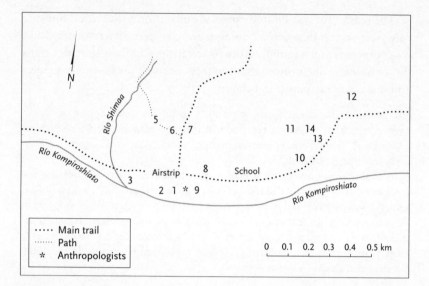

MAP 2. Households at Shimaa, 1972–73. Numbers correspond to the census (see table 25, chapter 4). Household 4 was abandoned at the time of study.

occupy a natural shelf some fifteen meters above the level of the river, on the ridge rising between the two rivers.

Other extended-family clusters or hamlets are scattered up the Río Shimaa and down the Río Kompiroshiato from the school community at Shimaa. Most of the households from these hamlets send their children to school, even though in some cases they have up to an hour's walk each way. Yet the adult members of these communities remain rather distant from adults in other hamlets, tending to conduct business separately with Maestro rather than with one another. Although social relations are peaceful and courteous, in private a good deal of suspicion and accusation is leveled against members of other hamlets. Individuals are reluctant to pass casually along the smaller paths that link unrelated households with their gardens, where one's motives for intruding might be suspect.

Compared with many other Matsigenka school communities I have visited, Shimaa is fragmented, and the people are somewhat aloof. Most school communities, especially those along the lower Río Urubamba, are larger, more compact, and appear to be more socially integrated. Visiting among households is more common, and the frequency of exchanges much greater, perhaps because of the greater abundance of meat and fish at the lower elevations. Life in those communities seems more casual and relaxed; people can be heard singing at almost any time, a rare occurrence in Shimaa (cf. Marcoy 1872: 1:587, 2:19).

Perhaps not all these differences reflect an upstream-downstream contrast. In fact, all sorts of differences in cultural detail are found from one Matsigenka community to the next. But, in some ways, life in Shimaa and other high-elevation Matsigenka communities is more difficult than it is at lower elevations, and these harsher circumstances are reflected in the smaller effective community size and a certain closed-off, inward-looking attitude found in the separate hamlets along the Río Kompiroshiato and neighboring rivers. Despite this attitude, or perhaps even because of it, I found Shimaa and its surroundings a wonderful place to live and do fieldwork. If people there are less sociable in large groups, they are more courteous and thoughtful in individual interactions. They are less attracted to the lure of commerce and new value systems. Their commitment to the freedom of the family unit is truly remarkable.

Prehistory and History of the Matsigenka

Contemporary understanding of the peopling of the Americas is in flux (Agenbroad 1988; Bryan 1983; Gibbons 1996; Nichols and Peterson 1996). The weight of opinion has favored the idea that bands of hunters, preferring open country occupied by large mammals, spread across the landscape in search of game (Lynch 1978). Evidence of large mammal extinctions by "explosive overkill" suggests that this population expansion occurred rapidly around 11,000 B.P. (Long and Martin 1974). Although such hunters may have avoided tropical forests because of the overall scarcity of wild foods (Lanning 1967: 39; Bailey et al. 1989), the discovery of occupation of a tropical forest site at Monte Alegre in the Brazilian Amazon dating to between 10,000 and 11,000 B.P. has established that rich riverine environments could sustain early settlement in the rainforest without horticulture (Roosevelt et al. 1996; cf. Gibbons 1995). Roosevelt (Roosevelt et al. 1991) also found eight-thousand-year-old pottery in the lower Amazon, made by a stable, settled preagricultural community that depended on rich shell-fish supplies along the river. Their pottery pre-dates by three thousand years the earliest pottery found in the Andes and Mesoamerica. People similar to these early potters likely spread along the banks of the larger tributaries and took the first steps to domesticate or experiment with borrowed crops suitable for cultivation in the Amazon rainforest (Lathrap 1987: 355). The presence of domesticated crops in Central and South America eight thousand to ten thousand years ago indicates that an incipient horticultural adaptation to the tropical forest had at least become possible (Bruhns 1994: 86, 91; Kaplan, Lynch, and Smith 1973; Roush 1997; Smith 1997).

THE ARAWAKANS

At the time of the Conquest, Arawakan was the most widespread of all language families in the Americas, "probably the only linguistic family that was represented in the three parts of the New World" (Pericot Y Garcia 1936: 614). During the Age of Discovery, Europeans came to know Arawakans primarily as the Caribbean Islanders who lived in towns with elaborately feathered chiefs, lounged in hammocks smoking pipes, and traveled throughout the islands in large dugout canoes. Among the words they contributed to world vocabulary were *canoe, tobacco, barbecue, hammock, yucca, maize, papaya, iguana, savanna,* and *hurricane.* They portrayed themselves to Europeans as noble and warm-hearted in contrast to their enemies the Caribs, who, partly owing to this ethnic bad press, became the prototype for cannibalistic savages (Leon-Portilla 1992).

But these Arawakan speakers were relatively late arrivals, having migrated into the Caribbean around the time of Christ. It is a sign of our ignorance of linguistic prehistory in Amazonia that the origins of Arawakan have been placed in such various locations as northwestern South America near the Caribbean coast (Schwerin 1972), the central Amazon (Lathrap 1970), and present-day Matsigenka territory (Noble 1965; Migliazza 1982; Urban 1992: 95). The last theory is of obvious importance to Matsigenka history. According to Noble (1965: 107), "By applying lexicostatistics and methods of determining probable geographical locations for earlier languages, [the differentiation of proto-Arawakan into the seven main language groups of Arawakan] most likely occurred near the headwaters of the Ucayali and Madre de Dios in what is now southeast Peru some 3500 to 5000 years ago. It is more plausible to suppose that they spread from a central point than that they travelled independently any distance in the same direction." Matsigenka, Campa, and Piro, the languages spoken in these headwaters today, are all members of pre-Andean Arawakan (Wise 1986), which is part of the Maipuran language group, generally considered to be the main branch of Arawakan languages (Matteson 1972).

Migliazza (1982) argues that the period six thousand to four thousand years ago, during which Noble supposed the differentiation of Arawakan to take place, was a dry period when much of the Amazon basin was savanna and only pockets of tropical forest persisted, including the wetter montaña of southeastern Peru (cf. Kerr 1996). As tropical forest expanded in the wetter climate from four thousand to two thousand years ago, the Arawakans of southeastern Peru—now adapted to a tropical-forest subsistence with a range of appropriate cultigens—would have spread out and differentiated, accounting for the vast distribution of Arawakan seen at the time of the Conquest.

In this respect it is significant that the eastern slopes of the Andes, and in particular the Urubamba region, have been identified as likely sites of early crop experimentation and domestication; these crops included maize (Lathrap 1987: 354), coca (Goodspeed 1961), and tobacco (Wilbert 1973: 440). And the headwaters of the Ríos Urubamba and Madre de Dios are known as one of the more extensive areas of petroglyph clustering in the Amazon basin: the motifs of the petroglyphs that have so far been described show a clear affinity to Amazonian as opposed to Andean motifs, but whether Arawakan speakers specifically carved them cannot be determined, and they have not been dated (Baer 1984: 288–91).

In any case, it seems likely that by four or five thousand years ago the first proto-Arawakan speakers already possessed the basic Amazonian culture pattern. A flow of information and crop varieties extending from coastal Peru to the northern Amazon seems likely (Lathrap 1987: 356). The most economical assumption would be that direct ancestors of the Matsigenka were living in the headwaters of the Urubamba and Madre de Dios at that time and participated in these momentous prehistoric developments. Certainly, contemporary Arawakans of the area, such as the Piro (Matteson 1954) and the Campa (Denevan 1974; Weiss 1975), are strikingly similar to the Matsigenka in a broad array of economic, social, and cultural details.

THE MATSIGENKA AT THE TIME OF THE CONQUEST

According to Steward and Metraux (1949: 535), "The [Matsigenka and Campa] culture may be Proto-Arawakan and probably represents an early migration into the montaña." They consider the region a "refuge zone," with the implication that the Campa/Matsigenka fled or were pushed there because they could not stand the fierce competition along the main rivers (see also Lathrap 1970: 73). In light of the above history, however, it is likely that Matsigenka ancestors occupied the montaña early and that subsequent developments like expansionist warfare and complex social organization occurred downriver following migration out of the headwaters.

At the time of the Conquest, the Matsigenka occupied approximately the same territory as today, although perhaps at greater population density (Denevan 1980: 20–21). Centered around 12°S latitude and 73°W longitude, the territory extends "as far north as the Rio Mishagua, as far south as the Koribeni Mission on the upper Urubamba, as far west as the Rio Apurimac and the Rio Alto Picha, and as far east as the Madre de Dios and Manu rivers" (O. Johnson 1978: 24; Baksh 1984: 26; see map 1). Downriver to the north and east were the Arawakan-speaking Campa, Piro, and Amuesha. Farther downriver were a number of Panoan groups, including the Cashinahua, Amahuaca, Conibo, and Shipibo. Ethnohistorical evidence is that these downstream groups were engaged in frequent warfare, had a local-group-level (village) social organization, and tended to dominate Matsigenkas whenever they met. Of these groups, the Matsigenka of Shimaa spoke only of the Campa, whom they called Ashaninka. Baer (1984: 31) reports that Urubamba Matsigenkas also recognize Piros, whom they refer to as Simirinchi. The Piro presence in the upper Río Urubamba is probably ancient because the Piro were long-distance traders linking the Inka with downriver Amazonian communities (Myers 1983: 70; Camino 1977). Whatever the states of war or peace among these various groups, they were likely still part of a vast net of exchange relationships that was intact at the time of European arrival (Lathrap 1981; Myers 1983).

To the south and west, above the barrier of the cloud forest, were the Inkas. The Inkas, building on the statecraft of earlier empires, had integrated the Andean highlands and coast for thousands of kilometers along the mountain chain and traded regularly with the montaña. This exchange of technology and products between the Peruvian Amazon and the Pacific coast long predates the Inkas, going back at least three thousand years (Lyon 1981: 293). But the trade linking the montaña and the highlands, though important, did not bring about political integration (Lanning 1967: 186). The Inkas, presumably like their predecessors, had only partial success penetrating the tropical forest. To be sure, they had descended several mountain ridges and river valleys, most notably the province of Vilcabamba (Lyon 1981: 4), to elevations around eighteen hundred meters, below the upper limit of Matsigenka foraging

(Lathrap 1970: 176; Isbell 1968). In these comparatively warm elevations they could plant crops like maize for harvests that would ripen weeks or months before their highland counterparts, or they could raise coca, cotton, and chili peppers, which would not grow at higher elevations.

As the distances were often great, requiring many days of travel, highland villages established outposts at the margin of the tropical forest (Parsons and Hastings 1988: 214–15), on the "archipelago" pattern (Murra 1980; Raymond 1988). Well-worn footpaths—"In many places the trails have cut so deeply into the hillsides that they form V-shaped valleys twice the height of a man" (Isbell 1968: 114)—indicate an ancient pattern:

> In only four days on foot, one can travel from jungle villages where canoes ply the slow waters to the plateau of Lake Titicaca where nightly frosts permit the cultivation of only the hardiest crops. In a single day's walk, along the valleys of many tumbling rivers, the climatic transition is so dramatic that the traveler passes from cold, potato and oca producing country, down through corn and racacha fields into manioc and taro zones . . . [indicating] a considerable antiquity for the symbiotic relationship between the highlands and the Montaña and for the trade of dried meat, desiccated potato (chuñu) and other highland products for tropical yuca, fruit and the all important coca. Coca is among the earliest plant remains recovered from the distant Peruvian coast, and along with other plants of apparent Montaña origin, verifies the great antiquity of trade in Peru. (Isbell 1968: 109–110; cf. Stocks 1987: 2)

Archaeological evidence is that these outposts traded with tropical forest Indians. In exchange for forest products, including feathers, monkeys, and tropical crops, the Indians of the forest received stone and bronze tools, pottery, highland crops, and alpaca wool (Lanning 1967: 186).

Differences in style and technique, however, clearly show that this was not an area of cultural blending but a zone of contact between the fundamentally distinct Andean and Amazonian traditions (Hastings 1987). Two different Quechua loanwords in Matsigenka are suggestive of contact with a stratified society: ponyarona, "highlander," referring to the poor mestizo immigrants from the highlands, and virakocha, "lord" or "ruler" (< [derived from] Wira Kocha, an Inka creator god), referring to Euro-Americans. As we shall see, the Matsigenka believe both groups to be of evil origin.

Despite their power and civilization, the Inka could not control the montaña politically. They viewed the Indians there as wild and dangerous, and built the great fortress at Machu Picchu for protection. Admiring their fierceness, the Inkas did sometimes try to press Amazonians into military service. But these warriors could violently betray their erstwhile masters (e.g., Reynard-Casevitz and Saignes 1988) and then simply melt into the forest afterward; they were obviously unsuited to become loyal subjects of the realm.

The Amazon Indians closest to Cuzco, where the Inkas' court was located, were the Matsigenka. The Inka called them Anti and named the eastern quarter of their realm Anti Suyu after them (Steward and Metraux 1949: 535; Reynard-Casevitz and Saignes 1988). The Inka did exert some control over the forests of the Cordillera Vilcabamba, which includes the headwaters of the Río Kompiroshiato, where Inka ruins have been reported (Reynard-Casevitz and Saignes 1988). Inka ruins have also been reported in the headwaters of the Río Mantaro Chico, adjacent to the Río Kompiroshiato (Matthiessen 1961: 263). The Inkas controlled a peasant population of perhaps 160,000 along the upper Río Urubamba downstream past the fortress of Machu Picchu to Quillabamba, but not much farther (Gade 1967: 24–25). Snell (1964: 2) mentions a Matsigenka legend that Inka soldiers often attempted to conquer them, but they fled in fear into the forest, where the soldiers could not follow them.

The Río Paucartambo (which becomes the Río Yavero) also offers direct access to the selva alta from Cuzco. Far down this valley, nearly to the confluence of the Río Yavero, abandoned Inka terraces and roads are in evidence (von Hassel 1907), in a region now inhabited by scattered Matsigenka families. Still farther east, Inka ruins are also evident in the headwaters of the Río Madre de Dios, perhaps associated with coca plantations under direct Inka control. In such a headwaters area, adjacent to the Río Paucartambo drainage, ruins of an Inka "city" some two kilometers by twelve kilometers in extent have been reported. These ruins may be the city of Opotari (presumably an Arawakan name; Reynard-Casevitz and Saignes 1988). The French explorers who describe it, however, believe it to be the lost empire of the Inka, Paititi (Cartagena and Cartagena 1981).

The Inka were known as superb road builders who used strong bridges to cross impassable ravines. The roads likely followed long-standing prehistoric trails (Raymond 1988: 297–98). It is often believed that they went to the edge of the tropical forest and then stopped owing to difficulties of construction and maintenance (Hyslop 1984: 264–65). More likely, however, the roads continued into the forest but have been lost because they were made of earth, not stone, and have grown over. In the upper reaches of the Río Mantaro Chico at about fifteen hundred meters' altitude (not far from reputed Inka ruins), I walked with Matsigenkas on a smooth graded trail two to three meters wide, in places carved out of the surrounding hillside and made flat and broad, cleared of brush and branches overhead; my companions told me that it runs "far, far" up into the mountains. Like the trail along the crest between the Ríos Shimaa and Kompiroshiato, such thoroughfares in the past could have been linked to Inka roads. The likely limit to Inka transportation was not land but water, along the large rivers dominated by canoe travel, where the Inka were out of their element and exposed to powerful enemies (Lyon 1981: 8).

Thus, at the time of the Conquest the montaña was a frontier of contact, with rough edges, between the "Amazonian cultural tradition" (Willey 1971: 496) and the Andean civilizations of Peru. These contact zones were valuable enough economically and politically to the Inkas to justify major investments in fortresses, roads, platforms, and terraces. These constructions gave them a reliable zone of production over which they had control and an interface region where regular trade with Amazon Indians could be conducted.

The Río Urubamba was a main conduit of such trade (Gade 1972). Evidently, the Arawakan-speaking Piro were the principal traders linking the two zones, "the merchants of the montaña" (Camino 1977: 127). Each dry (low-water) season they made trading voyages, requiring weeks or months, from the lower Río Urubamba through the Pongo de Mainique to a trading post at El Enquentro (figure 5). In this contact zone downriver from Machu Picchu and Quillabamba, Quechuas came to exchange metal tools, gold and silver, and other highland goods for coca, monkeys, feathers, woods, dyes, medicines, resins, and, perhaps, women and children. Various trading entrepots have been mentioned in the same vicinity, roughly halfway between Quillabamba and the mouth of the Río Kompiroshiato. Marcoy (1872: 1:425) placed the "frontierline which separates civilization from barbarism" in the 1860s at Chahuaris, near El Enquentro and less than one hundred kilometers by river upstream from the mouth of the Río Kompiroshiato. Lyon (1981: 9) places the prehistoric trading center a short distance downriver from there, just below the confluence of the Río Yanatili (Río Lares) and the Río Urubamba.

Reports by early European travelers indicate that the Piros completely dominated the Matsigenkas, driving them inland from the banks of the Urubamba at least during low-water season. When they encountered Matsigenkas, Piros marauded their gardens and captured women

FIGURE 5. Men loading a balsa raft with parrots for trade downstream.

and children to be traded to highlanders. The Matsigenkas did not re-sist the Piros with force but may have allowed local leaders (*korakas*, a Quechua loanword) to negotiate deals to provide Piros with food and trade goods in order to minimize the disruption of ordinary Matsigenka families (Camino 1977: 133–36). Apart from the Piros, the Matsigenkas maintained their own low-key but steady trade with Quechuas (Gade 1972: 210).

Perhaps in this sense the Matsigenka can fairly be said to have occu-pied a refuge zone where they were protected from some of the fiercest military struggles of both the Inkas and the downriver tribes. They could occupy marginal foraging areas, possibly benefit from an umbrella of peace held over the region by the Inkas (Reynard-Casevitz and Saignes 1988), and trade directly with the Inkas. By occupying a marginal eco-logical zone that more powerful peoples did not covet, the Matsigenka appear to have found a quiet backwater in which to pursue their rela-tively tranquil, if frugal, existence.

AFTER THE CONQUEST

Francisco Pizarro invaded Peru in 1532. According to Peruvian history (or legend), after Pizarro murdered the Inka ruler Atawallpa, the em-pire collapsed and various Inka princes gathered their wealth and fled into the rainforest. In the early years of the twentieth century, Campa Indians told von Hassel (1907: 297) their legend: four thousand Inka soldiers, led by a "prince of the royal house," had descended the Río Urubamba fleeing the Spanish. Some believe they built Paititi, the City of Gold, somewhere near the headwaters of the Río Madre de Dios (cf. Gray 1987: 308–9). It is difficult to gauge what effect the collapse of the Inka might have had on the Matsigenka. With irrigation systems and roads falling into disrepair, Quechua-speaking populations would have declined in the montaña. They probably still would have found ways to trade: the Matsigenkas von Hassel met along the Río Paucartambo in 1900 could speak Quechua quite well. Powerful tribes were eliminated from the major rivers in the eighteenth and nineteenth centuries (Myers 1983), and even the neighboring Campa were heavily missionized, though at the cost of many Catholic martyrs. By 1667 some eighty-five hundred Campas had been missionized, and towns grew in support of commercial farms that produced sugar cane, coca, tobacco, and cacao (Peru 1987: 74). Apparently, the Matsigenka felt the impact less (Ferrero 1966: 42–43), and they were described by early Peruvian explorers as "friendly" (Grain 1939: 239). Later, Manko Inka organized resistance among the Quechuas and dominated much of the Urubamba, including the valley of La Convención. Although Manko Inka's movement was destroyed, it was not until persistent growth in the number of haciendas in the area from the late seventeenth century through the nineteenth century that the general resistance of the descendants of the Inkas to Spanish rule in Matsigenka territory was steadily undermined in favor of commerce.

For a period in the eighteenth century, Campa resistance also hardened around the messianic figure of Juan Santos Atawallpa, who claimed to be descended both from the Inkas and from God (Varese 1973). The Campa, who had begun by befriending missionaries and ranchers, suffered so much from disease and exploitation that they rebelled. Santos Atawallpa and his followers sought to drive out the Spanish and restore the Inka empire to its former glory. They killed or drove out missionaries, ranchers, and townspeople and seized control of their territory. But by then they had already been transformed by their adoption of such crops as plantains and sugar cane. Even after one hundred years of isolation from the Spanish, they still had smithies using bellows and forges for making iron tools (Steward and Metraux 1949: 537–539).

Dominican, Jesuit, and Augustinian missionaries became active in the Matsigenka area after the beginning of the eighteenth century, usually without the violent outcomes that hindered their work among the

Campa. But their success with the Matsigenka was clearly superficial. They managed only to contact settlements, and these were so reluctant to change their ways that in the 1960s Padre Andrés Ferrero (1966: 85–87) wrote in frustration, "The Machiguenga permits neither repression nor criticism. Should someone, even the missionary whose moral authority he recognizes, try to orient, correct or prevent his behavior, he departs immediately with the phrase: 'Here one can't live; nothing but gossip and rumors; I'm going where no one will bother me and I will bother no one.'"

Following Peru's independence from Spain, missionary activity in the montaña was sharply curtailed by the secular government, but commerce increased as new roads were built. Downriver, Iquitos began to emerge as a major shipping port for moving forest products to European and North American markets. During the rubber extraction of the late nineteenth century Iquitos was transformed from a small village into a town of twenty thousand (Guinness 1909: 214), and by World War II, after successive economic cycles in fine woods, petroleum, animals and hides, barbasco, chicle, and cascarilla, it had grown into a city of thirty thousand (Martinez 1983: 11). But its orientation remained downriver: when the citizens of Iquitos decided to pave their streets, for example, twenty-eight hundred tons of gravel were loaded on a ship in the port of Callao near Lima on the Pacific coast and sent sailing twelve thousand kilometers through the Panama Canal and up the Amazon because no overland route covered the twelve hundred kilometers between Callao and Iquitos (McIntyre 1972: 465). A road from Lima to Pucallpa, completed in 1943, opened a floodgate of immigration into an area viewed by the government as underpopulated. Between 1940 and 1981 the population of the Peruvian Amazon grew from 400,000 to 1,800,000 (Butts and Bogue 1989: 165–66).

The treacherous rivers and trails of the selva alta, however, made the area difficult to control, as the Inka had found. The rebellion of Atawallpa, in fact, was only one in a series of resistance efforts by montaña communities that have continued into the present day (Varese 1973: 356; Brown 1994; Brown and Fernández 1991). Nonetheless, the national government devised and implemented ecologically naive development plans with the explicit goal of relieving the intense population pressure in the highlands by encouraging it to spill over into the montaña (Krebs 1960: 59), viewed as uninhabited and containing untold riches. It was estimated that by the start of the twenty-first century this unprecedented migration of highland farmers without knowledge of tropical horticulture would destroy twenty-four million hectares, or about one-third of the tropical forest of Peru (Martinez 1983: 12–13).

Like other forest communities (Varese 1972: 123–25), the Matsigenka of the Urubamba valley were subject to slave raids during and after the rubber boom of the late nineteenth century. A Peruvian, Justo Pereira, dominated the Urubamba until, according to legend, his son Fidel Pereira (born circa 1888), who was half Matsigenka, killed him in a dispute over a woman and took over his territory. By World War I, Fidel Pereira had over five hundred men working the rubber avenues and was greatly feared and held in awe throughout the region. He enforced his will through his control over *korakas* to recruit labor and coordinate trade.

As he aged, he began to set his children up as rulers of a string of communities along the Río Urubamba upriver from the Pongo de Mainique. The Matsigenka families living in these communities were dependent on the Pereiras, and it is said that they were tracked down and beaten if they tried to run away. When linguists with the SIL began to work in the area in 1953, they found these Matsigenkas to be passive and somewhat browbeaten by their Pereira masters (Snell 1973). Rosengren (1987a: 160–69) documents a history of harsh control and exploitation by these potentially violent rulers.

When Orna Johnson and I first arrived, these communities were still in place, and the Pereiras, while most courteous, were also protective and perhaps defensive: they cared about the well-being of the Matsigenkas in their communities but were paternalistic and did not welcome outside scrutiny. Orna and I did meet and converse with the eighty-four-year-old Fidel Pereira, a slight man with light brown skin and a thin white beard. Educated and thoughtful, he was a gracious and knowledgeable conversationalist, discussing the role of communist China in the United Nations and the policies of former U.S. president Lyndon Johnson. It was difficult to credit this frail old caballero with the ruthless acts attributed to him.

The Matsigenka did not take intrusions on their freedom lightly. Their resistance, which has most often taken the form of flight from exploitation, left the regions of the Río Tigompinia and Río Timpia unpopulated until the last few decades. Along with certain ecological factors (chapter 2), this is the most likely explanation for why overall population density in the Matsigenka area remains below precolonial levels. Resistance was not always peaceful however. Evidently the Matsigenka resorted to violence in resisting the ambitious explorer Carlos Fermín Fitzcarrald when he came after them with Piros and Campas armed with

Winchester rifles in the nineteenth century (Ferrero 1966: 39). And as recently as the 1960s, possibly coinciding with a guerilla uprising in the valley of La Convención, a Matsigenka man associated with one of the Pereira communities reportedly killed a white man as part of a millenarian movement aimed at killing all whites (including the Pereiras) and restoring a utopian rule by mysterious beings from downriver (see Pereira 1944). The movement fizzled out as soon as it began, and the man was never punished for the homicide (Snell 1973).

Along the eastern margins of Matsigenka territory, even recently the Matsigenkas faced homicidal raids by Panoan groups like the Yora (Shepard 1999: 34). Characteristically, and to the astonishment of the Yora, the Matsigenka did not attack Yora settlements or even seem to do much to defend themselves but flee when attacked (MacQuarrie 1991: 222–27). The Matsigenka pattern, therefore, has been to avoid violence and to express their resistance by locating away from the river, disguising their trails so that slaving crews traveling along the river would pass them by. From their locations on bluffs, hidden from below by vegetation, they could watch unobserved up and down along the river. Even during our fieldwork in the 1970s the fear was so great that, on long trips through the forest, we would usually find the homesteads we happened on empty, often with food smoking over the fire: the inhabitants had heard us coming and had fled silently to a safe place in the forest.

Although living scattered and well hidden was certainly adaptive during the slaving period, it was also profoundly in character. Rosengren (1987a) describes the Matsigenka of the upper Río Urubamba as "highly atomistic and amorphous. . . . They do not live in nucleated villages and have no fixed notions of territoriality. They are not divided into clans, lineages or moieties. . . . Their society is loosely structured and they themselves are generally individualistic. People are not arranged in hierarchies of any sort" (quoted in Davis 1994: 80). All evidence indicates that they have been this way during the indefinite past. Neither explorers' reports nor the Matsigenkas' own traditions indicate that they ever lived in more complex societies than that which Rosengren describes. All signs of intensification and social elaboration—terracing, roads, monumental architecture—are clearly of Andean origin. Even the outgoing sociability and frequent group rituals reported for some Panoan groups (Shepard 1991: 85) are largely absent among the Matsigenka.

That many Matsigenka families remained isolated for generations is attested to by the devastation caused by measles, influenza, and other epidemics that struck Matsigenka communities in the 1950s and 1960s on first contact with Peruvians and Euro-Americans (Wieseke 1965: 12,

35). Surely, their fear of disease was a powerful motivation to remain isolated. In fact, given the history of decimation of other tribes, disease may be an indicator of the degree of success with which different groups maintained isolation. Wieseke's (1965) medical study of Kamisea included migrants from the hinterlands of the Urubamba, Kamisea, and Manu rivers. Those from the Kamisea showed the least exposure to contact-related diseases (2.8 percent positive for tuberculosis, 5.5 percent for measles), whereas those who had come from the Urubamba had the highest exposure (54.5 percent positive for both diseases); the Manu immigrants were intermediate (33.3 percent positive for both). This might be evidence that the Urubamba region, closest to the old areas of trade with the highlands, had experienced more continuous contact with the outside than had the hinterlands of Kamisea and Manu. Although on a tributary of the Río Urubamba, the Matsigenka of the Río Kompiroshiato tended to avoid the big river, just as travelers along it passed by the mouth of the Río Kompiroshiato with scarcely a thought.

The old isolation is moderating as Peruvian laws, especially the Agrarian Reform Law and the Law of the Selva, protect the Matsigenka from the exploitative practices of the past and as new generations with immunities replace those lost to disease. Government offices and programs available to the Matsigenka, as to other forest tribes, allow them to register land titles and form "native communities" with official standing (Peru 1987). As difficult as these laws are to enforce, they do indicate change. The highland farmers who descend the mountain valleys and take up residence alongside Matsigenka families bring not only population pressure but also greater savvy about how the national political system works. And the growing density of farmers with products to sell encourages both infrastructural development and an increased government presence. For the most part, the Matsigenka in the 1970s were welcoming these new opportunities and the security they afforded.

In their school communities one generally finds an airstrip and a soccer field. Men and boys, and often girls, play soccer with cries of enthusiasm and are fiercely competitive in games with other communities. Schools with rows of desks impose new standards of personal comportment and hygiene, as well as the unfamiliar disciplines of study and homework. Corrugated metal roofs mark the exhaustion of the more comfortable palm leaves, and the sounds of Peruvian music on radios and tape recorders give further evidence of the growing commercial and cultural integration of the Matsigenka with the greater outside world (Izquierdo 2001).

CHAPTER 2

Making a Living

Over the millennia, each aboriginal group [in Amazonia] succeeded in developing a seasonal cycle that combines hunting, fishing, gathering, and agricultural activities of different kinds and relative intensities, but which in every case assures the availability of all essential nutrients indefinitely without endangering the equilibrium of the ecosystem.

Meggers 1971: 27

A single Matsigenka household is capable of meeting all its own subsistence needs with few exceptions. A hamlet of related households may develop a division of labor integrating the households economically, but such integration is rarely necessary, and the dissolution of a hamlet into separate single-family households is always possible. There is no economic basis, therefore, for social aggregates beyond the family, and this is certainly one of the conditions for the existence and viability of a family level society.

The Use of Time: An Overview

The members of a Matsigenka household potentially possess the complete array of skills needed to supply their basic needs. We seldom find the Matsigenka of Shimaa working in collaboration with other households, although for certain tasks, like barbasco fishing, they do. And wage

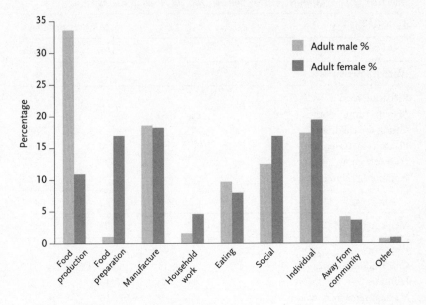

FIGURE 6. Adult division of labor, by sex.

labor and commercial activities count for little—in 1972–73 only 0.3 percent of adults' daytime activities (figure 6).

THE DIVISION OF LABOR

Based on systematic random observations of behavior (Johnson 1975, 1996; cf. Johnson and Sackett 1998), it is clear that a Matsigenka marriage is a partnership of two skilled individuals, each with a separate domain. Their behavior tells a story of clear and thoroughgoing differentiation, one that leads not to segregation and discrimination between the sexes but to mutual respect and interdependence (Johnson and Johnson 1975; cf. Rosengren 1987b: 341–42). Table 2 summarizes how adult men and women allocate their time to different activities over the thirteen-hour daytime period from 6 A.M. to 7 P.M.

Differences between men and women are sharp. Food preparation and cloth manufacture occupy women more than four hours a day, with childcare adding another hour, and other female tasks—plaiting mats and baskets from cane or palm leaves, cleaning house, and washing clothes and pots—fill out most of their day. Men dominate in all aspects of agriculture, although women and girls plant a few crops and

TABLE 2. Summary: Division of Labor by Sex

Allocation of Time (Minutes per Day) during Daylight Hours (6 A.M. to 7 P.M.)

Activity	Minutes per Day	
	Men	*Women*
Women's Activities		
Preparing food	18	141
Manufacturing cloth	1	108
Caring for children	3	63
Plaiting (mats, baskets)	0	13
Housecleaning	0	11
Washing (clothing, pots)	0	8
SUBTOTAL	22	344
Men's Activities		
Weeding	54	1
Constructing houses	47	1
Hunting	43	0
Making items from wood	40	4
Making items of fiber twine and netting	32	1
Planting	29	0
Preparing gardens	10	0
SUBTOTAL	255	7
Both Women's and Men's Activities		
Doing nothing, resting	76	112
Eating	61	59
Visiting in community	65	53
Harvesting	61	42
Fishing	44	21
Traveling outside community	33	29
Collecting wild foods	26	20
Engaging idly in recreational activities	28	15
Being ill	23	18
Caring for self	15	9
Caring for others (not children)	10	8
Chatting	7	8
Sleeping	8	4
Caring for yard	5	6
Making beads, ornaments	2	8
Other	39	17
SUBTOTAL	503	429
TOTAL	780	780

TABLE 3. Time-Allocation Patterns of Infants and Toddlers
Minutes per Day during Daylight Hours (6 A.M. to 7 P.M.)

	Infants		Toddlers	
Activity	*Male*	*Female*	*Male*	*Female*
Being idle	613	602	604	525
Eating	106	96	110	133
Being bathed, cleaned	23	55	11	46
Playing	8	14	22	43
Being ill	23	0	15	5
Engaging in productive tasks	0	0	9	19
Other	7	13	9	9
TOTAL	780	780	780	780

NOTE: Average age: infants, male = 0.5, female = 0.7; toddlers, male = 2.3, female = 3.8 years (weighted by number of observations).

contribute to harvesting. (The amount of planting by women and girls is so small it does not appear in the time-allocation random observations.) Hunting is an exclusively male occupation, and men also predominate in building houses, manufacturing wood objects of all kinds, and making net bags and other artifacts requiring fiber twine.

The general pattern, recognized by the Matsigenka, is that the house is the woman's domain and the garden is the man's. Because men's activities tend to be outside the house, hunting on steep trails or doing heavy garden work, men expend about one-third more energy per day than women do (Montgomery 1978: 63). Men and women spend the remainder of the time in activities that both regularly engage in, many of them involving collaboration or companionship between them. These activities include harvesting, fishing, and collecting wild products, as well as leisure and social activities.

Before the age of six, children of both sexes are very much alike in their use of time; they are engaged mostly in idleness, play, and eating (table 3). The situation changes, predictably, with older children (ages six to fourteen), who begin to act more like their parents, with older girls contributing to housekeeping and childcare while older boys contribute to food production (table 4). The older boys, however, are not completely like grown men: they do not hunt, and they spend much more time than men in food-preparation tasks, primarily collecting firewood and fetching water. They are also somewhat active as babysitters.

TABLE 4. Time-Allocation Patterns of Older Children
Minutes per Day during Daylight Hours (6 A.M. to 7 P.M.)

Activity	Male	Female
Being idle	434	454
Eating	78	104
Producing food	97	21
Manufacturing items	22	9
Preparing food	35	67
Engaging in housekeeping and hygiene	16	47
Caring for other children	11	24
Other (being ill, traveling, visiting)	87	54
TOTAL	780	780

NOTE: Average age: males = 9.0, females = 7.8 (weighted by number of observations).

THE DAILY ROUND

Men and women spend about half their daylight hours working, especially in food production, food preparation, and manufacture. They generally begin to wake at first light, around 5:30 A.M., but often do not rise until 6 or 6:30. Women are up before men, building the fire and going early to the river to fetch water for cooking. For men, and for women to a degree, this is a period of leisurely eating.

The transition to work is abrupt. A man simply says, "I'm going," and rises in one fluid motion to walk out the door. For a man, 8 A.M. to 2 P.M. is the peak period of heavy work, when agriculture and foraging dominate all other activities. The other common activity during these hours is manufacture. Some manufacturing, like house building, can dominate a man's daylight hours for days or weeks, during which he may do little foraging and may neglect his gardens. Other manufacturing activities, like making bows and arrows or net bags, can be done indoors and are favorite ways to spend time during rainy days, evenings, or simply a day off from heavy labor. Matsigenka men are steady laborers; they work briskly and with few breaks but tend to taper off by mid-afternoon. Thereafter, they are most likely to be found bathing, eating, and resting.

A woman's day has a different rhythm. She begins her day earlier than a man, but work does not dominate her mid-day period to the degree it does a man's, and her day is more varied with tasks, each taking less time. Women go to the garden but only briefly in the morning before the mid-day heat can affect their young children. During the day, women are often alone at home with their children, occupied with many tasks: food preparation, childcare, housekeeping, and manufacture.

For both men and women, the later part of the day is a time for social activities like visiting, drinking manioc beer, and recounting the events of the day. The house casts a long shadow as sunset approaches, and the whole family tends to gather on mats in the comfortable shade outdoors, eating, grooming, making artifacts, and chatting. At dusk, around 6 P.M., the level of productive activities drops off sharply. Visitors tend to return home, and men rarely work after dusk. In the most common evening scene, the household members are gathered near the fire, sometimes in the company of relatives from an adjacent house. Women may be spinning cotton thread, the comfortable whirl and knock of their wooden spindles punctuating the evening calm. Men work on net bags or other crafts that can be done in the dim firelight. Usually leftover ears of corn or pieces of manioc are warming for individuals to snack on. Quiet conversations reporting the day's events, discussing social problems, laying plans for the next day, and retelling folktales fill this important time of the day. Children begin to doze off soon after dark, and by 8 P.M. the household is settled for the night. Individuals may carry on conversations later, but they speak so softly that they cannot be overheard from the other side of the house.

People generally do not leave the house during the night, except for occasional night hunting from blinds in gardens. The family generally spends the night together, gathered near the fire when it is cold. Occasionally, someone gets up to stir the fire and add wood as needed. Women often tie pieces of cooked manioc to lengths of twine hung from the rafters as late night snacks. In the morning, only empty loops of twine remain.

Food Production

Adult men spend about a third of their daylight time and adult women about a tenth in food production (see figure 6); youths contribute at about a third of the rate of their adult counterparts. The main types of food production are horticulture, fishing, and foraging, with a small effort put into the care of domesticated animals (table 5). Gardening accounts for half the time spent in food production, most of the remainder being divided between foraging and fishing.

TABLE 5. Proportions of Food-Production Time Spent in Gardening, Foraging, and Fishing

	Gardening	Foraging	Fishing	Other	Total
Male adult	56.5%	26.4%	16.6%	0.55%	100%
Male youth	63.0	8.6	22.9	5.7	100
Female adult	47.7	21.5	23.8	6.9	100
Female youth	35.7	21.4	28.6	14.3	100
TOTAL[a]	53.55%	23.4%	20.25%	3.0%	100%

[a]Weighted by total number of observations.

TABLE 6. Stages of Matsigenka Garden Production

Matsigenka Description	Translation	Haney's Phases
nonkogakerora kametiri kipatsi	I will want (seek) good land	Selecting the site
nonkarasetakerora	I will clear it	Clearing the site
nompotakerora	I will burn it	Burning the slash
nompankitakerora	I will plant it	Planting
nontsamaitakotakerora	I will cultivate (weed) it	Weeding
nogakerora shinki	I harvest maize	Harvesting
nompireatakerora nogakerora ovatsa nogakemparora	I will cut and harvest manioc	—
nompankitairo pashini sekatsi	I will plant more manioc	—
tera nompankitairo aikyiro	I will not plant any more	Leaving fallow

SOURCES: Johnson 1983: 31; Haney 1968: 7.

GARDENING

On the basis of calories alone, a household's gardens are by far its most important source of food. Matsigenka gardens are remarkably productive and guarantee that starvation is a distant, perhaps insignificant, danger, even for isolated households. As a key part of the recurring cycle of household migration and resettlement, garden production is a complex and dynamic gradual transformation from first clearing to final abandonment.

The Matsigenka describe garden production as a series of discrete phases that correspond closely to the stages scientists use in discussing tropical horticulture (table 6). A farmer seeking to clear a new garden wants land with promising soils and no competing claims from other

TABLE 7. Matsigenka Soil Classification and Soil Characteristics

	Metsopatsari (soft soil)		Kusopatsari (hard soil)	
	Imvaneki (sand) (3)	Shimentya (gravel) (6)	Potsitari (black) (4)	Kiraari (red) (10)
Nutrients				
Organic matter[a]	3.3	8.0	5.2	5.2
Nitrogen[a]	0.16	0.38	0.26	0.24
pH	5.7	6.2	6.4	5.2
Phosphorus[b]	14.2	14.3	7.6	9.5
Potassium (K+)[c]	0.54	0.57	0.59	0.48
C.E.C.[c]	12.35	25.36	16.94	17.66
Texture				
Sand/gravel	61%	51%	32%	27%
Silt	29	31	40	43
Clay	10	18	28	30

NOTE: Twenty-three soil samples were analyzed.

[a] Percentage.
[b] Parts per million.
[c] Cation exchange capacity, in mil equivalents per 100 grams.

households (see chapter 4). The most preferred soils are dark and soft, and the least preferred are light-colored and hard. Laboratory analysis of a sample of Matsigenka soils shows that preferred soils are both rich in qualities that indicate good agricultural potential (e.g., amount of nitrogen and cation exchange capacity) and high in sand and gravel, which help make them soft and pliable (table 7). (*Imvaneki* are sandy soils near the river; they are preferred because such areas are easy to clear and cultivate. But these soils quickly lose fertility, as reflected in their low level of nitrogen.) In the vicinity of a household soils may be of distinct colors and hardness, and some of the best ones may be at a less convenient distance; thus the choice of where to start a new garden is complex and somewhat chancy (Wilshusen and Stone 1990: 107–8).

Overall, the soils available in Shimaa are good to excellent for tropical soils (Young 1976: 285–303; Landon 1984: 106–44; Sanchez et al. 1982: 821; Carneiro 1964: 16). Even the poorer sandy soils are reasonably fertile for a year or two. Being easy to clear and work, sandy patches near the river's edge may have played a larger role in the past, when local population densities were lower, total garden investments were lower, steel tools were more scarce, and abandoning a garden after a year or two was more likely than it has become today (Shepard 1999: 48).

Men usually clear a new garden every year, most commonly at the start of the low-water season, from April through July, so there will be time during the least rainy part of the year to let the field dry for burning. Garden clearing is often a lonely, grinding, day-in day-out labor that is a relief to finish. Men must watch out for snakes and sharp thorns and falling branches, and many suffer cuts and broken bones from the work. The forest is so tied together by vines that smaller trees, even when cut through at the base, cannot fall. Of necessity, a man cuts all the small trees in an area of several hundred square meters, leaving them dangling, then cuts wedges facing downhill in the trunks of the large trees just to the point where they are close to falling. Finally, by felling the largest tree in the group, he causes them all to topple together with a thunderous crash—an exciting moment that makes anyone around laugh, whistle, and jump.

In the less wet months of low-water season, the intense sun for days on end dries the slash despite occasional rain. A good burn requires little labor and cleans most of the rubbish out of a garden, leaving only larger trunks and ash. To burn well, a field should dry for two or three months, capped off by several straight days of bright sunshine and steady winds. Several men and boys work together, using firebrands to start fires at the downwind border of the garden. There is no danger of starting a forest fire: even intensely hot fires with flames leaping twenty meters in the air barely singe the wall of forest bordering the garden.

Nervousness that the rainy season may start early sometimes leads men to burn gardens prematurely. The resulting bad burn puts them in a foul mood, for they fully appreciate what unpleasant work awaits them. A second burn requires piling rubbish and burning each pile separately, several days of hot and dirty work. And a bad burn fails to kill weeds that have grown up while the field was drying, increasing the future labor of weeding. A field that has burned badly will probably be abandoned a year or two before a well-burned field.

The day after burning, while logs are still smoldering in the new garden, a man begins planting manioc, followed by maize. The spacing of these two basic crops, which is careful and not at all haphazard (contra Anderson 1952: 136–42), creates a grid in which other crops will be planted. Although women then make a series of short visits to the field to plant cuttings throughout the grid, the first-year garden is designed mainly to produce as much maize as possible and to establish new manioc plants that begin producing only after the maize has been harvested. The other crops certainly add to the diversity of the diet, but the mix of crops found at the outset is less diverse than that found in older gardens that lack maize (see table 12, later in this chapter).

In Shimaa, sweet manioc *(Manihot esculenta)* is far and away the major food in the diet. In fact, the Matsigenka word for sweet manioc, *sekatsi,* derives from the root *-seka-,* "eat," and is best translated as "that which is eaten" or, simply, "food." It accounts for two-thirds of all calories produced in gardens, and much is left behind when gardens are abandoned. Manioc plants differ in appearance: some have dark green leaves, others are shot with red; some have short, thick stalks, others long thin ones; and so on. My records contain fifteen named varieties of manioc, and the more people you ask, the more names you get. Although different names do not necessarily mean different varieties, the Matsigenka themselves relish diversity and request cuttings from others' gardens to try out. Their usual explanation for this practice: "Because we like to." One man, however, said, "I plant these varieties because I am afraid otherwise they will die out." Diversity is an adaptive aspect of Matsigenka horticulture and characterizes even minor crops (Johnson 1972; cf. Hames 1983).

Although maize, *shinki (Zea mays),* is second to manioc as the most important food crop, it is the dominant crop in first-year gardens, accounting for well over half of all plants in the field. Because the Matsigenka believe that a newly cleared field has a limited capacity to grow maize, they plant it only once and harvest it first. Thereafter, gardens take on a much different appearance; they are dominated by root crops and herbs until they are abandoned. Being an important source of oil and protein in the diet, maize is the main reason for clearing at least one new garden per household each year.

In any garden, although a favorite variety of maize may predominate, other varieties are found also. When I asked for maize seed to plant my new garden, men were immediately willing to give me some seed, even a dusty and insect-riddled handful of grains Omenko had kept around as seed for years. I also planted some hybrid corn I had brought with me from a garden store in Massachusetts. When they learned I had my own seed, men offered me all sorts of gifts of food in exchange for some. Knowing that all seeds of a given variety of hybrid corn are genetically identical, I was startled by the great differences in growth of individual plants of the hybrid corn in different parts of my garden. I could con-

FIGURE 7. Planting women's crops.

clude only that differences in soils in my garden accounted for the differences in plant growth. But the Matsigenka did not see it that way. Although they recognized the possible influence of soil qualities, as discussed above, within a single garden they downplayed such influences, preferring two other explanations. They believe, first, that magical and spiritual forces are at work and, second, that there are differences in the strength and vitality of the seeds themselves, such that only some will sprout and thrive.

In addition to manioc and maize, men are associated with such crops as bananas (*poseiro, Musa* sp.), plantains *(parianti, Musa paradisiaca),* coffee *(kapiki, Coffea arabica),* rice *(aroshi, Oryza sativa),* and peanuts *(inke, Arachis hypogaea).* In Shimaa these were minor crops; coffee was growing in importance as a possible source of cash, which Maestro, as the representative of a modernizing world, was promoting.

A fair characterization would be that Matsigenka men plant a few cultigens in large amounts, whereas women plant many cultigens in small amounts. The men's contribution is the staple food supply, the women's a diversity in taste and nutrients. When a woman goes to plant, she carries a grab bag of bulbs and cuttings that she plants selectively in appropriate spots, like squash in a small pocket of ash. When you ask, "What do women plant?" the most common answer is *onko,* "cocoyam" (*Xanthosoma nigra;* similar to taro and arrowroot), and *magona,* "yam"

(*Dioscorea* sp.). Other popular crops generally associated with women are *tsirianti*, "pineapple" *(Ananas comosus); tinti*, "papaya" *(Carica papaya); impogo*, "sugar cane" *(Saccharum officinarum);* and *ampei*, "cotton" *(Gossypium* sp.). All these crops are important to the household economy throughout the year.

Many other crops are planted here and there, with low frequency, including some that in other tropical regions are of major importance, like bean, pepper, squash, peanut, sweet potato, avocado, lemon, onion, orange, cacao, and tobacco (table 8). Despite their rarity, most people like these crops, but many require much labor or take so long to mature that the household will be ready to move away by the time they begin to bear fruit. None of them add elements to the diet that are not already provided in other ways.

Aging gardens become smaller but contain a greater diversity of crops (table 9). Typically, the house garden (*novankireshi*, "my plants") is part of the first garden planted in a new settlement. Even after two or three years it remains an important source of food by virtue of the root crops grown there, especially manioc and cocoyam. Also, all family members are free to plant varieties they find interesting, which add spice to the standard diet; here, they can experiment with new plants at low risk (Johnson 1972), such as rice, which two men planted experimentally in 1973 and which was widely planted within two years. The house garden is also a medicine chest of herbal remedies like lemon grass, moonflower, hibiscus, coca, tobacco, cedar, and the all-important medicinal sedges (*ivenkiki;* chapter 5). In addition to fruit trees, house gardens also contain palms for construction of weapons and houses. Not domesticates, they are deliberately left standing in a garden clearing and survive the fire to grow until they are harvested.

Starting within weeks of planting, men must weed continuously: "We are always weeding; weeds don't wait." The word for weeding, *notsamaitakotakerora*, derives from the word for garden, *tsamairintsi*, and it is apt that weeding should be designated the generic garden work since it occupies so much time. Weeding every six weeks or so in soft soils is preferable: a man can weed over five hundred square meters an hour under such favorable conditions. But when weeds become entrenched or where the soil is hard, the work can increase tenfold and may lead a man to abandon a garden: a hectare of new garden can be cleared in roughly two hundred hours, so why continue to weed an older garden several times a year at a cost of one hundred or more hours of muscle-knotting work?

A new garden receives a major weeding at the time of the maize

TABLE 8. Plant Species Identified in Shimaa Gardens, 1972–75

English (Spanish) Name	Matsigenka Name	Scientific Name	Comment
achiote	*potsoti*	*Bixa orellana*	Cosmetic, dye
arrow cane	*chakopi*	*Gynerium saccharoides*	
avocado	*tsivi*	*Persea americana*	
balsa	*paroto*	*Ochroma lagopus* Sw.	
banana	*poseiro*	*Musa paradisiaca*	
barbasco	*kogi*	*Lonchocarpus* sp.	
barbasco	*kogi kiripeshianiri*	*Tephrosia toxicaria*	
bean, kidney	*maroro tyongipa*	*Phaseolus vulgaris*	
bottle gourd	*piarintsi*	*Lagenaria siceraria*	
cacao	*kakao*	*Theobroma cacao*	
calabash tree	*pamoko*	*Crescentia cujete*	
chonta *(pijuayo)*	*kuri*	*Bactris gasipaes*	
coca	*koka*	*Erythroxylon coca*	
cocoyam	*onko*	*Xanthosoma (nigra?)*	
coffee	*kapiki*	*Coffea arabica*	
cotton	*ampei*	*Gossypium barbadense*	
daledale	*shovnaki*	*Calathea allouia*	
gourd	*tsota*	*Lagenaria siceraria*	
granadilla	*tsimoritoki*	*Passiflora cuadrangularis*	
(guamo)	*intsipa kepiripari*	*Inga* sp.	
guava	*komashiki*	*Psidium guajava*	
hibiscus	*ashi merentsi*	*Hibiscus* sp.	"For flu"
lemon	*irimoki*	*Citrus limon*	
lemon grass	*kasankari*	*Cymbopogon citratus*	Herbal tea
maize	*shinki*	*Zea mays*	
mango	*manko*	*Mangifera indica*	
manioc	*sekatsi*	*Manihot esculenta*	
mint	*menta*	*Mentha* sp.	
moonflower	*saaro*	*Brugmansia* sp.	
(ojé)	*potogo*	*Ficus* sp.	Medicinal herb
(oncocha)	*onko makato*	*Anthurium* sp.	Relative of arrowroot
onion	*seboya*	*Allium* sp.	
orange	*naranja*	*Citrus sinensus*	
(pandro)	*pashiroki*	*Trema micrantha*	Lashing fiber
papaya	*tinti*	*Carica papaya*	
peanut	*iinge*	*Arachis hypogaea*	
pepper, red	*tsitikana*	*Capsicum* sp.	
(pifayo)	*manataro*	*Bactris chaetochlamys*	Useful palm
pigeon pea	*miminkoki, tsitsita*	*Cajanus cajan*	

TABLE 8. *(continued)*

English (Spanish) Name	Matsigenka Name	Scientific Name	Comment
pineapple	*tsirianti*	*Ananus comosus*	
plantain	*parianti*	*Musa paradisiaca*	
rice	*aroshi*	*Oryza sativa*	
sedge *(piripiri)*	*ivenkiki*	*Dichromena ciliata, Cyperus* sp.	
soursop *(chirimoya)*	*anona*	*Annona* sp.	
spearmint	*ivinishi*	*Menta spicata*	Aphrodisiac
squash	*kemi*	*Cucurbita* sp.	
sugar cane	*imvogo*	*Saccharum officinarum*	
sweet potato	*koriti*	*Ipomoea batatas*	
tangerine	*mandarina?*	*Citrus reticulata*	
tobacco	*seri*	*Nicotiana tabacum*	
(tomate del monte)	*mananeroki*	*Solanum* sp.	Magical plant
yam	*magona*	*Dioscorea* sp.	
(yarina)	*kompiro*	*Phytelephas microcarpa*	
?	*koviriki*	*Spilanthes ocymifolia*	Medicinal herb
?	*poe*	*Phaseolus* sp.	Fruit/tuber
?	*shimasheri*	*Cassia* sp., *Caesalpinia* sp.	Decorative flower
?	*tivana*	*Bromelia* sp.	Net-bag fiber
?	*tsigaro*	*Scheelea cephalotes*	Useful palm

NOTE: In addition to the species listed here, garden surveys turned up another twenty-five named plants for which I lack identification. They include some minor edible species, many medicinal herbs, and some magical or decorative plants: *choritoshi*, *inchoviki* (leaves for steaming fish), *iratsipini* (protects males from female pollution), *iseka ataava* ("chicken food"), *kepina*, *kokama*, *korama*, *korinti* (fruit), *kuro* (manioc magic), *pankogiririra poreatsiri* (flower), *pantiariki* (seed; Spanish, *pan de arbol*), *pao* (tubers, *calabaza*), *pocharoki* (fruit), *porenki* (fruit, *palillo*), *porotoki* (bean), *sankonka* (medicinal herb), *santari* (medicinal herb), *sarioki* (bead for necklace), *sharovantareki* (gourd), *shikovana* (medicinal herb), *shimanteki* (fruit), *shinti* (medicinal herb), *shirina* (tuber), *tamviapini* (ornament), and *tareko* (dye).

TABLE 9. Age of Garden and Species Diversity

Garden Age (n)	Average Size (ha)	Average Number of Species
One year (5)	0.67	7
Two years (2)	0.44	11
Three+ years (2)	0.18	22

TABLE 10. Annual Food-Crop Yields by Type of Garden,
Average Downstream Household, 1972–73

Crop	First-Year Hill (0.56 ha)	Second-Year+ Hill (0.36 ha)	Riverside (0.06 ha)	Total (0.98 ha)
Manioc	1,149	4,687	526	6,362
Pineapple	443	780	0	1,223
Maize	731	0	0	731
Plantain, banana	207	380	0	587
Papaya	35	274	0	309
Cocoyam	21	210	11	242
Sugar cane[a]	17	201	0	218
Yam	12	26	0	38
Cacao	0	22	0	22
Pigeon pea	2	9	0	11
Guava	0	0	11	11
Beans	0	6	0	6
Coffee[b]	0	0	0	0

SOURCE: Johnson 1983: 55.

NOTE: Except where otherwise indicated, measurements are in edible kilograms.
[a] In liters of liquid.
[b] Immature.

harvest, after which it is devoted to root crops and perhaps some bananas or barbasco fish poison. A household's many gardens are like a
huge market where fresh produce is always available. Harvesting from
Matsigenka gardens has much in common with household shopping in
market economies: perhaps twice a week you fill your bag with staples
and some specialties and go home to prepare dinner. For special products—cotton, barbasco, fiber—you go to a specific garden where these
materials are growing and harvest what you need. Throughout the year
a few hours of work each day, steadily applied, are all that is required to
maintain this abundance indefinitely (table 10).

The system practiced in Shimaa employs fallow periods so lengthy
(twenty years or more) that men rarely could say anything at all about
who might have last farmed the land they were about to clear. The first
garden cleared at a new homestead is most likely in forest next to a
stream of clean water (i.e., no upstream neighbors). By the time it is
producing maize, the family has moved into a new house in the middle
of this garden. After the maize harvest, work starts on clearing a new

TABLE 11. Decline in Soil Fertility with Garden Age

Garden Age (n)	Organic Matter (%)	Nitrogen (%)	Cation Exchange Capacity (mil equivalents/100 gr)
Primary forest (4)	6.8%	0.32%	19.4
One year (12)	6.7	0.31	21.4
Two years (2)	6.2	0.30	19.4
Three+ years/ house garden (5)	4.3	0.20	16.1
Abandoned (4)	3.2	0.14	13.8

TABLE 12. Densities of Selected Crops in Older Gardens

Garden Age (n)	Size (ha)	Species (#)	Densities per Hectare				
			Maize	Manioc	Cocoyam	Cotton	Pineapple
One year (5)	0.67	7	7,650	3,915	625	285	760
Two years (2)	0.44	11	0	6,020	2,615	680	1,305
House garden (2)	0.18	22	280	3,470	3,610	140	280

garden for the next year. Ideally, each new garden is adjacent to the previous one so that they slowly encircle the original garden, which has become a house garden. As gardens age, they tend to be abandoned because of either weeds or a decline in soil fertility (table 11); fertility decline is sharpest after the second year, when the tendency to abandon gardens increases. Although men told me that older gardens are fine for all crops except maize, their behavior suggests otherwise: they tend to plant their crops farther apart after two years, as if responding to lower fertility (table 12).

The abandonment of a garden begins with a state of semi-abandonment known as "it belongs to peccary," *ashi shintori,* when a garden still has much manioc, bananas, plantains, papaya, and barbasco. For several months such a garden may be reclaimed through only a few weedings per year, but then most crops die off and secondary growth takes over.

Overall, the Matsigenka of Shimaa have an effective technology for producing ample basic foods with modest effort. The agricultural work of an average household, with a total of about one hectare of gardens in production, produces over thirteen million calories per year (Johnson 1983: 62), or about twenty calories of food energy for every calorie of energy put into gardening. This good return to labor results in an overabundance of food energy compared with household nutritional needs and an abundance of most other dietary essentials.

FORAGING

Foraging, which occupies slightly more of a person's day than fishing, includes both hunting and collecting; these activities are distinct in the sense that real hunting is serious man's business, whereas collecting tends to be a family affair and feels like a hike and picnic. But the two activities are related because trips into the forest always include the possibility of both.

Matsigenka men like to hunt—as Maestro put it, "I don't work on Sundays; I go hunting"—and they do so at every opportunity. If a man hears a bird near the house, he quickly grabs a slingshot or bow and bird arrow and tries his luck. If, while gathering materials in the forest, he hears a bird sing, he imitates its song to lure it within range. The men vary widely in their aptitude for hunting. Some, like Oscar, are powerfully built and fearless hunters who go to great lengths and face any adversary, confident that their skill with bow and arrow will protect them from injury. Others, like Aretoro, tend to stay closer to home and to pursue smaller game, using a slingshot as often as bow and arrow; but these men are crafty hunters and keep a steady flow of small game coming into the household. Still others, like Evaristo and Santiago, seem ill at ease hunting and are generally somewhat ineffectual in the male role.

The hunt is the core of a man's view of himself, his relationship with his wife and family, and his place in his social network. All these levels are activated impressively when he brings in enough game to share widely. Animals, creatures that "have breath" and are animate, are abundant in the forest, but those that are considered edible (*piratsi*, "game") are few and far between. Meat is rare in the diet, and, as everyone loves it, they gratefully acknowledge the successful hunter. The main species of game in the Shimaa area, those actually hunted, are listed in table 13.

Collared peccary *(shintori)* is the prototypical game: ask a hunter where he is going, and he will answer, "I am going to hunt *shintori*"; his highest praise for another place is, "They have *shintori* there." And, in view of the fact that all meat is scarce, peccary does contribute the greatest amount to the diet. The Matsigenka believe peccary to travel in

TABLE 13. Major Game Species

Matsigenka	English	Spanish	Scientific Name
Mammals			
etini	armadillo	*carachupa*	*Dasypus novemcinctus*
kemari	tapir	*sachavaca*	*Tapirus terrestris*
maeni	bear	*oso*	*Tremarctos ornatus*
maniro	deer	*venado*	*Mazama americana*
matsontsori potsonari	puma	*tigre*	*Felis concolor*
megiri	squirrel	*ardilla*	*Sciurus* sp.
oati	tayra	*zorro negro*	*Eira barbara*
osheto	spider monkey	*maquisapo*	*Ateles paniscus*
parari	otter	*nutria*	*Lutra longicaudis*
samani	paca	*majaz*	*Agouti paca*
santaviri	white-lipped peccary	*huangana*	*Tayasu pecari*
sharoni	agouti	*añuje*	*Dasyprocta* sp.
shiani	anteater	*oso hormiguero*	*Myrmecophaga tridactyla*
shintori	collared peccary	*sajino*	*Tayasu tajacu*
shito	capuchin?	*mono negro*	*Cebus* sp.?
yaniri	howler monkey	*cotomono*	*Alouatta seniculus*
Birds			
chakami	pale-winged trumpeter	*trompetero*	*Psophia leucoptera*
chompari	snowy egret	*garza*	*Egretta thula*
kanari	guan	*pava de monte*	*Penelope* sp., *Pipile pipile*
katsari	crested oropendola	*paucar*	*Psarocolius decumanus*
kentsori	white-throated tinamou	*perdiz*	*Tinamus guttatus*
kintaro	scaly-naped parrot	*loro*	*Amazona mercenaria*
mamaro	owl	*lechuza*	*Otus choliba?*
mamviro	pigeon	*paloma*	*Columba* sp.
marini	Amazonian black-tyrant	*papamosca*	*Phaeotriccus poecilocercus*
oe	Andean cock-of-the-rock	*pajaro de roca*	*Rupicola peruviana*
pareto	parakeet	*loro pequeño*	*Aratinga mitrata*
pishiti	Cuvier's toucan	*tucán grande*	*Ramphastos cuvieri*
sankati	Spix's guan	*pucacunga*	*Penelope jacquacu*
shirinti	tinamou	*perdiz pequeña*	*Crypturellus (bartletti?)*

(continued on page 56)

TABLE 13. *(continued)*

Matsigenka	English	Spanish	Scientific Name
Birds			
shiromega	white-tipped dove	*paloma*	*Leptotila verreauxi*
tetsini	brown mandibled aracari	?	*Pteroglossus mariae*
tsamiri	curassow	*paujil*	*Mitu mitu*
tserepato	Amazon kingfisher	*martin pescador*	*Chloroceryle amazona*
tsivini	fasciated tiger-heron	*martin pescador*	*Tigrisoma fasciatum*
yonkororoni	red-winged tinamou	*perdiz*	*Rynchotus rufescens*
yotoni	channel-billed toucan	*tucán grande*	*Ramphastos vitellinus*

SOURCES: Identifications are from Eisenberg 1989; Schauensee 1970.

NOTE: Spanish names are those used locally.

small family groups similar to human nuclear and extended families. From observation they have learned what seeds and fruits peccaries eat, and recent evidence of such feeding or other spoor, such as still-muddy footprints, is impetus for the hunter to leave the trail and explore the neighborhood. If spoor is old, no one bothers because peccaries are always on the move. A wounded peccary may charge a hunter, as happened to Julio's father, who was badly bitten in the leg but recovered.

Other large mammals are desirable but rare, including white-lipped peccary, spectacled bear, deer, great anteater, sloth, and tapir. Of these, I have seen only white-lipped peccary, deer, and tapir roasting over the fire. But men have stories to tell of their own or their relatives' encounters with the other large game in the past. They have a good idea of what these animals look like, the sounds they make, their feeding habits, and the dangers they pose to a careless hunter. My sense is that a man could go through life without killing some of these animals but that he is bound to come across their spoor, have encounters with some, and perhaps enjoy their meat as a gift from another hunter.

Monkeys, especially *osheto,* "spider monkey," are also desirable, inferior to peccary only because they provide less meat. Spider monkeys feed on fruits and seeds in the forest canopy, the falling waste a clue to their presence. When they spot hunters below, they flee at great speed, and it is difficult to keep up with them on the ground. An equally large but less favored monkey is *yaniri,* "howler monkey." In contrast to the spider monkey, the howler, a leaf eater, moves sluggishly in the trees, and it thus has a reputation as lazy *(peranti);* it even sits still and peers down at hunters who are taking aim, only moving off slowly after the first arrow is released. But the Matsigenka of Shimaa complain that its meat has an unpalatable smell and can cause indigestion. The male also has the reputation of being a shaman. Many people, but by no means all, refuse to eat its flesh.

Fowl are also highly desirable game, less subject to food restrictions than most others. Frequently, guan, curassow, and tinamou are flushed during hunts, as are less common fowl like heron, egret, trumpeter, and cock-of-the-rock. Although most arrows miss their mark, over the course of a year these fowl provide about as much meat as monkeys do. A number of small mammals are also known to exist in the forest but are rarely seen: armadillo, squirrel, paca, agouti, and tayra.

A man's average daily allocation of time to hunting is less than forty-five minutes, but most hunting is done on dedicated trips every few days. The hunting party is usually small, one or two men with a boy to serve as bearer. Starting in the mist of early morning, they strike out on a main trail that will take them far from the crowded vicinity of Shimaa. Owing to game depletion in the vicinity of Shimaa, for perhaps two hours they are far from stealthy, crashing through underbrush, talking, joking, and singing as much as the strenuous pace of the march permits. Once beyond the depleted zone, hunters become more earnest. Alert to their surroundings, employing sight, smell, and sound, they pick up cues to the presence of game and other wild foods.

Hunters always pause to collect whatever food presents itself: insect larvae, bird nests, ripe fruit, palm hearts. For this reason a hunter leaves home equipped for generalized food getting (figure 8). In addition to his bow, he carries ten or twelve arrows of various types: broad-bladed bamboo-tipped arrows for large game, jagged-edged palm-wood-tipped ones for monkeys and large fowl, and knob-headed ones for smaller birds. Around his neck he drapes a length of sturdy cord, looped like a many-stranded necklace, that he can wrap around his ankles to help him scale trees. Across his shoulder is a net carrying bag and in it a broad knife for lopping off branches full of fruit or felling palm trees to get at their fruit and hearts. Thus outfitted, he can hunt every animal he encounters and collect all but the least accessible wild fruits, nuts, insects, and vegetables the forest has to offer.

In addition to hunting trips, other techniques are commonly used to bag game. Hunting blinds may be placed in trees (*kutorintsi,* intended for birds) or alongside trails (*mankorarintsi,* intended for mammals). It

FIGURE 8. Omenko with bow and arrows.

is also common to set snares *(iviri)* in the forest in the vicinity of the homestead. These are of two types. *Tameshirintsi* consists of one or more twine nooses draped between two tightly strung, adjacent horizontal cords, between either two stakes straddling a trail or two upright twigs on a branch. A bird running along the trail or landing on the branch to peck at fruit will run its head into the noose, which will tighten as it struggles. *Samogarintsi* is a noose tied to the end of a bent sapling and tripped by an animal attracted to the bait in the center of the noose. Both types of snare can be made in smaller or larger versions, depending on the size of the game being sought.

Finally, boys and some men always keep a slingshot with them. Most common is the Y-slingshot with a rubber sling *(konoritsa)*. While sitting idly alone or with companions, they practice with stones against nearby targets. On trails or in gardens, they take potshots at whatever birds they see, occasionally hitting them. At night, men take a flashlight (when they can get one) and stalk birds in fruit trees in the house garden. Many men also know how to make a bola-type slingshot *(varakatsa)*, but I have not seen it in use.

Because I owned a shotgun, I was an attractive hunting partner, but my shortcomings in skill and endurance certainly affected the strategy of the hunt, and the shotgun affected the outcome. There were two other shotguns in the vicinity of Shimaa, and most of the larger game in my records were killed by shotgun: eleven of eleven monkeys, seventeen of twenty fowl, eleven of twelve peccary, and one of two tapir. Altogether, shotguns brought in about 80 percent of all large game animals I knew of. Yet of the thirteen households in the time-allocation sample, none owned a shotgun. As my fieldwork progressed, I came to feel that I, as an outsider, had no business killing animals in the rainforest, and Maestro took over use of my shotgun.

My best estimate is that the supply of meat from hunting for the average household in Shimaa during the period of my study amounted to only about 16 kilograms per year (dressed weight), or about 0.2 kilograms per person per month (equivalent to two or three hamburgers). Our frequent visits to households during the time-allocation observations established that meat was only occasionally present, and this finding was confirmed during the periods when we lived in Felipe's downstream household for periods of time. In all households, meat was treated like a precious commodity to be eaten in tiny portions, so that even a spider monkey yielding five kilograms of edible meat could last a family of seven for many days; it was smoked over the fire and doled out in nibbles with each meal.

Men speak with nostalgia of the pre-school past when the big three —peccary, spider monkey, and guan—were common. They blame the shotgun hunter Italiano, from the farthest downstream hamlet, for scaring off the game. This is one example of a number of similar explanations of resource scarcity that emphasize the agency of the resources (animals are scared) rather than overuse by humans (animals have been hunted out). The explanations do not take into account that local human population density is much greater and residence more permanent than in the past or that the shotgun is much more effective than the bow and arrow once game have been sighted.

Hunting returns are so meager they sometimes seem hardly worth the effort, but they are not the only rewards of hunting trips. For those who know where to look, the forest is a storehouse of desirable foods, and a hunter's return at day's end is anticipated with excitement by his family, even if he has bagged no game. Whole families often spend the day in the forest, collecting rather than hunting. A man brings his bow and arrows and may have snares in the area that he checks, but the goal of such trips is to locate seasonal sources of wild food and to draw on the labor of the whole family to harvest as much of this supply as possible before another family shows up on the scene and, courteously but inevitably, joins the harvest.

The three main collected foods by quantity are larvae, palm hearts, and fruits/seeds. Of these, the most important nutritionally are caterpillars (larvae of butterflies and moths) and grubs (larvae of beetles). The Matsigenka distinguish at least forty-six different caterpillars, each of which tends to be abundant for a week or two, especially during April and May, sometimes in groups of many hundreds clustered together on a tree or marching in columns along the forest floor. Grubs are the larvae of beetles that live inside trees and eat bark and wood. Grubs have soft, white, corrugated bodies with a small brown head. The largest grubs, *pagiri,* are six centimeters long and weigh ten to fifteen grams. They can be found in rotten logs that can be detected by a foul odor from ten or twenty meters away by a forager walking a forest path. Smaller grubs are found in living trees, sugar cane, and *caña brava* (uva grass). The Matsigenka distinguish nine such grubs, varying greatly in size from *pagiri* down to *tegyoki,* which are less than two centimeters long and weigh only a third of a gram; they may be eaten raw or boiled.

Other insects make a minor contribution to the diet. Adults and children fish a termite hill with a blade of grass moistened with saliva, either eating the termites raw or taking them home to share (figure 9). Of particular interest are the tiny larvae, *kaun,* which weigh only about 0.1 gram apiece but can be raised in large quantities in the fibrous mash that remains after manioc beer is strained. Kept in a trough or gourd, after a week the swarming *kaun* can be harvested and served as a side dish with manioc, a practice that blurs the boundary between wild and

FIGURE 9. Rosa termite fishing with her son,
Apa, and her infant daughter.

domesticated food. Other consumption of insects occurs opportunistically. Children use brooms to bat down swarming butterflies and eat
them on the spot. Most often, when an edible insect is found, it is eaten
immediately as a between-meal snack. Altogether, insects add up to a
significant dietary contribution, nearly twice as much as game at thirty
kilograms per household per year.

The second main source of collected foods is heart of palm, the ten-
der white shoot at the top of the tree that will become its next leaf. Palm
hearts weigh up to one kilogram and together add nearly sixty kilograms of vegetable food to the household diet each year. Whenever a
palm is felled to supply raw materials for manufacture, its heart is removed and saved for a family meal. But foragers frequently fell a palm
tree only for its heart and leave the tree to rot even though the men at

TABLE 14. Foraging Returns, Average Household, Shimaa, 1972–73

Source	Kilograms/ Year	Kilocalories/ Kilogram	Kilocalories/ Year
Game	15.8	1.93	30.5
Insects	30.3	0.93	28.2
Palm heart	59.0	0.26	15.3
Fruit	82.0	0.76	62.3
Nuts	7.0	4.96	34.7
TOTAL	194.1		171.0

Shimaa continually complained about the scarcity of palms for their various construction needs. Such waste may have been less costly when families lived as scattered homesteads and hamlets. But the Matsigenka have not yet conceptualized the need for resource conservation, and the old practices can be devastating in multifamily settlements like the school communities (Johnson 1989).

Many other fruits and vegetables appear in the forest at different times of the year. Most common are sweet or sweet-sour fruits and palm fruits. When fruits are in season, families frequently return from foraging with their net carrying bags (tseoki) stretched to capacity. Palm fruits come in many varieties, several of which are like coconuts in that they have hard shells containing a milky liquid and a white edible meat. Mostly consumed opportunistically as snacks, they can form the basis of a soup for the whole family when they are available in large quantities. Apart from the occasional walnut and seeds that may be consumed in the course of eating fruit, other nuts and seeds play almost no role in the Matsigenka diet. A household consumes nearly ninety kilograms of wild fruits and vegetables each year, of which only seven kilograms are nuts and seeds (table 14).

Altogether an average household takes in a total of 194 kilograms of foraged foods in a year, or about 30 kilograms for each member, well under a kilo a week. Although game, insects, and nuts are nutritionally rich, the whole package of foraged foods provides a household with only about 75 percent of the energy they expend in getting it, perhaps the lowest returns found among any Amazonian peoples (Hames 1988: 55). It is not calories that the Matsigenka seek from foraged foods but good taste, which is most probably provided by fats, protein, and general dietary diversity.

TABLE 15. Fishing Time and Yields, Average Household per Year

Method	Yield (kg/hr)	Time (%)	Hours/ Year	Total (kg/year)
Poison	0.635	43	330	210
Hand	0.228	30	230	52
Hook/line	0.136	16	123	17
Net	0.228	11	84	19
TOTAL		100	767	298

FISHING

Fish have a central place in Matsigenka life. When one meets a stranger, the most likely question (after the obligatory *ainyo piniro,* "Is there your mother?") is, "Are there fish in the river where you live?" The name of the Río Shimaa itself derives from *shima* (boquichico, *Pruchilodus nigricans*), the most common fish in the Matsigenka diet. The most common methods are poison, net, hook-and-line, and hand fishing. Poison fishing is much more productive than the other methods, but the methods are complementary rather than competitive and together make full use of meager resources (table 15).

Fish poisoning employs two cultigens of the general class known as *barbasco: kogi* (*Lonchocarpus* sp.) and *kogi kiripeshianiri* (*Tephrosia toxicaria*). When crushed, their roots release into the water poisons (primarily rotenone) that stun the fish and inhibit their ability to breathe; they then float or swim dazedly along the surface. Although lethal to humans when ingested in concentrated amounts—*kogi* was reportedly used in one Matsigenka suicide attempt—it is harmless when used in fishing.

In the selva alta, the swift rivers require dams to slow the current if barbasco is to be effective. The usual method is to locate a channel partially separated from the rest of the river by a sand bar (figure 10a). Men build a log dam upstream from the sandbar, to divert the strong current away from the channel, and a second dam of logs, dirt, and leaves running from the riverbank to the upstream end of the sand bar to slow the water to a trickle. The crushed barbasco roots are washed in the trickle and as the milky poison spreads downstream, stunned fish begin to surface and are easily collected.

Meanwhile, at the downstream end of the channel, women begin work on their own dam. When the water has been slowed, it is enough for the women to use small rocks, dirt, and leaves to channel the remaining water in the stream toward a mid-point where they place a

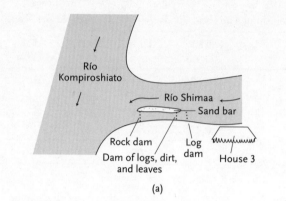

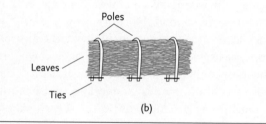

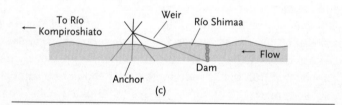

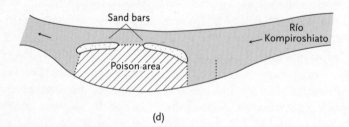

FIGURE 10. Poison-fishing dams and weirs. *(a)* Single-family effort. *(b)* Caña brava mat for dam. *(c)* Río Shimaa weir, April 19, 1973. *(d)* Río Kompiroshiato, July 26, 1975.

FIGURE 11. Weir under construction for Río Shimaa poison fishing, April 19, 1973.

woman's net and gather the stunned fish that drift into it. Owing to this division of labor by sex, the upstream end of the channel is all men and boys, while the downstream end is all women and girls.

After the introduction of the poison the men spread out downstream as the women move upstream. As the two groups intermingle, households aggregate out of the flux, each focusing on a different section of the channel. Families may share their catch with other families, but there is no guarantee that the take of fish will be proportional to the amount of labor individuals contribute to the project. Afterward, neighboring households gather for communal meals so that everyone gets to eat, regardless of effort.

Building a dam is heavy work. Few natural channels in the river are small enough to be exploited by a single family, so barbasco fishing fosters multihousehold cooperation, the largest cooperative ventures I observed in Shimaa. Because of the need for coordination, barbasco fishing also calls forth an unusual degree of leadership. The need for leadership, and its limits, were illustrated in one major venture that went seriously awry. In 1973 Maestro conceived a bold plan to construct a weir of rushes in three sections that, when installed side by side, would be wide enough to span the entire Río Shimaa near its mouth (figure 10c, figure 11). The idea was to introduce barbasco about a kilometer upstream from the weir and harvest the whole stretch of river in one fell swoop, a technique once observed by Farabee (1922: 4–5). To this end, from four to thirteen men had been up at various hours of the night pounding twenty kilograms of barbasco roots into a coarse mash, at the rate of about one hard pounding hour of work per kilo. But the men who packed the mashed roots upstream failed to wait for Maestro's signal that the weirs were ready, and they poisoned the stream too soon. It would have been a rich harvest, but instead the bulk of the stunned fish were swept away downstream through an uncompleted portion of the weir and were lost. The effort nevertheless paid off with a good yield of 1.3 kilograms of fish per hour of labor, yet such a scale of organization was clearly beyond the collaborative skills of the participants.

The largest cooperative effort I observed was a barbasco-fishing expedition in 1975 (figure 10d). Only about two years after the attempt described above, the expedition yielded just 4 percent as much fish per hour of labor. The main difference was the depletion of fish through continuous barbasco fishing over the two-year period. For the river fauna, a barbasco expedition is a catastrophe from which it requires months, if not years, to recover. By stepping up the pressure with frequent use of barbasco, the Matsigenka were depleting all the available fishing opportunities in the vicinity of Shimaa. We know from Baksh's (1995: 192) careful studies at Camaná that this process is inevitable in this region wherever there are permanent settlements and populations larger than an extended-family hamlet. As with hunting depletion, however, the Matsigenka explanation is that the fish are "hiding."

Net fishing is complementary in that it takes advantage of the muddy turbulence following heavy rain, when poison fishing is impossible and the fish cannot see or hear the net coming. Men and women use different nets and techniques. The men's net, *kitsari,* is a broad rectangular net strung between two poles that a man holds in front of himself as he works alone waist deep against the current, scooping his net upstream against the bottom then up to the surface. The women's net, *shiriti,* is smaller and round. A woman uses it in shallow water and works close to the bottom, usually in tandem with children or other women who walk backward upstream from her, loosening rocks and sending the creatures hidden around them scurrying, to be carried into the net by the current.

The remainder of fishing time is split between hand and hook-and-line fishing. The method of hand fishing is to prowl close to shore in muddy, turbulent water, feeling for small fish and water creatures around and under rocks. It requires no equipment and is a frequent occupation of children and adults during or after rain. Although the yields are low, the effort is rarely without some reward. Hook-and-line fishing occupies only about 16 percent of fishing time, and its yields are poor. Like net and hand fishing, however, it remains relatively popular because it occupies a niche of time that is not filled with other food-procurement strategies. Line fishing generally exploits the main current of the river unsuitable for other methods and is a relaxed sort of fishing one can combine with bathing to end the day on a pleasant note.

Fishing with dynamite was common downriver along the Urubamba River, but was new in Shimaa when Maestro used it several times during the month of September 1972. At first his yields were good, forty or fifty fish at once. But by the end of the month his last two ventures with dynamite brought in two fish and no fish, respectively. Again, the explanation was that the fish were hiding.

RAISING DOMESTIC ANIMALS

Domesticated animals are minor in the household economy in Shimaa, and they probably played an even smaller role in the past. Many households raised a few chickens *(ataava)* and Muscovy ducks *(pandyo)*, but because many others did not, the average numbers per household were 5.5 chickens and 1.0 duck, including chicks and ducklings. Fowl are allowed to forage for insects and seeds in the vicinity of the household during the day and are fed an ear or two of maize in season. At night they are protected in chicken coops that are frequently broken into by wildcats or, perhaps, humans. The labor involved is minimal and is usually handled by a child.

Dogs *(otsiti)* and cats *(mishi)* were occasionally brought into the community during 1972–73, but all died despite affectionate care. The cats had an unfortunate tendency to eat a kind of lizard that left them paralyzed, and the one dog was bitten by a wildcat and died after Maestro applied insecticide to the wound to keep the flies off. In other Matsigenka settlements we saw parrots and monkeys that were leashed and appeared tame, but in Shimaa only Kasimira kept pets, two wrenlike birds with clipped wings that flew in and out of her house freely and were handled affectionately by all members of the household. Perched on a rafter or outside in the papaya tree, they sang different songs, often simultaneously. By December 1974 she had also managed to raise the first litter of kittens in Shimaa.

Food Preparation and Consumption

Matsigenkas eat many foods raw, especially on collecting trips and while hand fishing. Most of the diet, however, is made up of starchy staples that must be cooked. Every married woman and every grown woman with children has her own hearth. It is very much her center of operations, and her young children stay in close orbit around it. The hearth, especially when inside the house, is kept going almost constantly, although it may be banked when the woman plans to be away for most of the day. A woman can restore a fire from embers even after several days, and although today they prefer matches, most Matsigenka men still know how to make a fire with sparks from striking rocks together or by means of a fire drill. The Matsigenka hearth is simply a place on the floor, perhaps slightly hollowed out and ringed with stones, where the fire is built. The fire itself (tsitsi) is in a star pattern, with logs pointed toward the fire in the center. Building and maintaining a good fire is a true art, requiring knowledge of the burning properties of different woods and of how to maneuver logs and kindling to attain the desired heat.

Notwithstanding the surrounding forest, maintaining a supply of firewood is a constant chore, one that gets progressively more difficult the longer a household remains in one location. Each day an average household needs about 0.15 cubic meters of large logs (about twenty centimeters in diameter), and another 0.05 cubic meters of small branches to do all its cooking. Ideally, a household obtains firewood from unburned logs in its surrounding gardens. At first, appropriate pieces are close at hand, but rather soon the choice becomes whether to range farther from the house to drag back heavy wood or to begin to chop up the larger trunks close to home. Since either alternative involves additional work, the longer the residence is in one place, the greater the cost of obtaining firewood. By 1972 firewood was periodically scarce near the school community. We begged men to help us get firewood but still fell short of our needs because they, too, were having difficulties.

Men butcher the large animals like tapirs and peccaries, but women tend to skin monkeys, pluck fowl, clean fish and caterpillars, and remove the husks, skins, and seeds from fruits and vegetables. Most commonly they boil foods in an aluminum pot without seasonings; if it is an animal, they retain the broth to be served as a soup dotted with droplets of fat and pervaded by the flavor of the animal. Women also occasionally boil a pot of red peppers along with wild and cultivated vegetables or make a sticky soup by boiling plantains together with some fish.

Other common methods of preparation include roasting directly in the coals—which imparts an entirely different flavor and may add a helpful dose of ash to the diet (Ohno and Erich 1990; cf. Mertz 1981)—and steaming foods like larvae and fish in their own juices by wrapping them in banana leaves or corn husks and placing them in the coals. Finally, when the harvest of fish or game is abundant, meat is smoked slowly on a babracot over a smoldering fire for several days until finished; the urge to snack on these delicacies between meals is strong and must be controlled to preserve the harmony of the household.

Women spend significant time preparing manioc beer. They begin by placing ears of maize in a stream for a few days until the kernels begin to sprout, which, as Eva explained, "sweetens it for beer" *(opochati ashi shitea);* adding mashed sweet potato also helps start the fermentation process. Matsigenka brewers do not usually chew and spit manioc into the pot to add saliva enzymes for fermentation, but they are familiar with the technique, and Orna Johnson has seen them use it when maize is unavailable. The fermentation underway, they boil and mash quantities of manioc, mix it with water in the large canoe-shaped trough found in every home, and strain the coarse mash through a plaited strainer, setting the fibrous residue aside. Children sometimes suck on the residue without swallowing it, but its main value is as a breeding place for the edible larvae, *kaun.* The strained liquid, the consistency of buttermilk, is then covered with banana leaves and left to ferment. Initially fresh and sweet tasting, the fermenting liquid becomes progressively more sour *(kacho)* as its alcohol content rises; it also becomes lightly carbonated. I would guess that a medium-strong manioc beer, fermented about two days, has an alcohol content in the 4 to 6 percent range. The labor cost of brewing beer, not counting the harvest of manioc, is about fifteen minutes per liter (O. Johnson 1978: 60).

Children spend about 15 percent of their daylight hours eating, but by the time they become adults this number falls below 10 percent. Snacking can take place at any time. Children left alone pop and eat popcorn or warm manioc left from breakfast; on rainy days the whole family works near the fire and snacks on ears of roasted corn or caterpillars; late at night someone may heat up food left over from dinner; and, of course, foragers help themselves to portions of whatever they find in the field.

The whole family commonly eats a meal together at around seven in the morning and again in mid or late afternoon. These meals consist most often of manioc and, when available, meat, fish, or grubs in small quantities. When animal food is not available to garnish the manioc, the Matsigenka consider the meal boring and apologize for it to a guest. Baksh (1984: 67) found that when there is no meat, the Matsigenka at Camaná eat less manioc and increase their consumption of beer. Typically, an abundant food like manioc is eaten at will, but special foods like meat or grubs are centrally distributed by household heads to ensure that everyone gets an equal portion.

When the households of a hamlet gather to share a special food like fish, they separate into men's and women's groups. The husband of the host family distributes the fish to the men and older boys, while the wife distributes to the women, girls, and young boys. They are quite careful to give out equal portions, even of the broth. Once the meal is over, there is some shifting of seating mats so that, just as in group fishing, sex segregation lasts only during the communal phase of the activity, then evaporates as individual families reform (Johnson 1980). After the meal, guests may stay on into the evening, chatting and telling stories.

After a period of adjustment of several weeks, I came to enjoy Matsigenka food. With salt scarce I had to allow my palate time to become sensitive to the natural flavors. Once accustomed to the lack of spices, I discovered that the natural flavor of the fish or meat was satisfying in itself. Several varieties of maize were so sweet that the cob itself was sweet, and people chewed it to a pulp before discarding it. Manioc, when prepared well, is a fine staple food. A single portion of meat for a meal would be no larger than I was used to eating in one mouthful, but I learned to break off tiny pieces to eat with each bite of manioc.

Dependent as they are on the bounty of nature, the Matsigenka enjoy a constantly varying supply of wild foods. Just when they seem about to run out of everything interesting, something new comes into season. The great diversity of foods, a tendency to eat even tough, dry, bony and crunchy parts, and the regular addition of dirt and ash make it highly unlikely that any specific nutritional deficiencies could occur. Only manioc beer, made by the women, seemed too scarce to please the men, while everyone would have been delighted to have more meat.

Analysis of Matsigenka food production shows it to be an ample source of a well-balanced diet (Johnson and Behrens 1982: 178; Baksh 1984: 380–93). In table 16, the last column compares the nutritional needs of a household with the nutrients available to it. It shows that the Matsigenka produce an abundance of every nutrient listed, generally about three times the recommended allowance. Their overall health (see later in this chapter) also indicates that malnutrition is rarely a problem.

TABLE 16. Comparison of Nutrients Produced and Nutritional Requirements, Average Household per Year

(1) Nutrient	(2) Foraging (194 kg/year)	(3) Fishing (298 kg/year)	(4) Farming (9,800 kg/year)	(5) Total Produced (10,292 kg/year)	(6) Recommended	(7) Produced/ Recommended: (5) ÷ (6) [a] (%)
Calories (kcal)	171	301	13,034	13,506	4,541	297%
Protein (g)	10,670	55,342	147,000	213,012	66,978	318
Calcium (mg)	114,460	59,600	3,528,000	3,702,060	2,044,000	181
Phosphorus (mg)	141,620	536,400	4,802,000	5,480,020	2,044,000	268
Iron (mg)	2,910	2,086	127,400	132,396	37,230	356
Vitamin A (retinol equivalent; mg)	203,700	0	1,862,000	2,065,700	1,700,900	121
Thiamine (mg)	175	89	6,860	7,124	2,190	325
Riboflavin (mg)	155	238	3,920	4,313	2,592	166
Niacin (mg)	2,910	8,940	58,800	70,650	28,762	246
Vitamin C (mg)	67,900	0	2,058,000	2,125,900	124,100	1,713

SOURCE: Johnson and Behrens 1982: 178.

[a] Amount produced as percentage of recommended allowance.

Manufacture

Barely participating in the market economy, the Matsigenka of Shimaa in 1972–73 made nearly all the material items they used in their daily lives, the notable exceptions being knives of various sizes and aluminum pots. Although they are skilled at making what they need and take pride in well-fashioned products, the skill involved is not beyond an ordinary person's capacity with practice and some guidance. A complementary distribution of skills between males and females ensures that a married couple can be self-sufficient, capable of long-term isolation without lacking essential technology.

POSSESSIONS

Matsigenkas keep careful track of their possessions (table 17). Those they do not manufacture themselves they receive as gifts from friends and relatives. A few items did not appear in our surveys. These included the assistant schoolteacher's broken shotgun; a portable record player acquired by Maestro during our first year of research; notebooks, textbooks, pencils, and paper belonging to some of the schoolchildren; Peruvian currency; slingshots; and flutes. There may also have been ritual paraphernalia like the sorcerer's stone *(serepitontsi)* that people would not have admitted to owning.

MATERIALS

Aside from food, the most important items in the Matsigenka environment are raw materials *(ovetsikantaganirira)*, especially woods, canes, and fibers; animal parts are rarely used, except for hides used in drumheads and teeth and bones used in necklaces and ornaments.

Palms are the most widely useful of all raw materials. There is no general term for palm, although the name of one, *kamona (Iriartea exhorriza)*, sometimes refers to several similar palms that provide hardwood and have edible palm hearts. But each palm is known specifically and in detail for uses as summarized in table 18. Trunks serve as house posts and beams; leaves provide roofing and strips for plaiting; hardwoods are used for bows, arrowheads, and spindles; and palm hearts, fruits, and seeds make a significant contribution to the diet. Although palms may serve many purposes, there is generally a preferred palm for any given use: *kapashi* for roofing leaves, *kuri* for bows and arrowheads, *sega* for

TABLE 17. Matsigenkas' Possessions

Almost Every Man	Almost Every Woman
Cushma	Cushma
Shorts *	Shorts *
Needles */thread	Aluminum pots *
Achiote face paint	Achiote face paint
Machete *	Kitchen knife *
Fishhooks */line *	Baby sling
Bow and arrows	Shoulder ornaments
Digging stick	Cane boxes
	Gourd bowls

Most Men	Most Women
Net carrying bag	Spinning/weaving set-up
Cloth carrying bag	Plates *
Kitchen knife *	Spoons *
Shirt *	Needles */thread
Coca	
Flashlight *	
Panpipes	

Some Men	Some Women
Axe *	Women's fishnet
Pants *	Net carrying bag
Woven wristbands	Woven wristbands
Climbing rope	Grinding board and stone
Mirror *	Dress *
Broad knife *	
Scissors *	
Traps	
Oar	
Soap *	
Drum	
Matches *	
Gourd bowl	

Few Men	Few Women
Men's fishnet	Mirror *
Beads	Sewing machine * (1)
Feather headband	Shoes/sandals *
Balsa raft	Beer trough
Shoes *	
Pocketknife *	

* Items the Matsigenka do not themselves manufacture.

TABLE 18. Palms Used in Manufacture

Matsigenka Name	Scientific Name	1	2	3	4	5	6	7	8	9	10	11	12	13
chorina	*Euterpe ensiformis, E. precatoria*	✓	✓	✓			✓			✓	✓		✓	
kamona	*Iriartea exorrhiza*	✓	✓	✓	✓	✓	✓	✓				✓	✓	
kapashi	*Hyospathe tessmannii*			✓				✓					✓	
kompiro	*Phytelephas microcarpa*			✓						✓			✓	✓
kontiri	*Iriartea* sp.		✓		✓	✓		✓					✓	
kuri	*Bactris ciliata, B. gasipaes*						✓	✓			✓	✓	✓	✓
manataro	*Bactris chaetochlamys*						✓						✓	
sega	*Jessenia bataua*			✓					✓	✓		✓	✓	
tiroti	*Oenocarpus multicaulis*	✓						✓		✓				
tsigaro	*Scheelea cephalotes*			✓					✓				✓	

SOURCES: For identifications, see MacBride 1960; Henderson 1995; and also Ferreyra 1970.

1. House post	6. Bow
2. House beam	7. Arrowhead
3. Roofing	8. Mats
4. Wall slats	9. Basket/sieve
5. Flooring	10. Spindle

11. Batten
12. Edible heart
13. Edible fruit/seed

seating mats. Because these trees are planted in gardens only rarely (cf. Balée 1988), they must be found in the forest, and shortages arise almost immediately in the vicinity of a new settlement.

Apart from palms, a few hardwood species like walnut (*Juglans neotropica*) and *kamuia* (Rubinacea) supply most other household needs for wood. The main uses are for house posts and beams; planks for doors, mortars, and oars; and trunks for beer troughs and canoes. Caña brava (*Gynerium sagittatum*, uva grass), a large, sturdy cane that grows wild in stands along the river, is a main source of poles for walls, rafters, and temporary shelters; its cousin, arrow reed (*Gynerium saccharoides*), is a slender cane sometimes cultivated in gardens as shafts for arrows (cf. Rutter 1990: 103).

The most important fiber is a cultigen, *tivana* (*Bromelia* sp.), which is processed into twine for nets and traps. Other wild fibers are extracted from bark and used in bowstrings (*tamarotsa*, *Cecropia* sp.) and lashings (balsa, *Ochroma lagopus*, and *pashirokitsa*, *Trema micanthra*). Because the only nails the Matsigenka have are the palm-wood spikes they use to build balsa rafts, lashing is the main method by which manufactures are held together. Much of the maintenance work needed on older houses is repairing worn lashings.

MEN'S PRODUCTS

In all areas of activity there is a sharp differentiation between what women and men do. These differences are recognized in the sense that questions like *tatoita ovetsikakero tsinani* ("What do women make?") elicit specific activities with high reliability. Men's manufacturing time is dominated by four products: *tivana* twine and netting (34 percent), wood products (e.g., drums, spindles, beer troughs, and balsa rafts; 25 percent), houses (19 percent), and bows and arrows (10 percent). So clear is the division of labor by sex that men spend 88 percent of their manufacturing time on these tasks compared with 1 percent for women.

The Matsigenka bow is of medium size and is made from *kuri*. This wood is much too hard to drive a nail into and rarely splinters. Unless a man has a *kuri* palm growing in his garden, as some men do, he must locate a tree in the forest of perhaps 25 centimeters in diameter, from which, using an axe or machete, he can extract a few planks 3 centimeters thick, 4 centimeters wide, and 150 centimeters long. He may also take a few smaller pieces of the palm for manufacturing arrowheads, but, unless he is collaborating with other men (which is unlikely), he leaves the greater part of the trunk to rot in the forest.

Using a machete, he roughly shapes the bow, then uses a knife as a scraper to give the bow its final shape: broader at the handgrip in the middle (2.5 to 4.0 centimeters), narrowing to the nocks at the ends (1.0 to 1.3 centimeters). When unstrung, the bow is perfectly straight and of a uniform thickness (0.5 to 0.65 centimeters) along its length (115 to 135 centimeters), polished and well-proportioned, capable of sustaining a pull of about 25 to 30 kilograms. It does not lose its spring with time and can last up to five years without breaking.

A Matsigenka hunter needs four main kinds of arrows, all employing a shaft of arrow cane *(Gynerium saccharoides)* that is straight, about 1 centimeter in diameter, and over 110 to 120 centimeters long, often with feathers secured to the butt end (*otiokike,* "anus") with wax or pitch and thread to bind them. Viewed looking down the shaft from the butt end, the feathers spiral to the right at about a 30° angle.

The arrowhead distinguishes one Matsigenka arrow from another; it may be made of either palm wood or bamboo. Of the two basic palm-wood arrows, the palm shaft *(kurikii)*, also called spider monkey's *(irashi osheto)*, is fifty centimeters long, sharpened to a point, and serrated along its mid-section to increase the tissue damage and bleeding as the monkey tries to remove the arrow. The foreshaft is heated and rubbed with wax, jammed tightly into the forward end of the shaft, and wrapped with waxed thread. The barbed arrow *(tsegontorintsi)*, also known as guan's *(irashi kanari)*, is intended primarily for fowl. Much smaller than spider monkey's arrow, it has four barbs inserted into the shaft along with the foreshaft in order to broaden the area of damage done by the arrow and to increase the probability that a vital part of the bird will be hit.

The bamboo-tipped arrow *(kapiro)*, also known as peccary's *(irashi shintori)*, is lanceolate, sharp-edged, and broad; it is designed to do as much internal damage and to cause as much bleeding as possible. Baksh (1984: 316) reports that men believe bamboo to be naturally poisonous, and they use taste and smell to select the most venomous bamboo stalks from which to make their arrows. A piece of bamboo two centimeters wide and ten to fifteen centimeters long is shaved to a point, given sharp edges along its length, split edgewise at the butt end to admit a palm-wood foreshaft, and bound to the foreshaft by careful waxing and wrapping with thread for five centimeters.

A less common type of arrow is *tyongarintsi*, made from one of several hardwoods with a point expanding to a bulb, for stunning small birds. Of twenty arrows, only one or two will be of this type. Other uncommon arrows include a long, thin palm-wood point for shooting fish (*irashi shima*, "boquichico's"), and a detachable harpoon point *(kat-sarori)* made of *kuri* and attached to the foreshaft by twine, also used in fishing.

Every man has some knowledge of how to make bows and arrows, but in this and other areas, skill is not distributed equally and so there is some specializing and sharing (Johnson 1998). The men found it easy to distinguish their arrows from those of other men, although most could not tell me how they were different, saying simply, "He makes his arrows, and I make mine." Style differences that stand out for these experts include the length of the shaft, the color and manner of thread binding, and whether feathers are split in half or used whole; they can also distinguish bows by their size and strength. The Matsigenka of Shimaa hunt so rarely in groups that there is seldom any need to keep track of arrows to determine who killed an animal.

Time and energy measurements show that a man can make a bow and ten arrows in about one eight-hour workday (Montgomery and Johnson 1973: 6). Pope ([1923] 1974) studied a large number of native American bows and arrows, and found the bows "heavy and jarring," and the arrows wobbly. My observation of Matsigenka bow hunters does not contradict Pope's technical assessment. Their arrows tended to wobble noticeably in flight and to miss their targets most of the time. However, the men are good stalkers; by imitating calls and using forest cover as camouflage, they can get surprisingly close to game before taking a shot, often within ten meters. Ever hopeful, men take their bows and arrows with them on nearly all forest journeys. In 1972–73, bow hunters in Shimaa succeeded in bagging virtually every kind of game, including fowl, monkeys, peccaries, tapir, deer, and one puma.

Men have much need for twine. *Tivana,* the source of twine commonly used in making fishnets and net bags, is a cultigen whose long succulent leaves, similar in appearance to those of the pineapple plant, have fibers running from tip to base. With the acquired knack one can pull the fibers from the leaf cleanly in one sweeping motion, then leave the moist green pulp aside and drape the white fibers to dry for two days in strong sun. The fibers are fine but strong and may be twined by rubbing them between palm and inner thigh with a downward motion several times until tightly wound and of an even thickness of about one millimeter. The whole process of producing this single-ply twine— including harvesting, stripping, cleaning, drying, and twining—takes about twenty-five minutes per meter. Completing two-ply twine takes only an additional three minutes per meter because it involves only twining together two lengths of single-ply twine using the same palm-thigh motion. By selecting two strands of different length, a man ensures that one runs out before the other. When this happens, he frays the ends of the shorter piece and the new piece and feathers them together as he twines them with the longer piece. Repeating this step each time one strand runs out, he is able to produce a continuous twine, thin, flexible, and strong, that he winds into a ball very much like string or yarn.

The basic principle of netting is to start with a row of meshes tied by knots to a loop of twine. An additional row of meshes is then knotted onto the first row, and so on (figure 12). A man adds rows of meshes until his net is of the desired length and width. When he gets to the last row, he weaves the mesh into a tightly woven border six millimeters wide. The knots prevent the loops from slipping or separating too far. Although knotting adds a laborious step to the process, the resulting

(a) 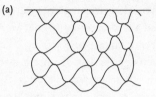 Starting thread
Row 1
Row 2
Row 3
Row 4
Etc.

(b) 1. Bring twine under knotting stick.   2. Bring loop of twine through mesh in previous row.

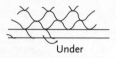 Under

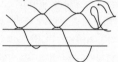

3. Start knot.   4. Pull knot tight.

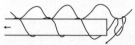

Ball of twine

Pull stick back to free knot.   Pull to tighten.

FIGURE 12. Making netting from twine. *(a)* Making a net. *(b)* Making a knot.

net will hold even small objects. The net bags have a surprising capacity, for they can stretch to hold a volume double the size they appear when empty. And, being netting, they can be crushed into a small size and easily carried out of the way until needed. It requires about fifty hours to make a man's net bag, one hundred hours to make a wide-mesh men's fishing net, and two hundred hours to make a fine-mesh women's fishing net.

In spite of their frequent moves to new settlements, the Matsigenka expend much energy building houses that are sturdy, secure, and dry, although, like many aspects of Matsigenka technology, they must be used to be fully appreciated (cf. Barriales 1977: 24). Matsigenka architecture is undoubtedly an ancient art and appears almost identical to that of related groups (Matteson 1954: 41–42).

A man begins with four corner posts of dense hardwood set in holes with dirt compacted so solidly that they cannot be budged; he uses a stone attached to twine as a plumb bob to assure that they are precisely vertical. He carves notches in the top of each post to cradle the main beams that become the two long sides of the rectangular base on which

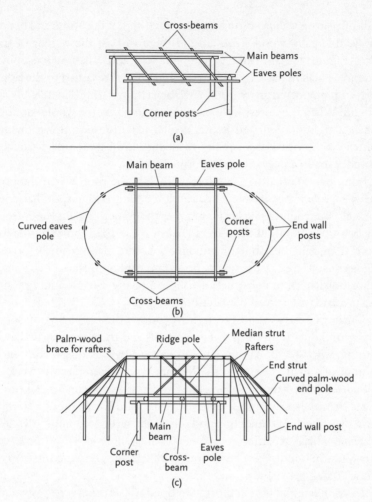

FIGURE 13. House construction. *(a)* Basic house frame. *(b)* Basic frame with rounded ends: top view. *(c)* House ready for palm-leaf roofing: side view.

the roof will ultimately rest (figure 13a), then lays three cross-beams unlashed across the main beams. At right angles to these, parallel to but outside the main beams, are two small eaves poles lashed to the cross-beams to form a rigid frame resting on the main beams. Lashed to the eaves poles and rising at a slope to the ridge pole are the rafters that will support the palm-leaf roofing. Occasionally a man stops with this basic pattern and settles for a rectangular house, but he usually adds elliptical ends by placing wall posts on a curve at each end of the house and bending flexible palm-wood strips around them to bear the weight of the rafters (figure 13b). A ridge pole, about four and a half meters above ground, is held in place by four struts, and rafters are lashed to the ridge pole and supported by a horizontal brace about three meters above ground. When the rafters have been lashed in place, the whole roof becomes a tightly integrated frame, a solid mass pressing down on the corner posts, with no possibility of being blown away or fractionally moved, even in a heavy thunderstorm (figure 13c).

Palm leaves lashed to the rafters complete the roof. When the preferred *kapashi* leaves are used, the result is a long-lasting roof that does not leak. But roofing one house requires thousands of palm leaves from perhaps three hundred palm trees (Baksh 1984: 294) and accounts for more than half the labor of building a house. Because these prized palms are scattered in the forest, providing roofing material becomes a major bottleneck in construction, and supplying a community of any size involves widespread destruction of *kapashi*.

A man can carry at most forty leaves at one time, and making some ninety round trips up steep mountain trails and then down again laden with an awkward, bulky burden of roofing leaves is one of the most arduous of a man's tasks. For the Matsigenka, it resembles the work of leaf-cutter ants tottering in long lines under leaf segments several times larger than themselves; they believe the ants are hauling leaves to roof their own dwellings underground. In more settled communities like Camaná, where depletion forced people to walk twice as far for leaves as in Shimaa, hundreds of hours were added to the construction of each house (Baksh 1984: 298).

To complete the house, most men build walls *(tantarintsi)* of palm-wood staves or caña brava poles. In the middle of one long wall they place an opening where a hardwood plank on hinges made from strips of hide or bark serves as a door *(sotsimoro)*. Some may add a raised sleeping area *(menkotsi);* flattened palm-wood planks laid over a framework of poles make a flexible, slightly bouncy floor or bed. A similar construction, but above in the cross-beams, creates a platform where a shaman does his singing.

In Shimaa in 1972 it took only 430 hours of labor to build a typical house ten meters long and five meters wide; the required time rose to 600 hours in 1973 because of the increased difficulty of obtaining roofing leaves. It usually takes more than three months to build a house, even when a man cuts back on all other activities. Mariano began his house on September 9 and had the rafters ready for roofing by September 18. But he was still roofing in November and finished his wall only in mid-December, nearly three and a half months after starting. Despite help from his brother and other family members, during this period Mariano fell far behind in his garden maintenance. This was the house his son Apa set on fire two years later (chapter 3).

The Matsigenka build simpler shelters when away from home. If caught in a rainstorm while hunting, a man cuts a few palm fronds and sticks them in the ground next to a tree to make a temporary lean-to. When his family moves to the river during the low-water season, he requires about two hours to build a more durable shelter (*savorovanko*), an A-frame of caña brava poles over which he layers a roof of caña brava leaves battened down with braces. More than a lean-to, this tent-like hut is large enough for a family, although when everyone is asleep there is no free floor space. Because it is the low-water season, a storm-proof house is not needed. The temporary residence at the river has the feel of a camp; wild foods are plentiful, and everyone tolerates with a sense of adventure the missing comforts of home.

Beyond these male-dominated activities, men do all the work with wood in Shimaa. At beer feasts, men pass the time making drums and drumsticks or fashioning toys. They make a balsa raft in less than an hour by felling a balsa tree, stripping the bark, and using palm-wood spikes and balsa lashing to bind the logs together. Such a raft, made of green balsa, is slow and heavy and rides low in the water; allowed to dry a few days, it becomes a light, high-floating raft. A few men have made dugout canoes (*pitotsi*), but, because of the arduous shaping required and the problems posed by swift, rocky mountain streams, most use rafts.

WOMEN'S PRODUCTS

Women's manufacturing is dominated by a single activity, the making of cloth. The Matsigenka grow their own cotton, an activity in which both men and women participate, but women tend to harvest it and prepare it for spinning by removing seeds and carding. Using a palm-wood spindle (made by men) set in a clay base (made by women), a woman twirls with her right hand while feeding cotton with her left. As thread accumulates, she rolls it into a ball. When she has two softball-sized balls of thread, she takes both and spins them into a two-ply thread to be used for weaving. Spinning cotton accounts for half of the work associated with cloth.

FIGURE 14. Setting up a loom. Although herself a mother of two children, the daughter *(left)* still seeks her mother's advice. (Thread provided by O. Johnson.)

Weaving is a skill for which women are greatly admired. The tool is the backstrap loom (Rowe 1977; Baksh 1984: 305). The warp is laid out by winding a continuous ball of thread in a figure-eight pattern around stakes set in the ground and attached to loom bars at each end, the far one being tied to a house beam, the near one attached to a strap around the weaver's waist (figure 14). Using a batten made of polished palm wood, the woman beats the weft into place across the warp. Stripes and small checkerboard patterns, made of variously dyed thread, are built into the design when the loom is set up. The quality of the finished cloth depends on how evenly the thread has been spun, the care with which the loom is set up, and the evenness with which tension is maintained by the weaver's leaning backward or forward while working.

A woman acquires the skill through years of collaboration with her mother; it is not uncommon to see a grown woman with children of her own turn to her mother for advice in setting up the loom or in determining the design for the weave. Some young women who do not know how to weave are regarded as lazy and less desirable as wives. Other girls already know the rudiments of spinning by age eight and produce a coarse cotton string that will find some use in the household.

Women in Shimaa on average spend over an hour and a half per day making cloth, both spinning and weaving. Spinning occupies a woman in times that might otherwise be considered leisure, much like knitting does for women elsewhere. Weaving is more demanding work. Sometimes, two women set up their looms facing one another in the same house for companionship during the long hours of repetitive labor. Orna Johnson (1978: 188) estimates ten weeks of spinning and three weeks of weaving to make a cushma (cotton gown, *manchakintsi*), about 120 hours of work. By this estimate a cushma costs at least one-fourth as much as a new house. No wonder when Western clothing becomes available, Matsigenkas eagerly seek to obtain it.

The cushma is the main goal of cloth making. Everyone in the family requires at least one, and the desirable state is to have three: an everyday cushma that is not torn, frayed, or worn through; an old, ragged one used for heavy or dirty work, and a brand-new one to be worn only on special occasions, like beer feasts. In a large family, a woman must make cloth manufacture a major commitment. She is always spinning, always weaving, and each family member knows where he or she stands in the line waiting to receive the next cushma. Although children's cushmas are easier to make than adults' because they require less cloth, if a woman has a large family with older children in it, younger children may have to go naked or wear mended hand-me-downs because their overburdened mother cannot get out from under the backlog of demand from the older members of her family.

Baby slings *(tsagomburontsi)*, cloth bags *(tsagi)*, and other small items take up the remaining 20 percent of a woman's cloth-making time. Like cushmas, these smaller items are always decorated with simple linear patterns. Making these designs requires considerable skill, and women peer closely at the designs in other women's cushmas, curious about the details.

Cloth manufacture altogether occupies three-fourths of a woman's manufacturing time. The remaining fourth of her time is split between plaiting, beadwork, and other activities like mending torn or broken items and making gourd bowls and face paint. Plaiting includes making items woven from palm leaves and cane strips, including sitting mats *(shitatsi)*, sieves *(tsiveta)*, and baskets *(morinto, tsimenkorita)*. Women also plait sieves for straining the fibers out of manioc beer, and baskets with lids for storing spinning materials and a few other possessions. Sitting mats wear out after a few months but are easy to make; the other items may last for years, so their manufacture is an occasional, not a regular, activity.

TABLE 19. Division of Labor by Sex: Manufacture
Minutes per Day

Product	Adult Men	Adult Women
Cotton cloth	1.5	103
Plaited items	0	13
Beadwork	1.5	8
Twine/netting	31	2
Wooden artifacts	31	3
Houses	47	1
Bows and arrows	9	1
Other	6	7
TOTAL	127	138

NOTE: Totals differ slightly from those in table 2 because of small differences in the method of calculation.

The division of labor by sex is summarized in table 19. In those tasks associated with women, women spend 124 minutes per day compared with 3 for men, whereas in those associated with men, men spend 118 minutes per day compared with 7 for women. These numbers emphasize how much a marriage is a joining of two half-skilled partners to create a fully skilled team.

Input-Output: Household Self-Sufficiency

Elsewhere (Johnson 1999a) I have explored in quantitative detail the question of the degree to which an average Matsigenka household—essentially a monogamous nuclear family living together under one roof—can supply its own needs from its own efforts. Answering this question is fundamental to appreciating both how and why the Matsigenka live at the family level of sociocultural integration. Figure 15 describes the flow of energy expended by members of an average downstream household in the course of their daily living. The numbers are actual figures based on studies of time allocation and energy expenditure.

The most interesting question for present purposes is the degree to which all this effort produces a supply of goods and services sufficient to meet the needs of the household members. The analysis shows that foraging and horticulture provide more than adequate nutrients to the

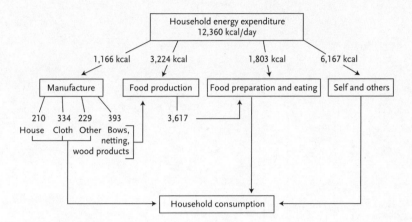

FIGURE 15. Household input-output: overview.

household, that men's labor amply provides housing, netting, and other men's products, and that women's labor provides adequate cloth, mats, and so forth. Although in the past it was more difficult to acquire machetes and aluminum pots than it is today, the Matsigenka clearly had in the past and have presently the knowledge and resources to support themselves as individual households, even though there may be some advantages to hamlet life that compensate for the additional inconvenience of living in groups and depleting important resources more quickly than a single household would. The Matsigenka have little economic incentive to form larger groups, certainly not the village-sized settlements missionaries, the government, and development agencies are promoting.

Health

Table 16, earlier in this chapter, showed that a household produces a surplus of key nutrients. Overall, the height-for-weight ratios are good (table 20). In 1972–73 there were only two unambiguous cases of malnutrition, one a thirteen-year-old boy with a marked pigeon chest, indicative of vitamin D deficiency, the other a six-month-old boy with symptoms of protein deficiency (moon face, faded dry hair); the younger boy was healthy when checked several months later, and a possible cause for the older boy's vitamin D deficiency was never discovered. Wieseke's

TABLE 20. Observed Weights Compared with Standard Weights for Height

| | Male | | | Female | | | |
| | Average Height (cm) | Average Weight (kg) | Standard Weight (kg) | % of Standard | Average Height (cm) | Average Weight (kg) | Standard Weight (kg) | % of Standard |
Age								
Adult	157.4	53.3	58.9	90	143.2	45.2	43.2	105
Youth	119.6	25.0	22.7	110	108.5	18.5	18.2	102
Toddler	79.1	11.2	10.8	104	85.0	12.1	12.0	101
Infant	70.0	6.7	8.7	77	64.2	6.8	7.0	97

SOURCE: Standard weights for height from Jelliffe 1966: 224–40.

NOTE: Average heights and weights are for people in time-allocation sample.

(1965) study of health in Kamisea confirms a picture of overall nutritional health.

Few social or religious taboos inhibit the Matsigenka diet (Johnson and Baksh 1989). The most powerful is the taboo against snake meat, which no one ever eats. Because snakes are killed often, the taboo means a small but probably not trivial loss of fat and protein throughout the year. Most other food taboos concern red meat and tend to be sporadically observed except by pregnant women. Apart from the loss of snake, therefore, and a small reduction in the amount of meat in the diets of pregnant women—which may have the possible beneficial effect (to mothers) of keeping birth weights low (Speth 1990)—magicoreligious beliefs have a minimal effect on overall patterns of food consumption.

Nonetheless, the Matsigenka of Shimaa face many challenges to maintaining overall good health, and not for lack of trying. They have standards of cleanliness to which they adhere, and they respond to injury and illness with all the tools at their command. But their technology for dealing with health threats, and particularly with infectious diseases, is of limited effectiveness.

HYGIENE

The Matsigenka work at keeping themselves, their homes, and their clothing clean. Naturally, sitting on dirt floors, working in forest or garden, and preparing unprocessed foods get people, their houses, and their patios dirty. But they do not usually sit on the ground without a mat beneath them; they bathe daily, wash their cushmas frequently, and wash their hands in clear water before preparing food. They do not go around encrusted in dirt or smelling bad. They are careful with waste, confining garbage *(kaara)* to designated areas away from the homestead, which they regularly sweep and weed. Strict rules govern bodily wastes, and people are especially disgusted by feces *(itiga)*, not only of other people but of any animal. The feces of toddlers, not yet toilet trained, are quickly collected into a leaf and disposed of. Paths are moved if members of any household begin to defecate regularly near one. In Camaná, chickens that were known to feed in community outhouses were not eaten but were sold downriver to non-Matsigenkas instead. The evil odor of feces is believed to invade the body and cause illness (Shepard 1999: 160).

Everyone carries some parasite burden. In contrast to the debilitating effects of amebas on me, it seemed that the Matsigenka lived with ameba without being much affected. Occasionally someone complained

TABLE 21. Parasites in Stool Samples in Kamisea, 1964

Parasite	Percentage of Stool Samples
Ameba *(E. histolytica)*	32%
Whipworm *(Trichuris t.)*	53
Strongloides s.	15
Hookworm *(Necator am.)*	57
Ascaris	62

SOURCE: Wieseke 1965: 23.

of anemia, weakness, tinnitus, dizziness, and sleeplessness, symptoms that I associated with amebiasis, but not often. Perhaps they come to biological terms with amebas early in life or die in the attempt. Wieseke (1965: 35) found parasitoses to be nearly universal in Kamisea (only 8 out of 167 stool samples had no parasites; table 21). To those we may add lice, which are the subject of frequent grooming by the people of Shimaa; they stir the lice up by slapping the head of the groomee and then pick the lice out and eat them or set them aside. But efforts at hygiene are in a sense a losing battle in Shimaa. In addition to parasites, infections pass freely among members of a household or hamlet because of the continual affectionate touching and sharing.

ILLNESS AND INJURY

First greetings after a period of absence usually include statements or questions about health, as when Evaristo greeted me: *Pokakevi novisarite tera nomantsigatake,* "You have arrived, Nephew. I am not sick." The question *tera pimantsigate* ("Not you-are-sick?") can elicit a lengthy description of complaints, to which courteous listeners respond with *je'ee,* "yes," and *ario,* "Is that so?" The most debilitating infections are colds and conjunctivitis, which hit the community in waves and quickly spread to everyone. Afraid of contagion, people routinely flee the community when word of infection reaches them, and they do not return until the infection has left the community. The reaction is most powerful in the case of influenza, *merentsi,* also known as *kamagantsi* (literally "death-thing" or "that which kills"). Wieseke (1965: 12) reports, "Just before their migration [to Kamisea], those from the Manu had seen many of their people, especially the older ones, wiped out by white man's influenza."

Wieseke's (1965) detailed health survey of Kamisea is probably appli-
cable in general terms to Shimaa in 1972. She found that the most common complaints were cough, cold, stomach ache, and diarrhea. Low-
grade skin infections were frequent; several people displayed evidence of
old or acute pinta; and many had respiratory infections. Common also
were dental problems, heart murmurs, and liver enlargement, although
high blood pressure was rare. In Shimaa, other infections like earache
occurred sporadically, but more likely were snake bites and accidents,
including cuts or wounds sustained during work. One of the snake bites
required our intervention with antivenin injection, but the other two
were likened to the bites of the large black ant, *maiini*—painful, but
survivable. As people actively engaging a wilderness, the Matsigenka
frequently suffer injuries.

Most health complaints came to our attention because people believed the medicines we had with us were more effective than Matsigenka remedies. Our house became a center where people stopped to
tell us their symptoms and ask for treatment. They were pragmatic
about accepting this help, seeing much illness and injury as more or less
naturally occurring. Some of the illnesses were seen as spiritual in origin, however, and I return to this crucial topic in chapter 5.

During 1972–73 in Shimaa, no infants died, but this situation was
fortuitous. We did medicate many children and sewed up the cut scalp
of a victim of an infanticide attempt. But Baksh was equally attentive
during his research in Camaná, yet six children died. At least four children also died in Shimaa during our absences from the field between
1973 and 1975: one was sat on by accident while sleeping in a pile of rags,
one was stillborn, and two who were doing fine suddenly died.

REMEDIES

When people are really ill, they lie quietly on a mat while the rest of
the household goes on as usual, ignoring the sick person (see figure 28
in chapter 5). Because the Matsigenka see any serious illness as life-
threatening (chapter 3), members of the family are worried about the
sick person but do not shower attention on him or her. This distancing
also reflects ambivalence arising from fear that the sick person is dangerous. That the sick loved one may have brought spiritual danger into
the household arouses a self-preserving avoidance, which strengthens
the idea that illness is primarily the sufferer's own business.

The Matsigenka have a host of herbal remedies for illnesses of all
kinds: teas, poultices, aromatic vapors, rendered concentrates. But

when spiritual danger is present, their most common practice is to bathe the endangered with very hot water and cut their hair as short as possible. Snakebite and pneumonia, both of which are seen as resulting from being shot with spirit arrows, are treated this way, as are a whole range of bodily aches and pains. Shepard (1999) and Izquierdo (2001) have thoroughly described and analyzed Matsigenka herbal medicine.

The most common herbal remedies are the many varieties of *ivenkiki* (chapter 5), each specific to a different ailment like stomachache, sore throat, or headache. But many other plants provide remedies as well. Some of these no doubt have pharmacological effects appropriate to the illness, like the vitamin C in peppers (*Capsicum* sp.), lemons *(Citrus limon)*, and hibiscus (*Hibiscus* sp.), all of which are used for colds. The powerful drug *potogo* (*Ficus* sp., Spanish, *ojé;* cf. Matteson 1954: 61) is an effective abortifacient; it was blamed for Serafina's death (chapter 3) and was reported to have had near-fatal effects elsewhere (Pereira 1970). Even such practical remedies as these, however, have their spiritual side, and others, like datura and tobacco, are profoundly spiritual. I reserve full discussion of the spiritual side of healing, including taboos, for chapter 5.

CHAPTER 3

Family Life

The concept of a social contract is not, apparently, unique
to Locke and other Western thinkers. In South America the
notion is commonly held that human beings must constrain
their animal desires to enjoy the fruits of living together. The
problem seems to be how to reconcile oneself to the fact that
man is a solitary animal condemned to live in herds.

Roe 1982: 229–30

Judging from the favorite stories told around the evening fire, the main
dilemma of Matsigenka family life is balancing the selfish and willful desires of the individual against the compromises required for life in household and hamlet (Johnson 1999b). Somehow, individual adults must be
fully self-reliant and take independent action, and yet at the same time
be unselfish and avoid the impulsive actions that can threaten even the
strongest family ties.

The Matsigenka emphasis on the independence of individuals and
nuclear families runs counter to the common anthropological position
that "individualism" is an egocentric, Western cultural bias (d'Ans 1974:
346; Hsu 1972; Kurtz 1992: 101). This dichotomy of the egocentric West
versus the sociocentric rest overlooks the degree of individual autonomy
and self-centeredness in even the most sociocentric societies (Kuwayama 1989; Johnson 1995: 459–60). Such a view, if applied to the Matsigenka, would unilaterally emphasize their deep sense of connection to
family at the expense of their equally strong sense of individual self-

hood, a culturally constructed acknowledgement of individual willfulness and responsibility.

The Married Couple

Not only are a husband and wife a complementary pair economically, but when nuclear families live on their own, they may be the only two adults anywhere nearby, a situation that increases their psychological and social dependence on one another. Behaviorally, husbands and wives are highly supportive:

Owing to the intensity of the relationship, I had expected husbands and wives to show less supportive behavior toward one another, but the expression of antagonistic feelings appears to be restrained in daily household interactions. This must be understood in light of the fact that animosity has its outlet: husbands and wives do periodically fight; drunken husbands do sometimes vent hostility on their wives; and in consequence wives sometimes leave their husbands. (O. Johnson 1978: 233–34)

When asked for information or some kind of help, husbands and wives are compliant with each other over 90 percent of the time, a much higher rate than that exhibited by other dyads in the household.

When one is contemplating marriage, one looks above all for someone who will be hardworking. The worst mistake is to marry a lazy person *(peranti)*, for such a spouse will not only fail to hold up his or her end of the division of labor but also will tend to be stingy and dissatisfied. Most Matsigenkas in fact are industrious. In addition to putting in long and often grueling workdays, men and women, after dark or on rainy days when mobility is limited, occupy themselves with manufactures while enjoying affectionate interactions and story telling.

Men are associated with strength and courage. For example, husbands inevitably precede their wives (and their children) when walking through the forest. I learned early in fieldwork that my ethnocentric tendency to be courteous by pausing to let "ladies go first" on the path led only to comical impasses. A man goes first on the trail because he is armed and prepared to defend the rest of his family in any dangerous encounter. Women are described as "fearful" *(tsaronti)*. Indeed, the word for brave, *iseraritake*, literally means "he-male-is." It is not a compliment, however, but a label for men who fight too much. When I asked men whether they were brave, they would say *tera nonserarikake*,

"I'm not brave," but might mention one or two other men who they thought were brave. The phrase *iseraritake,* therefore, may best translate as "he is hyper-masculine, fierce."

Men, however, must be strong. A man's life is said to be dangerous, and men are expected to do the heaviest labor and carry the heaviest burdens. A woman cries at a harsh word, but a man does not cry even when struck. If a man encounters a demon in the forest, he shoots it, whereas a woman can only scream. A man who cries easily or is perceived as weak is described as womanly (*tsinaneshinianka,* literally "female soul"). A complementary term for women who spend too much time outside the house and who avoid women's work (especially spinning cotton) is *serarishinianka,* "manly."

Men see hunting as exclusively their domain. "Women have a negative influence on hunting and they are therefore not allowed to accompany men on hunting trips. Sexual abstinence the night before staging a hunt is a necessary prerequisite if the hunter shall have any success. Even merely dreaming of women is considered to be devastating for the outcome of the hunting" (Rosengren 1987a: 61). Hunting is also an opportunity for men to go off alone, to "stretch their legs" away from the importunities of life in the hamlet (cf. Kensinger 1995: 33).

Rosengren (1987b: 341; 1987a: 82–84) stresses the separation between the sexes, especially the man's control over hunting and aversion to the pollution of women's menstrual blood. He sees a general pattern of separateness, lack of cooperation, mutual avoidance, and male domination of women (1987b: 334). Although his generalizations may be too strong for Shimaa, tensions certainly can separate husbands and wives. Although it is kept under wraps, the disappointment husbands and wives feel in each other as providers is often palpable. Husbands are frequently impatient with their wives because they have run out of manioc beer. Men would drink more beer if only their wives would make more. They quickly drink up whatever beer is on hand and make a small face or dismayed noise when they peer into a gourd and find it empty. Some men also feel unfortunate because their wives are poor cloth makers. In such families, the children and even the adults must wear badly torn and patched cushmas because the wife does not keep up with the family's need for clothing, and this lack of decent clothing is a public embarrassment.

For their part, wives are often displeased with their husbands as providers of meat. Garden produce is ample, but fish and game are always too scarce, more scarce even than manioc beer. This lack of meat becomes a source of tension because people prefer drinking manioc beer to eating boiled manioc unimproved by meat. The problem intensifies as men demand more beer from women who are already angry because there is so little meat coming in, and the women know that when men get drunk on manioc beer, they are more likely to vent their frustrations on their wives.

Men fear contamination by women's menstrual blood, which can make them tired, weak, and ineffective—that is, the opposite of manly. Husband and wife should not lie near one another during her period, and he must not come into contact with her menstrual blood. "It makes him sleep all the time," Roberto said, "and when he hunts, his arrows miss the mark; he won't catch fish, won't want to work—like an old man." The menstruating woman enters and leaves the house by a separate door, so that the man can use the main entrance without risk of pollution.

Male strength also plays a role in the different ways husbands and wives manage anger. As a rule, both men and women contain anger as much as possible. For a married couple, the result is that many courtesies shape the way they make their wishes known. If a man wants beer, he asks, *aityo shitea* ("Is there beer?"), rather than saying, *makero shitea* ("Bring me beer!"). Likewise, if a woman wants her husband to hunt, she does not command, "Go hunt!" or criticize him as a poor hunter; it is enough for her to say quietly, "There is no meat." Men and women know what is expected of them, and they generally do it without having to be told.

But when anger breaks through, especially when men are drinking beer, they may beat their wives. The primary reasons a husband gives for anger are that he believes his wife to be lazy or unfaithful. He may become short-tempered with her if she is slow serving him, but unless there is a build-up of resentment over time, his anger is unlikely to turn violent. If he is deeply angry, he may leave (divorce) her, but the most likely outcome when he sobers up is that he feels remorse and asks her forgiveness.

The woman's response is different. If beaten, she becomes angry but does not fight back, fearing to make her husband's violence worse. Instead, she runs away (*oshiganaka*, "she flees"); this behavior is understood to be an expression of anger and not of fear. She may run to a brother or father if they are available: they are likely to come angrily to her defense, scolding the offending husband, "You married her; don't beat her now, or why did you marry her in the first place? If you don't want her, give her back and live alone."

As a measure of their hurt and rage, however, some women who have been beaten run alone into the forest. This is a bold and desperate act because women are far more vulnerable than men to spiritual attack in the forest. A husband who loves his wife becomes quite frantic at this turn of events and runs into the forest to find her. If he cannot find her, he must wait anxiously for her to show up somewhere (word reaches him quickly), then go and contritely ask her to come back to him.

Apart from the emphasis on male strength, love and desire between men and women is largely an egalitarian matter. In folktales, both men and women are portrayed as aggressive seducers. Both are assumed to feel sexual desire strongly, and both may take the initiative in courtship. In such a small society, finding appropriate mates is always a problem. In Shimaa in 1973, for example, three women in their late teens trekked from homestead to homestead throughout the greater Kompiroshiato watershed to scout eligible mates and advertise their own availability.

Both men and women can be objects of love magic. Shepard (1999: 143) found the Matsigenka to be anxious and secretive about love magic. Some "perfumed" *(okasankatake)* herbs, like spearmint *(Menta spicata),* are believed in even small quantities to drive either sex mad with desire. A small amount placed under one's sleeping mat can cause one to run around nude and shameless—like an animal—and can be used both to woo a lover and to punish an ex-lover. In Shimaa, a dangerous love magic is *matsatonkishi* (literally "weak bone leaf"), a leaf that can cause an individual to become listless by day yet active by night, an awful reversal by Matsigenka standards.

Further anxiety about the danger of overwhelming sexual desire is evident in stories that link lovers with demons. Many demons are thought to have the power to seduce and then kill by rape with their huge penises. Either a man or a woman can become such a demon, and both possess the deadly penis. Such demons embody unrestrained impulsive sexuality and longing. By blaming illness and death on such demons, the Matsigenka concretize the danger of sexual impulsiveness. The fear is not limited to illicit sex. Even intercourse with a spouse can be dangerous because spirits take the shape not only of lovers but of husbands or wives as well. This change in shape is especially true of deer *(maniro).* A *maniro* is believed to once have been a man who killed women. They say that now, when a deer is attacked by a jaguar, the deer appears to cry *Ina, Ina* ("Mama, Mama").

Despite the disappointments and the fears, Matsigenka husbands and wives spend much time together in evident harmony and enjoyment of each other's company. They frequently sit side by side at home, working quietly at separate tasks, talking and laughing together. At times they become playful and giggle or wrestle. They care for each other spiritually, by observing food taboos when the other is sick or vulnerable. They often depart from the house together also, leaving the children in the care of an older sibling or a kinsman from the hamlet, to go foraging or to work in the gardens. These are also their opportunities to have sex away from the crowded household.

Childhood and the Development of Matsigenka Selves

From an ecocultural perspective the self is an organization of motivations, skills, and expectations that enable an individual to do what must be done to ensure survival and reproduction under local conditions (Goldschmidt 1959; A. W. Johnson 1978: 120–21; Weisner 1996). The task for parents is to guide their children toward the kind of self organization they will need if they are to do well in the natural and cultural environments in which they must live as adults. Among the Matsigenka, adults must not only be able to live in nuclear-family isolation for much of their lives but must actually prefer to do so. The frustration of missionaries and schoolteachers who have failed to induce the Matsigenka to subscribe to community-building efforts is dramatic evidence that the Matsigenka are happiest when they are free from intrusions and constraints arising from others' agendas.

The Matsigenka take for granted that each person—adult and child—is a center of spontaneous, impulsive desire, and that this impulsiveness must be respected in the growing child even as it is gradually brought under control. Patterns of childcare, cultural beliefs about how children develop, and cautionary tales about adult misbehavior all show that the management of impulsive willfulness is the central problem of Matsigenka social life. A more or less pure representation of the impulsive individual can be found in their Trickster figure. As described in general terms by Radin (1956: xxiii), "Trickster is at one and the same time creator and destroyer, giver and negator, he who dupes others and who is always duped himself. *He wills nothing consciously. At all times he is constrained to behave as he does from impulses over which he has no control.* He knows neither good nor evil yet he is responsible for both. He possesses no values, yet through his actions all values come into being" (emphasis added). In Shimaa, the story of Tasorintsi, who created the good things on earth (chapter 5), is about a powerful and impulsive Trickster child who could transform the world. When frustrated, he turned his male cross-cousin into a rock and his female cross-cousin (his potential bride) into a tapir. He turned other cousins into a monkey, deer, and finally armadillo. No reasons are given in the narrative for these acts, which are partly in response to thwarted wishes and in part simply happen, *kogapai* (without reason).

In the version of this story collected by Shepard (1989), the hero is Kashibokani, "the self-created one." He transforms the world by blowing his breath, but without control, turning humans into beasts even he has never heard of. He is a grandiose, virtually omnipotent being who has no parents, owes no one anything, and has vast powers that he exercises impulsively, expanding the animal world—the world of impulsive beings—at the expense of humankind. His sister, a feminine civilizing force, recognizes the danger and arranges for him to be captured, beaten, impaled, bound, and removed to the edge of the sky, the most distant point on earth. There he must be kept as far away from humans as possible because if he sees a single human, even at a distance, he will flip over the world and collapse the sky. His gardens of maize and papaya are transformed into inedible wild plants, from which weapons will ultimately be forged for humans to use in hunting the wild animals that Kashibokani created from humans in the first place.

This and similar stories postulate the existence of a child-being so free from constraints that it can impulsively destroy humanity. This being grows itself, is willful and threatening even as an infant, and has an affinity to animals, especially monkeys. It is significant that this being is male and that his sister controls him because the Matsigenka see men as inherently less restrained and more violent than women. The message is that the grandiose, amoral, animal-like Trickster child must be immobilized and taken as far away as possible if humans are to live on this earth and gain mastery over animals. Still, the man-child has not been killed: he waits in the mouth of the sky for even the faintest of human contact, which could reactivate him and destroy the world.

BIRTH AND INFANCY

The Matsigenka believe that pregnancy is the result of sexual intercourse between a man and a woman and that a single act of intercourse is sufficient to cause pregnancy. Even if she has had more than one partner, a woman is always believed to know who the father of her baby is.

A fear of being deceived into having intercourse with a demon disguised as a lover counteracts impulses to engage in extramarital sex.

Although they recognize an herb, *inchapari,* which when brewed into a strong tea is said to prevent a woman from conceiving or even having periods again, women do not often practice birth control. Pregnancies are usually welcomed as among the most desirable events in life. A woman recognizes that she is pregnant when her period stops and when she feels the fetus growing inside her. She makes few changes in her life, pursuing her daily routine as before. On discovering she is pregnant, however, she quickly weans her toddler, if she has one, and avoids certain foods, especially red meat and certain species of fish. Members of her immediate household are also expected to reduce or eliminate these foods in their diets.

Some pregnancies, perhaps as many as one or two in ten, are not welcomed. If a woman conceives out of wedlock, has lost her husband, or is still nursing a child much younger than three years of age, she may seek to terminate the pregnancy. Various herbs (*potogo, igentiri,* and *seriavenkiki,* "hemorrhage sedge"), taken as teas or compresses, are believed to cause the fetus to rot or burn away and be aborted in a discharge of blood.

Birth is a private affair involving the immediate household and perhaps one or two adult siblings from neighboring households. We were able to observe the birth of Estepania's baby. Estepania, who was not married, lived with her brother, Julio; when she believed her labor to be beginning, however, she came to stay with our next-door neighbors, Aretoro and Pororinta, who were not her kin. This move was most likely intended to take advantage of Maestro's modern health remedies and knowledge, as well as our own. This was her first child, and the Matsigenka recognize that first births are the most difficult.

Estepania spent her time quietly for a few days and, when the birth did not begin, returned home. She was back a few days later, however, and that night, while she sang during a rainstorm, I could tell she was in labor by the regular alteration between tense, high-pitched singing and slower, relaxed singing. The next day, Aretoro set up in a shady spot a horizontal pole that she could hold and pull on during her last contractions. After she removed her cushma, Pororinta massaged her and rubbed her belly. She gave birth from a squatting position onto a plaited mat.

In most cases the procedure would be much the same. A woman's husband should be present to provide basic assistance, including suck-

FIGURE 16. Being bathed after giving birth.

ing on her belly and preparing teas to hasten birth, and helping hold her
in position so that the child is not harmed during birth. If her husband
is not available, then other members of her extended family can help. A
husband wants to help because he fears the loss of his mate in childbirth.
With characteristic Matsigenka directness he asks, "Where will I get another wife if this one dies?"

As is common, Estepania's newborn was left alone on the mat while
the mother was bathed and dressed (figure 16). The baby was breathing
but did not cry much, waving his arms and legs in the air and grimac-
ing. After about ten minutes, Pororinta turned her attention to the
baby, bringing a large bowl of water hot enough that even in the daytime shade it gave off visible steam. She bathed the baby by pouring a
stream of hot water onto a part of him, causing him to cringe and cry.

She rubbed and cleaned off one portion of the body before repeating the maneuver at an adjacent place until the baby was completely washed. Then she swaddled him in cloth and gave him to his mother to hold. About an hour later Estepania breast-fed him for the first time.

The cultural meaning of bathing the infant in hot water is that it will strengthen the baby for the hard life ahead. The hot-water bath for both mother and infant is part of a larger pattern of using hot, nearly scalding, baths for anyone who has been exposed to danger, especially spiritual danger. In fact, a husband who has assisted at the birth should himself be given a hot bath to prevent the appearance on his skin of black or white spots *(impatsatanakera)* or the occurrence of cracked soles and heels on his feet *(igarachate)*.

Even if a woman does not attempt an abortion, she may feel ambivalent toward the newborn. A small but significant proportion of women, again perhaps one in ten, contemplate killing their infants rather than raising them. Men may have opinions about doing so and may promote infanticide if they believe another man is the father, but killing a baby is primarily the woman's decision and her action. She may decide, for example, to kill her infant if it is a "bad" baby—that is, a baby who cannot be soothed (O. Johnson 1981). Estepania could not soothe her baby and, after several days, let it be known that she was thinking of killing him. Another woman said, "In that case, I'll take him." After a few more days, however, the volunteer returned the baby, admitting that she could not soothe him either and that she did not want him. But this time Estepania kept him and raised him herself. Geronimo's wife cut her infant daughter's scalp in despair at having been recently abandoned by her husband, but after we stitched her wound, her mother kept her, and she was a healthy toddler in her mother's company when I saw her again eighteen months later. In two other infant deaths described as accidental, extramarital paternity may have been an underlying factor. In some cases, the infanticide is done on orders: unwed Irima threw her baby in the river because her mother said, "I want you to work only for me." Justina did the same because her co-wife, who was first wife, said, "You are my servant [*nampiria*]; you can't raise children, only I can."

Often, relatives do not intervene in infanticide, regarding it as a mother's prerogative. But sometimes someone tells the mother, "You are responsible; raise the child." The general belief is that troublesome children should be bathed in hot water, not abandoned. We did not hear specifically of deformed children and how they are dealt with, but babies believed to result from demon attacks are often described as ugly at birth (hairy or with monstrous features) and are killed. Twins *(pite-*

tacharira), however, are not regarded as bad or dangerous, and there were teenage girl twins in Shimaa during our research.

A number of cultural elements surrounding conception and childbirth illustrate the themes of autonomy and individualism. In the difficult choices of abortion and infanticide, the mother has the ultimate say and performs the act, even when her husband or parent tries to influence her decision. The exceptions, where senior women order dependent junior women to kill their babies, show the willfulness, or selfishness, of the senior women, who do not want to lose control over the young women's labor. The observance of birth prohibitions and the participants in the actual birthing are restricted to the immediate household of the mother or her closest relatives.

Leaving the newborn alone while attending the mother first is a complex act. In the most obvious sense, it places the mother's value and importance first. But it also implies an attitude toward the infant: the belief that the hot-water bath strengthens the child is not unlike the slap on the bottom with which newborns are greeted in many hospitals, where the slap is culturally constructed as a benevolent effort to "strengthen" the child's lungs. In both cases, the cultural rationale may mask a harsher aggressive message to the effect, "You're not in the womb anymore!"

The Matsigenka pattern of leaving infants alone after birth also has an element of trusting to the babies' will to live or of testing whether they have a will to live before embracing them with a bath, swaddling, holding, and nursing. It is the inaugural instance of a lifelong pattern of letting individuals alone and expecting them to communicate their needs before intervening. In keeping with this principle, Matsigenka caretakers do not put infants on any kind of schedule. They attempt, instead, a subtle balancing act: on the one hand, infants learn that their cries are quickly met with nurturance because the Matsigenka do not believe that crying is good for a child; on the other hand, caretakers do not anticipate or impose care but wait for the child to signal distress before responding.

Infants spend most of their time rather firmly swaddled and against their mothers' bodies, in a sling during the day and by her side at night. Others may hold babies for shorter periods, either to help the mother out or because they want to hold and cuddle the baby. Babies may also be left on a mat near the mother for an hour or so to sleep or lie calmly awake, gurgling, waving, and looking around.

While carrying them in the sling, mothers perpetually rock, pat, and adjust their infants. If they cry, mothers first offer them the breast, then, if they cannot be consoled, check for soiling (mothers know quickly when their babies need to be cleaned because they do not use diapers). If these tactics fail, a caretaker bounces the baby or gently swings from side to side. The longest I heard an infant under six months of age crying without receiving any attention was five minutes. Infants cry for much longer periods but only in cases—usually illness—where efforts to soothe them have failed.

EARLY CHILDHOOD

Swaddling, breastfeeding on demand, and constant holding provide a kind of transitional womb that eases the Matsigenka newborn into life in this world. The goal is to raise children who are calm and contented: their needs should be met, but they should not be overindulged. After a few months, more is expected of an infant. Ordinary foods like manioc and banana begin to be offered, after being premasticated by the mother. It is considered dangerous, however, to feed a small child any of the meats prohibited to pregnant women (and girls in puberty seclusion) because they can cause bloody diarrhea. The same danger exists if either parent eats proscribed meats in the baby's first month of life. There is a parallel here with the prohibition on eating howler monkey in the early stages of maize growth (chapter 5). The parents, like the man who plants the maize, will endanger a child's healthy growth by eating howler monkey. Even later, as the child begins to eat the foods everyone else eats, red meat remains a serious concern. At most, small children are given red meat in limited quantities, lest they grow up to be lazy malcontents.

As children grow, mothers test their ability to tolerate discomfort by letting them cry briefly—if they calm down on their own, they are left untended. The Matsigenka allow a gradual lengthening of the gap between the child's clamor and the caretaker's response. To this end, early toys are provided, like the bright orange inedible fruit of the *mananeroki* (Spanish, *tomate del monte; Solanum* sp.) that dangles from a string over the baby's mat or a rattle sewn from nutshells and bright feathers attached to the shoulder of the mother's cushma near the child's sling. These toys hold the child's interest and encourage playful reaching and batting.

The Matsigenka overtly do little to hasten a child's development. Their style is best described as a gradual raising of expectations. They do not cajole a child to rise up and toddle toward them, but they welcome her when she does. And later, when she has become more competent, if it is time to go somewhere, the caretaker ignores her gesture to be picked up—arms upraised, eyes imploring, perhaps a whining "Unh! Unh!"—waiting instead to see whether the toddler will get up and follow along without being carried. If the child refuses or if after a few yards she stumbles and cries to be picked up, the caretaker responds. Such small lessons, repeated continuously, apply a subtle pressure, conveying the message, "Let's see what self-reliance you are capable of today!"

Children two or three years old often respond to the invitation to walk along but also continue to ask to spend time in their mother's sling. They learn to ride in the sling astride their mother's back, so that their faces are alongside hers, sharing her view over her shoulder as she walks along or converses with people. Or they ride on her hip, legs now dangling down to her knee. They still consider the breast their own possession, reaching down into their mother's cushma and pulling the breast to their mouths like an ice cream cone, slurping while watching with interest the world around them.

Despite the generally peaceful pattern of childcare to this point, there is an underlying tension in that the mother and other caretakers are testing the child's limits, expecting more and more self-reliance. The toddler may protest being left alone in the care of older siblings, but the mother becomes increasingly indifferent. Because the games and activities of older children are inherently interesting to the toddler, the mini-tantrums that mark this transition are brief and are not particularly disruptive. Sometimes the tension erupts as mothers impatiently jam their breasts into the mouths of crying toddlers or yell at them to be quiet.

As a toddler, a Matsigenka child is in great physical danger. Having what Fraiberg (1959) calls "a love affair with the world," toddlers engage in a ceaseless exploration of their surroundings. But the natural world is harsh, unforgiving, and close at hand. A toddler has little judgement and can wander into the fire or off the riverbank, can pick up a stinging insect or ingest lethal substances. For this reason limits are imposed on the toddler's freedom of movement. When working at home, mothers often tether their toddlers to a stake pounded into the floor. Like a leash, this tether, the Matsigenka version of a playpen, keeps toddlers from wandering into harm's way. Matsigenka caretakers are cognitively able to maintain unbroken awareness of their toddlers even while engaged in tasks like weaving or peeling manioc. When untethered toddlers come near some danger, mothers, apparently busy with something else, unerringly swoop down and lift the children away from the threat, holding them until they squirm away in their enthusiasm to resume exploration.

Matsigenka behavior during the second and third years of life includes what Mahler, Pine, and Bergman (1975) call *rapprochement* (A. W. Johnson 1981; cf. Weisner, Matheson, and Bernheimer 1996). The rapprochement child eagerly seeks to explore the world, but also now has the cognitive capacity to recognize the dangers of separation and exposure to nature. Hence, the child's desire for autonomous exploration is accompanied by a countervailing desire to check in and receive reassurance of safety and connection. The Matsigenka take for granted that their young children want to be on their own, yet they have a realistic awareness of the children's limitations: a child is "free" to explore "safely." Parents and older siblings neither encourage nor resent young children's desire to separate: they seem quite neutrally to accept what toddlers want as long as it does not put the children in danger or make it impossible for caretakers to complete other necessary tasks. When children return to their caretakers for holding or reassurance, they are welcomed, although usually after some hesitation to test how much they want it; often they return to their caretakers and touch them, then wander off again after receiving no apparent response:

A boy of 19 months is standing next to his mother, then approaches me as she comes near to see what I am doing. Several other children are around: the boy grabs an older boy's legs for a second, then goes to mother and hugs her legs, goes around behind her, comes out the other side and watches me, still holding her left leg with his right hand and leaning against her leg. The children run to the fire to pull out a roasting plantain, and the boy goes along to watch. His mother gets about five meters away, walking away from the house, when he turns and follows her. As she returns to the house, he holds her hand. Then he holds up both arms as if to be picked up; she does nothing and he turns away and rejoins the group of children near the fire. He sits with them picking at the plantain, while his mother remains nearby.

Compared with much parenting in the United States, parenting among the Matsigenka leads to few battles for control between young children and parents: neither the dramatically yearning child trying to drag the caretaker here or there nor the anxiously rushing caretaker crying, "No! Stop that! Get away from there!" I never saw struggles over feeding. Toddlers were free to wander among the family at mealtime and beg bits of what they wanted; they offered chewed bits of food to others, and these gifts were generally accepted. If they dribbled or spilled food, it was cleaned up. If they refused food, someone else ate it, and soon all the food was gone. Without evident anger, impatience, force-feeding, or scolding, caretakers teach toddlers the value of food

TABLE 22. Relationships of Caretakers to Infants and Toddlers

Relation	Number of Relationships Observed	Percentage
Mother only	394	50%
Mother and father	209	26
Sister	63	8
Nonkin caretaker	34	4
Other kin	30	4
Co-wife	20	3
Brother	17	2
Father only	12	2
Child is left alone	8	1
TOTAL	787	100%

and its real scarcity (no refrigerators or pantries to raid on demand). Snacks are often made available between meals and overnight, however, so the hungry toddler's wait to be fed is not usually overwhelming.

The Matsigenka allow very young children, even toddlers, to play with knives, machetes, and other potentially harmful tools. I have seen boys too young to walk peel an orange with a machete. This kind of freedom allows children to acquire facility with tools from an early age and is part of the general pattern of letting children explore their world even when it may expose them to some harm. Once I saw a toddler pick up a *maiini* ant (*Grandiponera* sp.), and before I could warn her, she was stung with a poison perhaps comparable to that of a black widow spider; she cried for hours and her hand was swollen for three days. The possibility always exists that this degree of freedom can be fatal: in Camaná in 1980 the beloved three-year-old son of Michael Baksh's adoptive family ate poisonous frog's eggs while his mother's back was turned and died within an hour (Baksh 1984: 336).

Behaviorally each mother is a center of gravity around which her children revolve in close orbits. They are rarely reprimanded for wandering out of orbit, but they discover in time that doing so is not encouraged. Because women are not overly generous with the children of other women, including their co-wives, it may simply be that the rewards for approaching other women are too slim to reinforce such behavior. Young children are found more than three-fourths of the time in the company of one or both of their parents (table 22). Indeed, 76 percent of the time children are with their mother, whether or not the father is present. By contrast, they are alone with their father only 2 percent of the time, an example of how mother occupies a social space between father and child.

The pattern of behavioral closeness between child and mother is especially dramatic in polygynous households, where the space is essentially divided into two or more sections, each centered around a woman's hearth (see chapter 4). Co-wives keep their possessions separate, and their children remain near their mother's space. Young children wander across the invisible divide into the co-wife's space, but older children and adults associated with one wife mostly remain on her side of the house. Even in polygynous households, children are cared for by their mother's co-wives only 7 percent of the time.

Mothers make many requests of their young children (O. Johnson 1978: 239). They ask them to do small useful tasks like picking up a spoon or chasing a chicken from the house. But children, especially toddlers, do not readily comply. At first it seemed as though mothers were barking out commands to recalcitrant children, using a stern high-speed delivery. But it became clear that mothers were not angry, just persistent. They repeat orders as often and in as peremptory a tone as needed to get compliance from children who they know are too young for ready obedience. The children, whose slowness to respond is tolerated by their parents, do not show resentment and eventually comply.

While mothers tend to request action from their children, children tend to request attention from their mothers. Small children especially ask their mothers to notice them, to see what they are doing—in short, to acknowledge them. But if mothers have to repeat in order to obtain compliance, children have to work even harder to get attention from their mothers. In fact, children comply with their mothers twice as often as mothers comply with their children. Still, mothers do comply with their children's requests more often than not, so the contrast between mothers and children must be viewed in the context of the overall supportiveness of household interactions (O. Johnson 1978: 231).

This permissive, accommodating pattern of childcare, including breast-feeding, lasts into the third or fourth year, albeit with the mother's increased reluctance. The level of expectations continues to rise. Toddlers are asked to fetch and carry; when they fail to comply they are repeatedly exhorted but seldom punished. As more compliance is expected, it is more willingly given: older toddlers reliably carry bowls of water, fetch items, and shoo chickens. Although children are rarely punished physically, threats certainly play a role in the increasing frequency of compliance. Standard phrases like "I will give you away" or "Jaguar will come and get you," although spoken lightly by caretakers, sow doubts in young children, judging by their frightened grins and ingratiating behavior when threatened. Stinging nettles are kept along one wall of the house as threats occasionally implemented. As much as the Matsigenka honor the child's free exploration and mastery of the environment, they are far from naively assuming that a child left to his or her own devices will naturally become compliant and responsible.

Overall, Matsigenka children of this age have a strong sense of entitlement. They enjoy both freedom and nurturance. Parents set expectations but at levels young children can tolerate. In this sense, Matsigenka child rearing approximates what Kohut (1977: 123–24) calls "optimum frustration": the children's needs are met but with a delay to see whether they can wait or can solve the problem themselves (cf. Winnicott 1965: 51–52). "Optimum frustration" does not imply no frustration: frustration is essential for growth, to encourage children to explore the full extent of their capacities. Caretakers must allow frustration to occur with a certain relentlessness. True, too much frustration is painful and may lead to excessive anger and mistrust. But too little frustration can lead to suffocating overprotectiveness and the possibility of what Kohut (1977: 124), tongue in cheek, calls a "pathological absence of paranoia."

TEMPER TANTRUM AS KEY TRANSITION

Reflecting their sense of entitlement, toddlers firmly demand what they want, as becomes dramatically evident with the shock of a new pregnancy. The child, center of his universe and to a degree master of all he surveys, is suddenly weaned and finds his mother substantially less generous. The new pregnancy forces the issue: it is time for this child to get used to being self-reliant.

The child's response is a powerful outrage and rejection of the new order. At this point Matsigenka children enter a temper-tantrum phase consisting of lengthy protests many times a day for periods of up to several months. Angry, especially at the mother, for weaning and for not picking her up, the child rushes at her, threatens to hit her, picks up twigs and dirt and throws them at her, falls to the ground screaming, refuses to budge, engages in long dramatic wailing, and in general uses the limited means at her disposal to show her rage and desire to hurt the offending mother.

Small issues that previously would have been resolved quickly, like being refused an item of clothing or a toy, now seed storms of protest. Mostly harmless, the tantrum child can occasionally cause great damage, as when Apa (forty-four months old) "accidentally" set fire to his house while his father was working in his garden: the house and all possessions in it burned to ashes, a devastating loss. This incident happened a few months after his baby sister was born.

The family's reaction to the tantrum phase is singular: with few exceptions, family members go on about their business through the multiple tantrums without acknowledging them or responding in any way. Of course, everyone is affected because it is impossible to ignore a weeping, screaming, agonistic child. But the family members remain calm and even talk across the raging child when they have business to transact. In between outbursts tantrum children may play with toys while whimpering and turning baleful eyes on their mother. That these tantrums can last for a half hour or more and be repeated throughout the day for weeks and months on end is a sign of the children's entrenched sense of entitlement—of deserving to get what they want and refusing to give in at this first real threat to their special position. Furthermore, because the family does not react angrily (rarely someone will snap, "Oh shut up!"), the child is allowed to protest more or less to exhaustion.

In one instance I had come back to the Matsigenka after a four-year absence to visit Mike Baksh in Camaná in 1980. As we sat going over his field notes that first afternoon, I noticed a four-year-old boy in a neighboring house wailing and making angry gestures. After about an hour, I asked Mike about the boy. "What boy?" he replied. He had become so used to his neighbor's tantrums that he had not noticed it as we worked. The boy had been throwing tantrums of several hours' duration each day for six months and showed no sign of abandoning the effort. No one in his family or among the neighboring households took any notice, and once I recognized what was going on, I no longer noticed either.

The temper-tantrum phase is a defining moment in Matsigenka child development, a fundamental separation when children learn with finality that they no longer command their caretakers, that they cannot intimidate and manipulate with tears (i.e., adults will no longer sympathize with the helpless child who needs to be cared for), and that their loss and rage are their own business.

I believe the child's main emotion during the temper-tantrum phase is not fear but anger. Fear of being alone and vulnerable is certainly present. Although Matsigenka children know for the most part that they are loved, there is always the subterranean awareness that real children have been killed as babies (infanticide) because no one wanted or could stand them and that older children have been given away through adoption *(nampiria)* when their parents no longer wanted them. But the main emotion is anger at the loss of privilege. Nothing I have observed of children during the tantrum phase or after suggests depression. Sadness, loss, anger, perhaps even mourning, but not the helplessness of depression. Between tantrum episodes, the child seems perfectly normal, playing, helping around the house, participating in meals.

LATE CHILDHOOD

After the tantrums have passed, children seem remarkably calm and self-reliant. Four- or five-year-olds, for example, although not yet ready to spend the whole day alone at home, can spend the entire day with a sibling only a few years their senior without seeing mother or father or other adult, yet not throw tantrums or express anxiety. And a seven-year-old can be left alone and trusted to watch over things, including younger siblings (figure 17). The following incident, concerning a seven-year-old boy, is an example of the degree to which children past the temper-tantrum phase are treated as essentially adult:

Fieldnote 09–27–72—Going by Antonio's house, we saw his son Raul sitting on the ground with a pool of blood 6 inches across in front of him, and his head bleeding. He was crying, but everyone else in the house was sitting around quietly minding their own business—including Maria and Antonio [parents]. After the bleeding stopped Maria washed the cut, which was not so serious. Raul was playing with his younger brother, the latter being the hunter and Raul being the jaguar. The hunter threw a rock at the jaguar and connected. This case may be evidence that children are permitted from an early age to have their bad moments and to take responsibility for their own foolishness, without overprotectiveness.

The state of being idle or cared for that dominates the life of children under six changes after the temper-tantrum phase is past and children begin to spend more time under the direction of their same-sex parent. Girls begin to make significant contributions to the women's work of the household, learning the rudiments of spinning, food preparation, and childcare. Boys begin to spend more time with their fathers, particularly in horticulture; they explore the garden while their fathers work, helping from time to time with simple tasks like bringing seed for planting or clearing rubbish to the edge of the garden.

FIGURE 17. A seven-year-old boy *(right)* pops corn, one kernel at a time, while caring for his four-year-old brother for most of the day.

Sons gradually grow away from their mother's sphere of influence as they adopt male work patterns, although even after marriage they remain deferential and generous to their mothers. Daughters, however, remain in a close and somewhat childlike relationship with their mothers as long as they live in the same house. Unless they marry or have children, they continue to eat from their mother's hearth, seek her advice, and follow her instructions (see figure 14 in chapter 2). Orna had only two adolescent daughters in her behavioral-observations sample, but the data showed that, in their interactions with their mothers, all their requests were for information, and most of these were requests for confirmation: "Is this how it is done?" (O. Johnson 1978: 255–56). This persistent need for assurance is both a sign of deference and the mature form of the smaller child's requests for mother's attention.

A strong identification with the same-sex parent thus intensifies during this period. Girls, learning work skills at their mother's side, remain close to their mother for many years, possibly for a lifetime. With the matrilocal bias implicit in bride service, several households in Shimaa included mothers and grown daughters—Kasimira and Viviana (household 3 in table 25 in chapter 4), Rosa and Erena (household 3), and the three-generation team of Camila, Beatriz, and Maria Rosa (household 15).

When groups segregate by gender for barbasco fishing or sharing a meal, girls and young boys stay with their mother, whereas the older boys (about age seven and above) join the men's group. Older boys range much farther from home than do girls. They may form wandering groups with two to four members who explore the safe trails near the settlement. They may be gone all day, eating sugar cane from relatives' gardens and foraging wild fruits and insects.

The Matsigenka sense of inheritance is largely a matter of what has been learned from the same-sex parent. When I asked men why they avoided certain foods, for example, they often responded, "Because my father didn't eat it and I never learned how." This answer refers to more than taste: it implies an ability to tolerate foods that might harm others. For example, when the Snell family got sick after eating a fish liver they had received from a Matsigenka woman, Betty Snell asked her why she hadn't warned them that it could make them sick. The woman explained, "Well, it makes us sick too, but we thought you knew how to eat it!" Fundamental aspects of character are inherited in this way; in the same way, the Matsigenka explain differences in *ivenkiki* (sedge) by their direct lineage rather than by their membership in a species or class (chapter 5). In other words, in Matsigenka terms, my nature comes to me not categorically, as a human or a male or a member of the Shimaa community, but as my father's son or my mother's daughter.

To say that children learn from their parents does not imply that they receive much in the way of instruction. Children are given freedom to watch and imitate parents with minimal interference. Orna and I, in trying to learn many elemental skills like cooking over an open fire or walking on mountain trails, received virtually no advice or instruction; people watched us flounder without showing us how it is done. To do otherwise (as we would have expected) would have been to anticipate, or second-guess, the needs of others rather than wait to be asked.

According to the Matsigenka, apart from gender differences, children should ideally be treated equally within the family. This is probably the case in intact families but is not necessarily so in cases of remarriage or adoption. The Matsigenka distinguish stepchildren *(nagakore)* and adopted children *(nampiria)* from full, or "true" *(sanorira)*, offspring. A woman entering a new marriage may be uncomfortable bringing along her children from previous marriages and so will place them with close relatives "while she settles in with her new husband" (O. Johnson 1978: 164). Because older children are an economic resource, parents do not have trouble placing them in foster care, and before they marry, stepchildren often seek opportunities to leave their household and join a relative's household.

The relationship between a caretaker and an adopted child is quite different. There is no pretense that the *nampiria* is offspring. Although adopted children are said ideally to be the same as true offspring, people do admit that they are expected to work more, and direct observations show that they work longer hours (O. Johnson 1978: 164). Adoption is a relationship conceived from the outset as a contract: the caretaker agrees to provide care and shelter, the *nampiria* agrees to provide labor while growing up and to care for the adoptive parent in old age. Sometimes men adopt girls to grow up to become wives for them. Whatever genuine affection may arise between the two in the course of a lifetime, the master-servant aspect of the relationship is always clearly present.

Behaviorally, mothers and fathers have different styles of interaction with their children. In Orna Johnson's (1978) videotape study, fathers initiated less interaction with their children than mothers did but received much higher rates of compliance when they did interact. The reason may be in part that fathers requested mainly information from their children, whereas mothers requested action, and it is easier to answer a question than to fetch and carry. But children seldom initiated requests of any sort with their fathers, and when they did, the requests were nearly always for information, not the requests for attention that they directed toward their mothers; children on the videotapes were never observed to request action from their fathers. Children received a fair rate of compliance from their fathers but offered three times as much compliance to their fathers' requests as they received.

As the overall pattern of interactions suggests, therefore, fathers are somewhat distant from their children, with mothers being the behavioral link between the two. This pattern persists into adult life. Once, when I wanted to measure Aradino's house but did not know how to say so in Matsigenka, I asked his school-age daughter in Spanish; she then translated my request, not to Aradino, who was sitting right there, but to her mother, who relayed the message to Aradino, who then answered me directly. Elements of behavior such as this, along with other aspects of Matsigenka society, lend it a "matrilineal" cast. For example, when a girl marries and brings her husband into her home for a year or two of bride service, it would be most accurate to say not that the groom is moving into her father's house but that she is remaining in her mother's household.

Matsigenka siblings are close and affectionate. They spend most of their childhood in each other's company and seldom interact with other children. There may, in fact, be few other children around, but this pattern is also a reflection of the nuclear-family-centered nature of Matsigenka behavior. Even when there are children present in the household who are not of the nuclear family, such as the child of an aunt, children from different families interact surprisingly little with one another. Of all videotape observations of children initiating interaction with other children, 94 percent were with full siblings. This bias toward siblings characterizes even polygynous households; children in them remain close to their biological mother's hearth and interact mostly with full siblings.

In quantitative terms, siblings interact with high frequency. They initiate interactions with each other as often as they do with their mothers. The difference is that they seek action from one another, not attention. In the videotape study, although children made no requests for action from fathers and only 12 percent of their interactions with their mothers involved requests for action, 60 percent of their interactions with siblings involved such a request (O. Johnson 1978: 322). Because requests for action are intrinsic to cooperative work, it is not surprising that older children have considerably greater authority (giving orders and receiving compliance) than younger children do (O. Johnson 1978: 258).

The Matsigenka do not consider incest, whether between siblings or between parents and children, as something that happens today. The closest they could recall were some instances of parallel cousin marriage, which in the classificatory kin system amounts to brother-sister incest. But they do tell incest stories (Johnson and Price-Williams 1996: 268–70, 311–13, 315–17), which follow the general emotional narrative line discussed below. Of particular note here, however, is that each of these stories explicitly blames a parent for the incest and for the tragedy that follows, with the children seen as helpless victims. Mother gets the worst of it, being blamed both for not letting go of her children and for excessive anger. In tone, therefore, the sympathies of the stories appear to be strongly with children (cf. Dundes 1985: 37).

ADOLESCENCE

Culturally, the transition from girl to woman is more clearly marked than that from boy to man. When a girl reaches puberty, she is secluded for a week nowadays (they say for much longer periods in the past). The purpose of this seclusion is to give her the opportunity to become light-skinned (out of the sun) and attractively plump. She is also instructed in the need for hard work and for generosity to her husband.

Puberty seclusion is regarded as a particularly vulnerable time in her life, and a host of restrictions must be observed:

She must be completely shut up indoors, a wall of mats separating her from her family.

She must not see the sky, or she will get spots.

If she eats: *etari* (armored fish), her feet will crack *(igarachate)*.

larvae *(pagiri, ponta)*, her mouth will rot and become foul.

tinamou *(kentsori)*, when she falls she will break her back (because *kentsori* has a soft back).

guan *(kanari)*, she will get white hair.

curassow *(tsamiri)*, she will get a red face.

peccary *(shintori)*, she will have a difficult birth; her child will kill her.

fish with teeth, she will become ill. (Toothless fish are all right in small quantities.)

She should not eat everything she is given, but should give part back *(pampuntapitsanavagetakempara)*, as a lesson in restraint/ generosity.

These prohibitions are similar to those imposed on pregnant women. The greatest number of them, as in pregnancy, guard against eating animal flesh (including fish and insects). As these prohibitions pertain to the scarcest and most desirable of all foods, this lesson in restraint impresses on the young woman the need to become a careful manager of such resources.

Although the earlier trauma of the temper-tantrum phase is a major watershed in Matsigenka child development, it does not have the effect of breaking the child's will. It does not force the child into submission but rather recognizes the child's passage into greater self-reliance, forever beyond the pampering of early childhood. Therefore, the matters of teaching the child hard work, restraint, and generosity remain. Not surprisingly, these are the lessons communicated in puberty seclusion. But boys must learn these lessons, too, and much of later childhood can be said to be devoted to such learning.

Among the Matsigenka, it is slow learning at best. Children, even early adolescents, wait to be told what to do and frequently dawdle and play away from the house. Perhaps they arrive early at the schoolhouse and stay late because at home they are expected to work. And some learn faster than others. Felipe's son Ekitoro often went fishing or hunting with a slingshot and provided small quantities of wild animal food for the family larder; by age fifteen he had already started his first garden. His cross-cousin Jorge, however, was an easy-going but lazy boy of Ekitoro's age; during our first year of fieldwork he resided in three separate households because people became irritated by his failure to contribute and asked him to move on. He knew his laziness was unacceptable to others but was avoiding change by testing different relatives. For their part, the relatives were saying to one another, "I can't do anything with him, why don't you try?"

Although puberty is not identified by the Matsigenka as a period of particular stress, and we found little evidence of acting-out or even of tension between adolescents and their parents, it is a time when the Matsigenkas' autonomy and sense of entitlement come up against their lack of choices in carving out adult lives for themselves. Although the majority of people we knew had managed to find stable and apparently satisfying marriages, several young people faced tough, poignant situations.

For example, Erena was fifteen in 1972. Her father had died many years earlier, and her mother, Rosa, had then married Aradino. In November Erena began to hang around our house, doing chores and ingratiating herself. Orna was surprised and a bit uncomfortable with this sudden approach. One night Erena stayed over, sleeping first on the floor in the public area of our house, then coming into our sleeping area for the rest of the night. We were about to explain to her the next day that she had to go home, when Rosa arrived and attempted to drag her home by force. But Erena resisted, and her mother abandoned the rather mild effort. The next day, Erena lingered around our house. By that evening, when Rosa came to get her, Erena had fled and was standing in the middle of the Río Kompiroshiato, up to her waist in water. Our neighbor Aretoro went out to fetch her, but she ran downstream to an island and hid in the dense foliage. Later that night, she went home.

As the story unfolded, Erena's behavior became explicable. Her stepfather, Aradino, had recently stopped calling her "daughter." This change clearly indicated that he was attempting to redefine their kinship relationship to allow for marriage (chapter 4). At forty-five, Aradino was one of the oldest men in the community. Erena clearly did not like what was happening. Probably as a result, she wrote a love letter to the

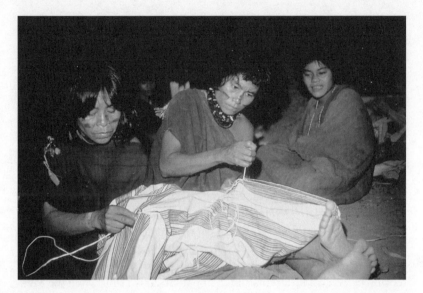

FIGURE 18. Aradino's co-wives, Kasimira and Rosa, sew, watched by Rosa's daughter, Erena, soon to be their third co-wife.

assistant schoolteacher, Antonio (a married Campa man from the community of Picha). She said she would marry him if he would leave his Matsigenka wife. Erena's half-sister Irima saw the note and told Erena's mother (figure 18).

Then the whole matter became public. Antonio's wife confronted Erena near the schoolhouse, and a crowd gathered. She berated Erena and told her she could not have her husband. Erena scowled and held her ground, but said little. She did not appear at all intimidated or ashamed. Aradino, meanwhile, complained to Maestro, "Is this what you teach our children in school?" Aradino, of course, had his own designs on the girl. Erena made clear that she still desired the assistant schoolteacher as a mate, but he did not encourage the relationship and, shortly after, moved his family back to Picha. By 1974 Erena was married to Aradino and had borne him a son.

Erena was in a bind. She did not want to marry an old man who had been in a father relationship to her throughout her later childhood. She tried to escape. She hoped that we would provide a safe haven for her and tried to win the handsome young schoolteacher's heart. She was not frightened or intimidated when her mother tried to use force to take her home or when the schoolteacher's wife challenged her in public. She firmly, and at times angrily, stood her ground. But her options were few. Her "father" would not approve her marriage elsewhere, and she would have to leave her mother in order to marry (an inappropriate, though possible, outcome). The assistant schoolteacher's salary and authority were strengths she hoped to use to extricate herself from the bind she was in, but he refused to play. So her protest went for naught, and she eventually accepted an outcome that, if not inevitable, was probably as much in her interest as the available alternatives.

In a case of late adolescence, Santiago was about twenty-three in 1972 and was married to Marina, age twenty; they had no children. Everyone agreed that he was lazy by nature, like the howler monkey. He became one of the earliest hangers-on at our household, taking advantage of our early efforts to build ties through generosity. His routine was to ask for things as frequently as possible because it took little effort and we might comply. Certainly, we gave him medicine, as we did anyone else who showed up asking for help, and in the beginning we gave out a multitude of small gifts like kerosene, matches, and fishhooks.

But Santiago never made any effort to reciprocate. He was among the first people we asked, "What will you give me in return?" He invariably answered, "Nothing," with such frankness that it was almost charming. Once, in January 1973, after I had given him many unreciprocated gifts, I asked him for some papaya, and he replied, "What will you give me?" After that, I wrote in my journal, "Santiago comes whenever he feels bored, apparently, and amuses himself by asking me for things for free and by pointing out all his sores and ailments, trying to bully me into giving him attention or medicine—he is a pest, and without doubt the laziest man in the community."

Santiago was believed to be sterile *(terira intomintempa)*. Everyone he had lived with agreed that he did not "know how to work" and that he hardly brought food home. He had planted a small garden in which he worked half-heartedly, and he earned staple crops from Maestro in return for field labor. An explanation for his laziness was his lack of potency. His nickname *otiovune,* perhaps a play on the words *otiomiani ishivu,* "little penis," indicated his inadequacy: not only sterile, he did not know how to have intercourse with a woman. When younger he had lived with a man named Asencio, who, when Santiago did not work, put chili pepper on his penis (cf. Roe 1982: 225). This remedy apparently led to a slight improvement in his industriousness.

Nevertheless, Santiago was accepted for what he was. He had a wife and a single woman (Maritina) who lived in his house and called him "Father." When accompanying other men on work tasks, he sat and whittled or shot his slingshot while they did the work, all the time carrying on a friendly conversation that seemed to contain no resentment

on the part of the hardworking companion. This tolerance for individual variation and responsibility is the flip side of Matsigenka efforts to
instill diligence, restraint, and generosity in growing children. If Santiago was the way he was, then so be it.

On the one hand, Santiago was a handsome young man with a pleasant manner. He was guileless and friendly. He was not ridiculed or os-
tracized. On the other hand, accepting him as he was did not mean that
people took on burdens on his behalf. They gave him the little he earned,
with which he appeared contented. One incident captures his marginal
situation. He came by to see me in late April 1973, drunk and asking for
soap and matches. When I asked what he would give me in return, he
said, "Nothing." At that moment Angel showed up offering me three
spinning tops for a bar of soap, which I gave him. Seeing this exchange,
Santiago left and returned later with some spinning tops, but I was
nearly out of soap and had enough tops, so I had to refuse the transaction. He was, in a sense, "a day late and a dollar short," but that was in
character. Also in character was his most serious miscalculation. He asked
another woman to become his second wife. Marina, already disappointed
in him for not giving her a child, stormed off to become another man's
second wife. Meanwhile, his prospective second wife refused, and Santiago was left without a mate.

Later childhood and adolescence elaborate on themes encountered at
the beginning of Matsigenka self-development. Children are not taught
but are allowed and expected to watch and learn, aided by an occasional
"Look, am I doing this right?" Their individuality is conceived as a cre-
ative response to their inheritance of qualities from their parents, especially their same-sex parent. Adolescents and young adults confront a
world in which the self-serving acts of others are taken for granted but
for which their own strong sense of self has prepared them, as seen in
the cases of Erena and Santiago. But strong self-centeredness also creates difficulties for the family group, and so the lessons of puberty seclusion emphasize self-restraint and generosity, and in this way they tackle
the problem of impulse control that is the central theme of Matsigenka
folktales and cautionary stories.

The Interpersonal World: The View from Folktales

The Matsigenka enjoy telling and listening to folktales, especially in the
evening. The audience is usually quite engaged, interrupting the narra-

tive to ask questions or to make comments. Sometimes, members of the audience show that they are emotionally affected by the story: Once, as she told the story of Kashiri (Moon), Pororinta mentioned that Kashiri's bride was big and her vagina was big. At this point Pororinta's husband, Aretoro, interrupted the story to exclaim, "If she were here now, I would sleep only with her!" He was obviously aroused by a story in which Kashiri marries a stereotypically desirable woman, and he could say so in front of his wife.

Folktales offer a unique window into the kinds of interpersonal situations—albeit stylized and fantastic in the stories—that Matsigenkas fear. An example is the story of Narani, a nocturnal bird (the common potoo, *Nyctibius griseus*).

Narani

There was a man who used to get drunk all the time and go off to drink by himself, leaving his wife alone at home. He said he did not want his wife to have children because he wanted her to work only for him. One night, when the woman was alone, Narani appeared as a man and called to her. She was afraid he would kill her, but then she told him to come and give her a child. Narani entered and spent the night until the husband returned. Then Narani assumed his bird shape and flew out.

Her husband brought back a tinamou [game bird]. When he asked her to open the door, she remained lying down. When he asked her to cook the tinamou, she said she was too sick. When he offered her food, she said that she was too sick to eat, that she had a toothache. He asked, "Why are you sick?" "Because you do not know how to give me a child," she replied. He said, "If I gave you a child, how would you work?" She said, "I could work." But the man knew from her illness that she had had intercourse with Narani and that his penis had broken her back.

That night, Narani came near the house [as a bird] and rested in a papaya tree. The man said, "I will shoot him." "Do not kill your brother," the woman said. "He is not my brother; he's a bird," the man said. His wife fell asleep, and he shot Narani. When she woke up, she was cured. She got angry and tried to kill her husband but could not. She said, "Now, kill me." He said, "Wait until I finish eating." Then he tied her to a tree and cut open her abdomen. Inside were thousands of tiny *narani* babies. The largest was a few inches long and ready to be born.

Narani took her away with him [i.e., her soul]. The man ran into the forest, until he came to the house of his classificatory daughter. "Where is my mother?" she asked. "She is dead," he replied. "Narani killed her. I want to sleep here."

After some time, he returned to his former home. Narani was sitting up in the tree, very sad. The man cut some sugar cane and sucked it. The day was cloudy, without sun. On the way back to his daughter's house, he encountered his wife's spirit. She said, "Why did you kill me before?" He said, "Because

Narani already killed you." She said, "Cut me open now," but the man fell unconscious because she was *ovegaga* (*kamagarini,* a very evil spirit). Later, he
came to and went to his daughter's house. He was very sick. He slept on a sandy
beach. He could not get up. "Why can't you get up?" his daughter asked. He
answered, "Because I saw your mother earlier and she killed me." In the morning, he was dead.

This economically told story offers a clear emotional narrative. In the
first two statements we learn of a man who drinks beer alone and wants
his wife to work only for him, two selfish and excessive desires that lead
to disaster. His wife, though fearful, assertively pursues her reproductive desire with the night bird, Narani, an act that in Matsigenka lore is
bound to be fatal, for her soul is taken by the spirit. If we count Narani's
implicit desire for the woman, the story begins with four instances of
desire, setting up a dangerous love triangle consisting of a selfish man,
his neglected wife, and the man-spirit who gets her pregnant. These
clashing desires are followed by a series of violent acts: husband shoots
bird-rival; wife attempts to kill husband; husband kills wife (cutting
open her belly to reveal the horrifying sight of hundreds of *narani* babies); demon-wife kills husband. The story presents us with a marriage
between two willful individuals whose conflicting desires lead to frustration, aggression, death/loss, and mourning.

To the Matsigenka, this story is not far-fetched but in fact entirely
plausible. The husband's selfish desire that his wife should not have children so that she can work only for him, while culturally inappropriate, is
not so different from the two actual cases in Shimaa, noted above, where
dominant women required subordinate women to kill their newborns
in order to have the subordinate women work for them.

Nor is the idea of a married woman seeking another man to impreg-
nate her far-fetched. In Shimaa, two men were reputed to be unable or
unwilling to have intercourse (*terira irogote ineerora tsinane,* "not he-
knows he-see-her woman," or *terira irogote iragantera,* "not he-knows
he-take-her"). As we saw, Santiago was impotent and lost his wife to a
man who could give her children. Evaristo, like the husband in the Narani story, was said to be capable of intercourse but did not want his
wife, Serafina, to become pregnant. When she died in childbirth, two
contrasting accounts were given.

The Death of Serafina (Version I)

Evaristo's wife, Serafina, had an affair with her cross-cousin Mauro and became
pregnant. When she felt the baby stirring in her, she believed she might have

been impregnated by a demon and went to Maestro for help. Using a stethoscope, he diagnosed a healthy pregnancy. After he left for teacher training in Yarina Cocha, she became anxious, believing she was in labor throughout the month of March. To hasten birth, a neighbor prepared the folk remedy, *potogo*, in a tea. But, not being familiar with the drug, he gave her several times the usual dose, and her diaphragm seized up and she died.

This version tells of a commonplace tragedy: a woman who dies unnecessarily of an overdose of a folk remedy. Her anxiety about the pregnancy, stemming from her fantasy that she had been impregnated by a demon, may have been partly anticipation of spiritual punishment for her extramarital liaison.

Another version of this story, however, is notably different:

The Death of Serafina (Version II)

In the fall of 1971 Evaristo and Serafina went on a collecting expedition to the headwaters of the Río Pogentimari and camped for the night along the riverbank, making a caña brava shelter. She left the house to defecate and encountered Segamairini, an evil spirit who chased her into the woods. When she got back, she told Evaristo. Some days or weeks later, she had a dream in which her father, who was dead, came to her and invited her to come live with him, saying, "I have my son-in-law here" *(notineri)*, but not meaning Evaristo. After that, although she had not had intercourse for some time, she began to feel the presence of a mature baby inside her. She believed it was the demon's child. When it was time to give birth, the child strangled her from inside. Serafina was buried downstream on an island that has since been swept away by the changing currents of the river. Evaristo burned their house down, and his remaining family, including two related households, fled upstream to escape her soul, which could be expected to return to the house to get her possessions (she was buried in only her cushma and beads). The burning of the house made it hard for the ghost to find its way, and after a few days the danger passed. Serafina was now transformed into Segamairini, a powerful and evil spirit with a large penis, who was capable of killing everyone in the vicinity of Evaristo's house. (The other relatives did not burn their houses and returned after four days.)

Version I minimizes supernatural involvement. There is no explicit connection between Serafina's extramarital love affair and her death by accidental overdose. But what about Version II? Her implicitly sexual encounter with a demon is clearly related to her death by strangulation by the demon-child inside her. In fact, Version II is remarkably similar to the Narani story: a wife whose husband refuses to make her pregnant has sex with a demon and is pregnant with a demon baby; she dies, and her husband and close relatives flee the house where she lived because she could return as a demon to kill them and drag them down into the underworld with her.

Because I collected the stories of Serafina early in fieldwork and the Narani story much later, I did not make the connection between them during my fieldwork. It is not so much that Serafina II replicates Narani but that both represent a natural storyline within the world-view of the Matsigenka. In fact, most of their folktales follow a common sequence of emotions and actions that can serve as a model for their greatest worries about interpersonal relations.

Matsigenka folktales are emotional narratives: a protagonist's strong emotions instigate emotional reactions and dangerous behavior in other protagonists. In almost all of twenty-nine Matsigenka tales I have examined in detail, the core dramatic narrative of the story repeats a common emotional progression: either someone desires something inappropriate (e.g., a man prefers the taste of human flesh to that of animal flesh), or someone inappropriately does not want someone else to have something they desire (e.g., a father opposes his daughter's desire to marry a blameless suitor). In either case the inappropriate desire makes someone else in the story angry (e.g., relatives of the cannibal's victims, the frustrated suitor). The anger is expressed in aggression: people are mutilated, killed, or transformed into animals or demons. Frequently, the tale ends with sorrow and blame, generally directed at one of the protagonists who got angry and caused all the violence and suffering. Analysis of many such tales reveals the common pattern summarized in figure 19.

The tale Narani exhibits this pattern in the flow of emotions: Desire 1 (husband wants to drink alone) and Desire 2 (husband wants to hoard wife's services) → Anger (wife's frustration) → Fear (wife's, of Narani) → Desire 3 (wife wants Narani to give her a child) → Desire 4 (implicit, Narani wants to give wife a child) → Suffering (wife sick) → Aggression 1 (husband shoots Narani) → Aggression 2 (wife attacks husband) → Aggression 3 (husband cuts/kills wife) → Loss (Narani mourns wife) → Aggression 4 (wife-demon kills husband).

Version II of Serafina's death may be regarded as a transformation of the coolly factual Version I into one consistent with the emotional message of the Narani tale. Serafina's husband does not want her to get pregnant, so she seeks a lover, but he turns out to be a demon. Her implied anger at and betrayal of her husband are contained in Version I; her belly swelling with the demon's offspring and her death are contained in Version II. Evaristo's terror at her likely return and spiritual at-

FIGURE 19. Common form of
the Matsigenka emotion story.

tack on him leads him to burn down the house and flee far away for as
long as it takes her spirit to give up and leave the area. The transformation from Version I to Version II "mythologizes" Serafina's death; it
turns a "just-the-facts" story, in which death is accidental, into a morality tale, in which death is the spiritual consequence of adultery.

Matsigenka folktales are rich stories full of details about all aspects
of ordinary life and spiritual existence. They nearly always portray emotional states and sometimes indicate their causes and consequences.
Table 23 lists the frequency with which emotions and emotionally
charged outcomes appear in the twenty-nine folktales I analyzed. Table
23 supports the conclusion that Matsigenka folktales are nearly always
tragedies. Only about 10 percent of the emotions and outcomes of the
tales reflect approval, gratification, and happiness. The other 90 percent
involve anger, fear, threat, aggression, and suffering, all as a consequence
of the clash of impulsive desire. The desire is usually but not always of a
man for a woman; sometimes it is of a woman for a man. Otherwise,
most often it is someone's desire for a particular food, especially meat,
that leads to anger and its terrible consequences. The Matsigenka conception of self as a powerful center of will goes hand in hand with a belief in the inevitability of anger when desire is thwarted. And anger be-
gets aggression. Sensing this ever-present potential for violence within
themselves and those with whom they live, Matsigenkas become anxious when anger is aroused. Stories present anxiety-provoking situa-

TABLE 23. Incidence of Emotions and Emotionally Charged
Outcomes in Twenty-Nine Matsigenka Folktales

Emotions/Emotional Outcomes	Number of Occurrences
Desire (especially for sex and meat)	81
Anger/frustration	51
Aggression	45
Admonition (includes warning, threat, suspicion)	27
Loss, sadness, remorse	21
Fear	19
Approval and gratification	19
Pain and suffering	16
Happiness/happy ending	12
TOTAL	291

tions over and over, showing how they are resolved with punishment
and frequently assigning blame.

Emotional Life

The Matsigenka tend to fear strong emotions (Shepard 2002). Ordinarily, they are calm, quiet, polite, and good-natured people—this is how
they present themselves in everyday behavior, certainly with strangers
but also throughout the daily routines of household life. Beer feasts are
an accepted opportunity to use alcohol to relax this emotional control,
but only to a degree. Even at a beer feast, if strong emotions result in
violence or destructive verbal attacks, they can leave a trail of lasting anger and regret. Strong emotions may also appear in dreams, *kisanirintsi*,
where they can be frightening and are often taken to be omens of im-
pending disaster.

DESIRE (*NOKOGAKE*, "I WANT")

The root *-koga-* refers to all kinds of desire, including the desire for
food, sex, companionship, and possessions. In my experience, the Matsigenka are strongly assertive people. They take it for granted that all
beings—animals, humans, spirits, even some plants—are willful selves

who shape their world through choice and action, like the self-creating Trickster Kashibokani. This attitude reappears in many domains: crops fail not because of the soil but because of the seed, the strength and capacities integral to the individual plant; when game are scarce, they have not been killed off but have fled the sound of shotguns; when fish are scarce after repeated applications of barbasco, they are not depleted but "hiding"; in a difficult birth, the child "doesn't want to be born." In these examples, crops, game, fish, and unborn children are all assumed to be active and responsible, not passive outcomes of their environment.

The notion of inheritance from the same-sex parent reinforces a sense of uniqueness. "I am as I am" is the underlying attitude, "and I do as I do." Such individuality is by itself a sufficient explanation for much behavior. I found it difficult to get people to speculate on the motives of others or even to talk about individual differences. Why did Karoroshi move his house? "*Kogapai* [no reason]." How do your arrows differ from Omenko's? "He makes his, and I make mine." Why do men plant many varieties of manioc instead of only one? "Because they want to." When I told people a version of a folktale different from the one they were familiar with, they would say, "Well, this is the way I heard it." They were not surprised that someone else heard it differently, nor was it a problem. The problem was mine, my wanting to discover explanations for and attitudes toward individual differences and discrepancies that—for the Matsigenka—required no further comment.

They do not often mask the self-centered motives of the individual, whether discussing themselves, others, or the protagonists of folktales. When Evaristo, for example, told me of his feelings about Serafina's death, he simply said, "I miss her. Who will cook for me, who will weave my cushma?" Similarly, in the folktale Matsiti (Ross 1947: 67), when a man discovers that a demon-woman (Matsiti) has killed his wife and taken her place, he kills her. He then has his mother take care of his son while he goes to find another wife. In a parenthesis, Ellen Ross commented, "Practical people, these men!" She must have been looking for a deeper sense of mourning from the widower, as I was from Evaristo. We will see below that the loss and mourning are there, but the self-centered needs behind the mourning are not ennobled with a social gloss.

I examine in chapter 4 how the Matsigenka taught me to identify in every transaction exactly what my self-interest was and to assert it clearly and firmly. If my interests were not met, I was to withdraw the hand of friendship, albeit without apparent anger, and simply stop dealing with someone who was, to use a most common Matsigenka word, *michanti* (stingy). I was required to be, by my standards, rude (if not arrogant). Rudeness was not far below the surface of the courteous Matsigenka, who changed dramatically when drunk:

Fieldnote 7–1–73—Getting drunk among Matsigenka, as among ourselves, exaggerates states of mind: pensiveness, affection, despair, anger. But the most striking effect is an increase in selfishness, or self-willedness: an increase in small impoliteness, demands for attention, and getting into activities (drumming, fluting) to the partial or complete exclusion of others.

Willful beings with varying degrees of supernatural power appear in many Matsigenka folktales. Osheto (Spider Monkey), for example, married his sister because, as he said, "There were no others. I wanted her. I took her." Later, driven from the house and living deep in the forest, he was invited to return home by his father. But he replied, "If I hadn't married my sister, perhaps I would come. But perhaps you have other daughters. If I came home, your daughters there, I might marry incestuously with them. So it is better that I don't come. So I won't marry them. So I won't marry all your daughters." He is describing himself as someone who cannot control his incestuous impulses.

Where the central clash of desires in a folktale does not concern sex, it is most likely to concern greed or gluttony over protein foods like game, fish, or beans. In the story of Yaniri (Howler Monkey), a man borrowed beans from his cross-cousin, Woolly Monkey, who was married to his sister. Woolly Monkey did not want to share his beans, but his wife talked him into it. But Howler became so entranced by the delicious taste that he cooked most of the beans and ate them, laughing, "He he he he he he he. O aroma of beans!" When Woolly Monkey found out, he was enraged at the deception and hit Howler in the throat, causing his throat pouch to appear. Howler Monkey then became a powerful and not so friendly shaman and now lives in the trees. This story appears to pinpoint the badness of Woolly Monkey's anger rather than Howler's gluttony. Had Woolly Monkey been generous, nothing bad need have happened.

It sheds an interesting light on Matsigenka individualism to learn that they are enthusiastic and competitive soccer players. They practice hard and play to win. Individuals strive to shine, and whenever someone scores a goal, the audience cheers and those who missed the point turn excitedly to their neighbors and say, *tiani igolatake,* "Who scored?" The predominance of grandstanding and a reluctance to pass or collaborate in strategy point to a strongly self-centered motivation on the players' part.

ANGER AND AGGRESSION (*NOKISAKE*, "I AM ANGRY")

Anger is far more prevalent in folktales than it is in everyday behavior. Anger is strongly associated with danger and fear because anger can get out of control and lead to aggression, injury, and death. In the cross-cultural "colors of emotions" study (Johnson, Johnson, and Baksh 1986), for example, the pattern that most distinguished the way Matsigenkas associate colors and emotions from other cultural groups pertained to anger: whereas for Maya, Spanish, and English subjects anger tended to be closely associated with strength (anger makes you strong), for Matsigenka subjects it was most closely associated with fear (anger is dangerous).

Disappointment, loss, theft, violence, and humiliation make the Matsigenka angry. And while some anger is vented in the heat of the moment and then passes, the Matsigenka can also carry a grudge, rekindling old anger even years after the event. Anger is the most common reason given for leaving a hamlet or community.

In everyday demeanor the Matsigenka approach some Apollonian ideal of calm and courtesy. People speak so softly they cannot be heard across the room. Rather than raise their voices, they send small children with messages. In Shimaa, social graces are carefully observed: visitors (including people with whom one has an old or current grudge) are always offered a mat, conversations begin safely with neutral topics, and all visitors are addressed individually on arrival and again on departure. For the most part, people answer questions with disarming frankness and usually with a smile. This was the pattern both in households where we were unfamiliar visitors and in those where we were regular and even live-in guests.

The sense of peace and tranquility of life with the Matsigenka is so wonderful that it comes as something of a shock when it is violated. For example, while on a hunting trip early in my fieldwork, when I was still willing to hunt animals with the shotgun I had brought, I was asked to bring down a howler monkey:

Fieldnote 1–24–73—. . . after I shot the first *yaniri*, it fell 30–40 feet out of a tree into a creek bed, but was still alive. The others seemed afraid of it, and Felipe asked if it was a *seripigari* [shaman]—it was female and without a howler pouch in its throat, and hence not a *seripigari*. After a few minutes they all began to stone it to death, laughing riotously at its attempts to escape.

The monkey was seriously injured and kept scrabbling out of the way of the pursuing men, who joked back and forth about her terrified screams and futile maneuvers.

This instance was not isolated. One afternoon Aretoro brought in a heron (trumpeter) he had caught in a trap. He had clipped its wings, and he laughed as it flopped ineffectually on the ground. A group of men and boys gathered to prod and taunt the bird, which attempted to strike back with its beak and thereby evoked roars of laughter and new taunts. Aretoro suddenly kicked the bird viciously into the air, then did so over and over to the laughter of the group. After a time, seemingly weary of the sport, he abruptly grabbed the bird and broke its neck. The crowd drifted away. Taunting the trumpeter was similar to the way many people played with our kitten, Mishi, by prodding her into a fury and then laughing.

The Matsigenka view anger as a powerful force capable of taking over an individual with disastrous results. Several stories contain an episode in which a violent man says, "Kill me before I kill you," or gives instructions for how his enemy may kill him (e.g., Kashibokani). For example, Julio believes the following to be a true story from the past:

Fieldnote 8–9–75—Kintiaro was a fierce *seripigari* [shaman] who wanted to wipe out Julio's ancestors. He was violent. He went hunting with his classificatory brothers and threatened to kill them: *"I will kill you. Kill me if you want, I don't care. If you don't, I will kill you."* They attacked him at night and killed him, even though he said it was a joke and begged them not to kill him. They left his body, but he cured himself, except that he remained blind. They attacked him again, and this time cut him up—his blood was black—and put him in the river. But again, with the help of *inetsane* [his spirit helpers], he reassembled himself, though still blind. After a long series of events, they managed to kill Kintiaro.

In this story and others like it is the idea of people being so uncontrollably violent that they must be killed. In one story, a man in Shimaa on two separate occasions lost his temper and hit someone. After the second incident, the men of the surrounding households said to him, "You must leave here. You are too angry and cannot live here anymore." The next morning, they found his cushma lying on the rocks at the edge of the river. According to one version, he drowned in the river. But, in another version, he still roams the forest on the other side of the river, naked like a wild animal.

When they are angry or distraught with loss, both men and women run into the forest to be alone. Men love nothing better than to go off hunting, alone or in pairs. Single households go to their distant gardens to enjoy the isolation for anywhere from a few days to many years. The social high that accompanies group events like fishing expeditions and beer feasts (see below) has its opposite in the fatigue with social relations that seeps in over time and results in withdrawal and escape.

When angry confrontation does occur, it is frightening to people, who try to intervene in the fighting, disarm the anger with humor and strained laughter, or leave the scene. The following angry outburst occurred in the context of beer drinking (a partial transcription is in O. Johnson 1978: 144–45):

Fieldnote 8–7–75—Felipe and Mariano working late today; Ekitoro was helping by cutting brush with a broad knife. Ekitoro comes in about 4:30. Then about 5 Felipe comes in. Both he and Mariano are drunk from a pot of *shitea* they had with them in the garden. When Mariano returned, he bawled his son out at great length about how hard he would have to work as a man. Then he came here [Felipe's house] and told us [Orna and me] how we were like a real father and mother to him. He reminded his son about the time he (Apa) burned down the house.

Later, we went to Mariano's house to drink beer. Julio was there with his family. Mariano and Felipe got very drunk. Still later, Mariano came here and sang [orated] in a high-pitched voice for a long time, getting angrier and angrier at Rosa (not clear for what). Felipe was also angry at Eva for not making beer.

Mariano jumped up and ran in and started slapping Rosa around. The other women got agitated, aroused Felipe who went out and had a long shouting match in which Mariano repeated how much he was working for Felipe (each slapped own self quite a bit). His anger about this was already reflected in his outburst against his son earlier.

8–8–75—Things still hairy in the morning. Felipe and Mariano are very mad at each other. Karoroshi says *tovaiti notsarogake—tera nonseraritake* (I'm scared, I'm not brave).

Karoroshi's expression means, literally, "plenty I-afraid-am—not I-masculine-am." The profound anger of his two brothers-in-law had him frightened, and he packed up his family and left the party early in the evening.

The fight itself was fairly well contained. Mariano's real anger was at the weeks of hard labor he had been putting into his brother's garden, but he first deflected it onto his son, addressing the real issue of hard work, then recalling how his son had burned down his house. Then he turned on his wife, finally unleashing abusive blows that agitated everyone and required his brother to intervene. Felipe was the real object of his wrath, and the two brothers carried on an intense high-pitched verbal duel outside the house, in which, interestingly, they refrained mostly from striking each other, slapping themselves on the body instead. This was a major fight. Mariano was sullen for days after and finally moved his family to a new site a kilometer downriver. The worst of the bad feeling between the two close brothers passed after some months, but Mariano continued to live separately. In this way anger brings about the social instability that the schoolteacher at Camaná had complained about: "They get angry and always want to leave." In many folktales where blame is assigned, the blame is placed on the one who got angry.

Actual physical aggression was quite rare in the vicinity of Shimaa in our experience. In addition to the infanticides and the violent man driven from the community, a homicide was reported to have happened over a love affair in the not-too-distant past, and we met a man whose face was disfigured by a suicide attempt with a shotgun in the mouth before the Shimaa school community was formed. But tales of infanticide, homicide, and suicide tended to blend into folk literature, so we were often unsure whether a death really happened or was a projection of violence into folktales.

Related to the process of projections is the way that the Matsigenka deal with death. Any death is upsetting and brings about discussion of possible causes, including violence. When children die, gossips are likely to recall that they were dropped or beaten sometime before the death. When women die in childbirth, supernatural aggression is suspected. When a man dies, it was a demon who took human form as his lover to steal his soul. A death becomes an opportunity to project onto others anger that is ordinarily contained, with some difficulty, in the individual.

Their fear of violence leads the Matsigenka to avoid anger like a contaminant. Shepard (1999: 54) provides a telling example of how the Matsigenka viewed Yora violence:

Though the two groups exchanged no information regarding medicinal plants directly, the Matsigenka became aware of some Yora medicines by observing the trail left in retreat after raiding expeditions. In 1987, long before I worked with the Yora, an older Matsigenka man, Quispe, pointed out to me a *Chondodendron* (Menispermaceae) species, saying it was a plant used by the Yora. He had observed that the Yora stripped the leaves from the plant, but did not know what they used it for. He had no interest in experimenting with the plant as a medicine, since he feared it might make the Matsigenka become warlike and violent like the Yora.

ANXIETY AND FEAR (*NOTSAROGAKE*, "I AM AFRAID"; *TSARONTI*, "COWARD, FEARFUL PERSON")

In stories, the sequence from desire to anger to aggression is followed often by someone expressing fear, a reasonable reaction. Still, I did not experience the Matsigenka as fearful people. Their peaceful faces were ready to break into smiles at any moment and lacked the haunted eyes or etched-in frowns of people who are plagued by anxiety. During a storm or while they awaited the arrival of relatives who were traveling on the river, their anxiety would become unmistakable as they cringed after a thunderclap or asked, "Where can they be?" But these moments passed when the storm ended or the relatives arrived safely, and the usual tranquility returned. When I surprised someone by coming close before they noticed me, their eyes would widen, followed by a pleased grin, rather than the startled jump and "Oh, you scared me!" I was familiar with in my own cultural world.

The words for fear describe immediate danger from other people (*notsarogake*, "I am afraid") or from dangerous animals and spirits (*nopinkake*, "I am afraid"). Anxiety or worry is rarely expressed, although *nokenkiake*, "I am thinking about," is sometimes used in this sense, as "I am thinking (wondering, worried) about my maize crop." A general absence of anxiety was among the most pleasant aspects of living among the Matsigenka, and I experienced a sharp drop in my own level of anxiety while among them. Watching my anxiety build back up to "normal" levels after my return to the United States gave me a keen appreciation of the truth of the description of ours as the Age of Anxiety. I attribute their relative lack of anxiety to a combination of a reality in which anger is well-controlled and unlikely to erupt without warning and to an inner life relatively free from intolerant self-judgments (a harsh superego). This lack of anxiety may seem strange after all the evidence we have seen for a fear of violence arising from out-of-control impulsiveness. But it is a matter of emphasis. In pointing out that Matsigenkas are concerned about impulsiveness, I do not imply that they are more concerned than other people. On the contrary, they seem to me to be far less judgmental of themselves and others than people are in the modern peasant and urban societies with which I am familiar.

Padre Andrés Ferrero complained that the Matsigenka "permits neither repression nor criticism" (chapter 1). This is certainly not true— they control lust, wrath, gluttony, sloth, and other "deadly sins" effectively in their own way, including through both criticism (via teaching and gossip) and repression (to the degree that they deny their own impulses and project them onto in-laws and folktale characters). But Ferrero is ethnocentrically pointing to a real difference between his own background and what he experienced among the Matsigenka—namely, the Matsigenka are not guilt-ridden. Padre Ferrero accurately saw their acceptance of the inevitability of appetites that will seek fulfillment as posing difficulties for effective missionization.

Fear appears in a number of dreams, like Roberto's anxiety dream on the eve of a bush-plane trip we were scheduled to take:

Fieldnote 8–24–75—Roberto told me his dream from last night; he was travelling down the Kompiroshiato on a raft with his whole family—Julio, Juana, Guillermo, Elva—and the trip was very rough and dangerous, with fast water and huge rocks looming. They were going "just for a visit."

We were indeed to be traveling in the downstream direction, albeit by air. In the dream Roberto's anxiety is represented by the rough, dangerous rapids and looming boulders. In addition to the understandable fears associated with travel by single-engine plane over the rainforest, there is also a complex meaning to the direction downstream *(kamatikya)*. It is at once the direction of modern Peruvian society, the direction in which ancient enemies dwelt, and the direction in which the soul must travel past Moon's weirs if it is to reach heaven. He understandably felt apprehension about traveling in that direction in a single-engine plane.

Perhaps most anxiety arises in relation to conflicts with other people and, no doubt sometimes, with oneself. For example, late in her pregnancy Eva became anxious that something was wrong, although subsequent events proved she was in perfect health. At this time, however, she had a hysteria-like attack in which she hallucinated a snake and fainted. Felipe rushed to her side. Pale, and cradling her in his arms, he whistled and blew on her head to recall her soul. When she came to, the family began a search for broken dietary taboos. They finally settled on Eva's co-wife, Amaria, who had eaten *shito* monkey during Eva's pregnancy. Having solved this frightening puzzle, Felipe drained off a whole liter of manioc beer in one draft. The anxiety behind Eva's attack likely had to do with her angry and competitive relationship with Amaria.

Breaking taboos, as Amaria was accused of doing, is willful and impulsive behavior. It is analogous to a common theme in folktales: disaster results when someone disobeys the leader or shaman. For example, tales explaining the origins of Quechua speakers *(ponyarona)* and of Euro-

Americans *(virakocha)* describe how someone ignored the shaman's advice and created a path or opening into this world from a lower plane of existence. In the tale of Anteater (Ross 1947: 36), a man disregards a shaman's warning and is killed. The shaman discovers the corpse and sadly announces, "I tried to call you. I told you to come, but you didn't. If you had, he likely wouldn't have killed you." Such lamentations are the usual accompaniment of disobedience in folktales, and they point to the underlying anxiety about transgressions, with the shaman playing the part of the authority figure.

Dreams often contain images that frighten the dreamers. Jaguars, snakes, a great wind, turbulent waters in the river frequently appear in dream accounts, signifying great danger. Matsigenkas are quite interested in their dreams and stress their vividness and realism. Emelio reported this dream in Camaná in 1976:

Now, I dreamt earlier. It was like daytime. As I went along there hunting, I came across jaguar sitting in the trail. He climbed a tree, guarding the trail. Then he jumped. He didn't come for me. Then I shot him. It was as bright as day, but it was a dream.

Then I woke up. I was here in my sleeping place. I was so frightened I was shaking. It didn't happen—it was a dream.

Then I slept again. I dreamt again. I dreamt about Brother. We went hunting peccary together. I shot one peccary and Brother shot one. I awoke. Nothing. It was a dream. Now, that's all.

And here is a dream of Leonidas's (in Camaná, 1976):

A while ago I dreamt many different dreams. In one the demon Kamagarini took human form. He carried me far away. He wanted to kill me quickly, but I took my arrows and shot and killed him. Then I went far away alone. Lots of Kamagarini came for me, they tried to stab me. But in my dream I wasn't afraid. I protected myself well. I was able to kill those demons. I was very frightened in my soul. I had no strength. But then I woke up, very frightened. I wondered what my dream had meant. I don't know.

I slept, I dreamt of rain. It fell heavily. I couldn't run away. Everything was a river of mud. It destroyed every living thing. But I had wings like a sparrow. It was as though my soul was flying through air. I took one man with me. I carried him up. Then I awoke. I was in my house here. That dream of mine, it was as if I were dead. All those others I saw in my dream were dead. But everything I have told of my dreams is nothing [*kogapage*]. I didn't really see them.

Then I slept again. I dreamt about jaguar. He came for me at my house, to get me. Then I shot him. I killed him.

Now, that's all.

The Matsigenka commonly believe that certain kinds of dreams portend death, a theme also found in folktales. If a man dreams of an encounter with a deer, he will encounter Deer (spirit) in the form of his wife or lover and have intercourse, not realizing that his soul is being broken up until later, when he becomes ill and then dies. This belief is an aspect of the fear that sexual desire makes one vulnerable to spiritual danger, and it is related to the belief that dead loved ones will (out of desire or longing) try to take their surviving spouses down into the underworld with them.

Most of these fears are ultimately about illness, suffering, and death. Because these are realities the Matsigenka experience directly throughout life, we may say that there is an undercurrent of anxiety ready to surface when omens of various kinds set them off. Seeing a vision (*notsavitetara,* "I have a vision") like Eva's snake can be such an omen. Others have reported seeing a butterfly *(notsavitetara pachantaro)* in the corner of their eye then finding it gone or mistaking a log in the forest for a person. These visions are glimpses of demons and carry mortal danger.

A portion of these fears postulate a malicious, possibly jealous, world of others. Men often avoid the trails near other settlements. Being away from their immediate neighborhood, they fear snakes or other dangerous animals that might attack them for encroaching on others' hunting territories. Or people fear the excessive tiredness that can be caused by magical herbs used against them by a spurned lover. Body aches and pains can also be caused by the wasp spirit that maliciously shoots an invisible arrow. Incidentally, excessive tiredness and body aches can be explained by amebiasis, but those invisible beings (amebas) are not recognized in Matsigenka folk medicine.

Baer (1983: 7) points out that, for the Matsigenka, fear is a common reaction to anything believed to be contaminating, such as exposure to menstrual blood, violation of food taboos, and dangerous feelings like anger and greed: "Contamination produces fright and this 'opens the body.' When frightened, a body opens, leaving it defenseless, easy prey for any witch sending off darts and menacing helping-spirits. . . . [However,] demons that bring illness and death can themselves be frightened away (by certain body-painting designs)."

In short, the Matsigenka weave a tapestry of danger in which realistic concerns about health and safety are linked to failures—one's own and others'—of impulse (desire) control. Although they are not anxiety-ridden, their tranquility is often disturbed by perceptions of danger both material (poisonous snakes really exist) and spiritual (snakes are the arrows of demons who hunt our souls for food). The impulses that move spirits to harm people are easily recognized because they are the same selfish, impulsive motives that humans try to control in everyday life. Although the Matsigenka have no exact word for guilt and show no evidence of the self-hate and self-condemnation that accompany full-blown guilt over sin, they do hold people responsible (*ipakagantanake;* Snell 1998: 175), and there is something guiltlike (conscience-stricken) about the accusations and punishments that accompany impulsive behavior in dreams and folktales.

The Matsigenka do have a word for shame (*nashiventaka,* "I am embarrassed or ashamed"), and it can be a source of anxiety, particularly when connected to public ridicule. The Matsigenka are no strangers to ridicule, but at the same time they appear to be relatively immune to its effects. With the exception of schoolchildren asked to sing or recite for holiday celebrations, people appear not to be uncomfortably shy or afraid in public settings. On the contrary, they seem self-possessed when in public, free to watch and comment, to participate in and frankly enjoy what is going on without embarrassment. Verbal assaults and ridicule in public involve some shaming, but, in the cases I observed, the recipients of the attack did not appear overly disturbed. They stoically "took their medicine" with a sheepish grin, attacked back with barbs of their own, or defiantly denied or justified the acts of which they were accused.

In short, it is not easy to shame a Matsigenka. One reason may be found in the way shame is used in child rearing. Children are constantly admonished to correct their behavior, and shame may be used as part of this larger process: "If you eat like that, you will grow up to be tapir" or "You are lazy like howler monkey." But, as we have seen, these admonishments are administered with little heat or danger. The young child appears more curious than abashed, and parents patiently accept the child's attitude.

JOY/HAPPINESS (*NOSHINETAKE,* "I AM HAPPY")

If the expression of anger is common in folktales but rare in everyday life, then the opposite is true of happiness. My deepest sense of the Matsigenka is that their ordinary existence, while physically hard, is one of peace and relative contentment, punctuated by moments of strong feeling that usually pass quickly. I discovered that, as I settled into fieldwork, I felt an unaccustomed tranquility, which I identified with happiness. I became most acutely aware of this feeling when I came home to the United States and found the stresses of my own life quickly engulfing me, leaving me with a longing for Shimaa, a mild case of nostalgia for paradise lost.

The Matsigenka, however, do not often use the term *noshinetake* to label this everyday contentment. They use it to describe feelings closer to elation and joy. For example, at a beer feast drunken men continually asked me, *pishinetake,* "Are you happy?" Regardless of my response, they informed me more than once that they were "very happy." They also use the term to label the delight when a special good happens, like a successful hunt or a return to health.

In the folktales, happiness is one of the least commonly described feelings. Usually, it occurs near the end of a story, after the trials have been endured and the heroes have achieved a happy ending. In some cases, the happiness occurs when a mother is reunited with her lost child. In others, it is when the heroes reach the promised land of the unseen ones. Of the twenty-nine tales I analyzed, only six have happy endings for some of the protagonists, and then only after much violence and suffering. Clearly, depicting happiness is not the main work of the folktales.

Here is one text that does depict a happy state (Ross 1947: 45–46):

Terira Ineero Igamane
(The Immortals [Not He-Sees His-Death])

They live in the forest. They have wives and children. When their wives give birth, they feel no pain. If they give birth at noon and cut the umbilical cord, by mid-afternoon the baby is sitting up, by evening he is walking, and by dawn he is fully grown up.

They take good people (from earth) when they die, but the bad ones they take not. They have long hair. When it is sunny, they walk about; when cloudy, they do not walk. They are unseen, they are invisible.

They eat boquichico fish, a little from the backbone, then throw it back in the water, where it goes on living. They do the same with its scales. Guan does not fear them, comes right to their houses. Jaguar does not attack them; they call jaguars their dogs. They pick fruit, eat it, by next morning a new one has grown back. They dig manioc tubers, next morning a new one has grown back. The plant does not die. When they harvest banana, they do not cut down the tree, they merely cut the stalk; next day a new one has grown back. They weed their gardens a little, the weeds do not grow back.

When they cut out the palm heart, the palm does not lie down but straightens back up. Whatever trees they cut down, they do not die; they grow again. Their houses never wear out, they are always new. The manioc beer they drink is never sour but always sweet. They have canoes that they pole strong and fast. Unlike people, they do not sleep while traveling—they arrive in one day.

Their cushmas never wear out, their teeth never fall out, they never get sick. They have flutes, they have string instruments *(igovoire)*, they always sing beautifully. They are different, not like people.

This story tells of the happy state of the perfect beings also known as the unseen ones (chapter 5).

In the real world, group events, with or without beer, occasion unusual happiness. As I describe in chapter 4, cooperative work events like barbasco fishing stimulate joviality, exaggerated courtesy, and playfulness. These social highs cannot be sustained for more than two or three days, but cooperative work rarely lasts that long. The obvious pleasure schoolchildren take in showing up for school early and staying late may also owe something to this kind of social high. Visits between communities, which are organized around soccer matches, have also become happy occasions. The host community provides food, and conversation is animated.

At larger beer feasts, where there is plenty of beer and festivities go on for forty-eight hours or more, the highs (and lows) are more extreme than at extended-family events within the hamlet. As drunkenness waxes, courtesy wanes. The man who asks "Are you happy?" pushes his face into yours and insists on an answer, grinning with wet lips. Requests for more beer become demands. Dancers dart and swirl nonstop, eyes half-closed, faces lighted in ecstasy or trance. Much of the hilarity now centers on jokes. Because much of the humor has an aggressive edge to it, a good person knows how to take the joke without showing irritation. A story of misfortune, which would elicit comments like "Oh?" or "Is that right?" if the victim were present, can sometimes cause fits of laughter if the victim is not around.

PAIN AND MOURNING

In describing myself as "happy" among the Matsigenka, I was comparing a stressful professional life at home with a relatively carefree, adventuresome field study during which I was either healthy or able to treat afflictions like amebiasis with effective medication. For all their good-natured calm, life for the Matsigenka is hard, and they suffer much. Their life histories are full of accounts of the early deaths of parents, spouses, and children. Their usual greeting, *tera pimantsigate* ("You're not sick?"), is a reminder of how illness is a central preoccupation. The most desired foods and materials are scarce, and much of work life is filled with arduous tasks like weeding and cloth manufacture. They are careful not to overindulge children so that they will not grow up to be lazy, stingy malcontents.

A nurse, Joan Lemke, once told me she found the Matsigenka to be among the most stoical of the tribal peoples she treated in her clinic at Yarina Cocha. Shepard (1999: 69) writes, "The Matsigenka take a stoic attitude, understating their pains and illnesses." Even very sick people who must have been in considerable pain came to our house but waited to be noticed rather than show their discomfort. They matter-of-factly described their problem and accepted treatment with few questions or comments.

The Matsigenka frequently say *choeni nokamake,* "I almost died," when describing an illness episode. Although this is often an exaggeration, it is primarily an appreciation of how fragile life is and of how often people die quickly from conditions that could be readily treated in a clinic or hospital. Many people also told of episodes of weeks, months, and in one case years in which infections and injuries kept them housebound in pain. Men with painful conditions (water on the knee, toe split by machete, foot wounded by shotgun) still limped to their fields every day. Pain and suffering are familiar conditions for everybody.

Although stoic in the face of suffering, the Matsigenka feel loss strongly and mourn long after the loss. Even when traveling, they speak of missing home (*nokenkiakero,* "I think about it"). They describe much more intense loss and grieving by combining the root *-kenki-* (think) with the word for soul *(-sure-)* to form *nokenkisuretaka,* "I grieve" (literally "my soul thinks"; cf. Shepard 1999: 89). Evaristo, who pragmatically lamented the loss of his Serafina's weaving skills, nonetheless also described to me how for more than a year after her death he could barely drag himself to work and could find no joy in life. And Mike Baksh found that his good friend Aurelio, months after the loss of his young son to poisonous frog's eggs, said that all he dreamt about was "my son, night and day" (Baksh, personal communication, 1980).

The following dream, reported by Casiano in Camaná in 1976, includes a poignant reflection of his feelings about the death of his four-year-old son.

Yesterday I dreamt again. I dreamt of a big wind. It blew *jiririririri.* As I watched, it knocked down a tree and carried it far away. It was as clear as day. Then I was going along with my daughter, the wind was no longer beating on us. Then I awoke. It was a dream, I was there in my sleeping place.

Then I fell asleep and dreamt again. Many men arrived from downstream. They said to me, "Let's all eat together." We prepared the food and ate it. Then one of the men gave me 1,000 Soles [about $15]. I bought ten knives. Then I said, "Give me that shotgun, so that I may shoot guan." He said, "It costs too much, you can't afford it." I said, "If it costs too much, forget it." Then I awoke, it was a dream.

Again I slept. I dreamt I went to Mantaro [where he lived before]. I dreamt that on arriving I saw my son who had died. He said, "Father, I miss you. Now where did you go?" I said, "I went to Parotori." He said, "Father, you got angry at me, you abandoned me." I said, "You died. If you hadn't died, I wouldn't have abandoned you. Like your sister, she didn't die and I didn't abandon her." Then he told me, he said, "Father, I'm coming." I said, "Let's go." He was really coming. Then I awoke: nothing. My head ached.

Then I slept again. I dreamt again of my son. I dreamt that, upon arriving, I saw him drinking beer there with his group [*itovaigavageti*]. He said, "Father, drink." He gave me some to drink. It was as clear as day. I saw that my son was grown, he had a wife. Then I said to him, "My son, I will come." He said, "You can't come." He could go where I, not being dead, could never go. I said to him, "Maybe later I will never see you again." He said, "Later, you will see me." He gave me arrows. He said, "Father, these are deadly to spider monkey." I took them and went home on the path. I slipped and fell down. I arrived here at my house.

I awoke. This was my dream. Now, that's all.

In this dream, Casiano wants to be reunited with his dead son. Significantly, his son says to him, "Father, you got angry with me. You abandoned me." Because it is Casiano's dream, we must ask why he has his son say such a thing. On the one hand, this may be a reversal and a projection: it was Casiano who was angry when his son "abandoned" him. On the other hand, Casiano may be feeling some guilt over his son's death, which he was unable to prevent. In either case, there is an accusation in his son's words, a sign of the anger that accompanies the loss of death. And the dream is moving evidence of how the boy's death still haunted Casiano more than a year later.

CHAPTER 4

Society and Politics

It would be easier to characterize Matsigenka society in terms
of what there is not than in terms of what there actually is.

Rosengren 1983: 48

In a family level society, the everyday social world varies between periods
of dispersed nuclear-family living and aggregation in extended-family
camps or hamlets. There is a larger social world, of course, but its structure is amorphous and ever-changing. Happenings beyond the household and hamlet are of great interest to family members. They want to
know where some kin reside, where spouses may be sought, where trade
goods and information come from, and so forth, but they do not experience the outside often. Interactions with this outside can be exciting but also dangerous and are usually for specific purposes and of short
duration.

The Household

COMPOSITION AND SETTLEMENT

The Matsigenka prefer to live in single-family dwellings, spaced well
away from their neighbors' houses. On average, the people of Shimaa
live in households with seven to eight members. Each household consists of a walled main house in a clearing, perhaps with an additional

kitchen or shed; this unit is physically and conceptually separate from other households. A husband and his wife or wives consider themselves to be independent of other households, even those in their own hamlet, and free to leave the house site for shorter or longer periods as they see fit. Of twenty-three households in the vicinity of the school at Shimaa in 1972, three-quarters (seventeen) consisted of a monogamous couple and their children, although seven of these had one or more additional household members, usually an unmarried kinsman. In three households the husband had two wives, and another three included widows with children.

The households in a new school community like Shimaa are generally similar to those found in more distant areas. But just as in the past powerful shamans acted like magnets drawing settlers and attracting unstable or transitional households, so today a schoolteacher and his aura of protection acts as a similar magnet. In Shimaa, as well as in the school community of Shimentaato, we found several households headed by widows, who in outlying areas would have to live with their father or brother for protection. We also found several young couples without children exploring the opportunities of the new settlement, whereas in outlying areas they would remain attached to the girl's natal family until they had children.

Considering the unusual preponderance of females in the Shimaa population (figure 20), it may be surprising that only three out of twenty-three households had polygynous marriages. This preponderance of females, however, was a local occurrence of chance origin: in the nearby community of Shimentaato, the ratio of males to females was virtually 1:1, and in Kamisea males outnumbered females 1.2:1. I return later to the question of why more of these available women were not absorbed into polygynous marriages.

Matsigenkas prefer to live either in single-family homesteads as small as four members or in extended-family hamlets of two to four households with no more than twenty-five members. Although this preference is giving way under pressure from the government to form native communities that will have official standing, the resistance of Matsigenka householders to such clustering is a perennial complaint of community leaders as they attempt to bring the Matsigenka into the modern world. As the schoolteacher at Camaná complained, "They can't handle community."

Even in the general neighborhood of the school community many families prefer to live alone at a distance of an hour or more from the

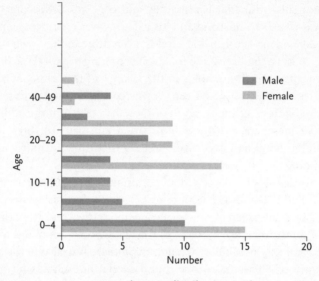

FIGURE 20. Age-sex distribution in the
time-allocation sample.

school itself. That this is close to the typical pattern became abundantly
clear when I had the opportunity in May 1973 to make a flight over the
watershed of the Río Kompiroshiato upstream from Shimaa. Apart from
the other two school communities at Shimentaato and Mantaro Chico,
we flew over twenty-two widely scattered settlements containing a total
of thirty-nine houses, an average of fewer than two houses per settlement. Half the settlements consisted of but one house, whereas only
one had as many as four (table 24), giving an estimated population density of 0.3 persons per square kilometer. The new-style community being promoted by the government could hardly provide more of a contrast: houses are close together, lined up in two rows with an open space
running between them. Such villages are common at the lower elevations, along the lower Río Urubamba, where travel in motorboats links
the Matsigenka more regularly to Peruvian society, and in communities
like Camaná that have strong progressive leadership.

Map 2 (chapter 1) shows the community at Shimaa. Farthest downstream along the Río Kompiroshiato (off the map to the right) were
the three households of Italiano's hamlet (households 17, 18, and 21 in
table 25); the children there walked forty-five minutes in good weather,
much longer in bad, to attend school each day. Moving up the Kompiroshiato toward the school, the next settlement was the downstream

TABLE 24. Number of Households per Settlement,
Upper Kompiroshiato Watershed, 1972–73

Number of Houses per Settlement	Number of Settlements Observed
1	11
2	6
3	4
4	1
TOTAL	22

(kamatikya) hamlet of Felipe's group, which had a core of five house-holds (households 10, 11, 12, 13, and 14). Household 10 belonged to Javier, a partial loner who moved his family a half-hour away from the downstream cluster during our fieldwork in 1973.

The school cluster, at the confluence of the Río Kompiroshiato and the Río Shimaa, itself was heterogeneous and quite unlike a traditional settlement. Households 5, 7, 8, and 9 were largely unrelated families living in various degrees of dependence on Maestro (household 6). Households 1 and 2 were really part of the upstream Shimaa hamlet, and household 3, while linked to the downstream hamlet, was another loner family that had a second residence far up the Río Shimaa and spent much of its time there. All in all, "not very united" is an apt description of this community.

The upstream *(katonko Shimaa)* hamlet consisted of households 19 and 20 in addition to households 1 and 2. It was difficult to get there during the rainy season, when the Río Shimaa was swollen and turbulent. Households 1 and 2 spent several weeks at a time upstream, where they planted gardens and went on foraging expeditions.

In sum, the larger community at Shimaa was an aggregate of three extended-family hamlets of two to four households each, in addition to the loose collection of households without close kin near the school. Beyond this aggregate, several isolated households lived far up the Ríos Shimaa and Kompiroshiato and did not send their children to the school. They visited Shimaa a few times a year to catch up on gossip and to trade a little but were otherwise averse to community life.

Selecting a House Site.   The school acts as both a magnet and a repellent for Matsigenka households. Attraction to the school, for trade

TABLE 25. Census of Households in the Greater Shimaa Area, 1972

Household	Name	ID[a]	Birth Year	Comment
1	Oscar	MHD	1945	
	Elisa	FHD	1946	
	Mariana	DA1	1969	b. August
	Artemio	SN1	1972	b. May
	Alicia	AF1	1956	
2	Omenko	MHD	1924	
	Victoria	FHD	1937	
	Lola	DA1	1957	Twin of Teresa
	Teresa	DA2	1957	Twin of Lola
	Pepe	SN1	1963	
	Rokash	SN2	1969	b. November
	Amelia	DA3	1972	b. May
	(Mauro)	AM1	1957	Usually in upstream Shimaa
3	Aradino	MHD	1927	
	Kasimira	FH1	1932	
	Rosa	FH2	1939	
	(Viviana)	DA1	1947	Daughter of FH1 (previous husband); mostly in household 20
	(Armando)	SN1	1966	Son of DA1
	(Jorge)	SN2	1969	Son of DA1
	Irima	DA2	1955	Daughter of FH1
	Erena	DA3	1957	Daughter of FH2 (previous husband)
	(Jorge)	AM1	1960	Son of FH2; lived in household 11
	Vinancio	SN1	1971	b. April; son of FH2 and MHD
4	Jacobo	MHD	1943	Whole family absent 8/72–8/73
	Celia	FHD	1939	
	Miguel	SN1	1960	
	Haroldo	SN2	1967	
	Olivia	DA1	1973	
5	Eduardo	MHD	1953	
	Inez	FHD	1947	
	Violeta	DA1	1968	
	Alberto	SN1	1971	
6	Pedro	MHD	1942	Maestro
	Adela	FHD	1942	
	Juan	SN1	1962	

TABLE 25. *(continued)*

Household	Name	ID[a]	Birth Year	Comment
	Raquel	DA1	1964	
	Delia	DA2	1968	b. March
	Melina	DA3	1969	b. August
	Delmira	DA4	1970	b. August
	Norma	DA5	1972	b. June
	Justina	AF1	1952	Servant
	Graciela	AF2	1956	Servant
	Teresita	AF3	1954	Servant
8	Santiago	MHD	1949	Composite household dependent on Maestro
	Marina	FHD	1952	
	Maritina	AF1	1952	Married to AM2
	Nieve	DA1	1965	Adopted
	Serequita	DA2	1967	Adopted daughter of sister of FHD
	Miriam	DA3	1969	Daughter of AF1
	Marita	AF4	1939	
	Vicky	AD1	1965	Daughter of AF4
	Delia	AD2	1968	Daughter of AF4
	Andrea	AD3	1970	Daughter of AF4
	Adela	AF3	1956	Sister of FHD, married to AM1
	Shoshovi	AM1	1956	Married to AF3
	Angel	AM2	1954	Married AF1 in 1973
9	Aretoro	MHD	1947	
	Pororinta	FHD	1948	
	Andres	SN1	1966	
	Moises	SN2	1967	
	Enriqueta	DA1	1970	
10	Javier	MHD	1930	
	Viviana	FHD	1937	
	Juanita	DA1	1954	
	Marosa	DA2	1962	
	Olga	DA3	1965	
	Elsa	DA4	1966	
	Erindina	DA5	1968	
	Silverio	SN1	1971	b. December
11	Felipe	MHD	1946	
	Eva	FH1	1940	

(continued on page 146)

TABLE 25. *(continued)*

Household	Name	ID[a]	Birth Year	Comment
	Amaria	FH2	1954	
	Manuela	DA1	1969	Daughter of FH1
	Aventura	DA2	1973	Daughter of FH1
	Ekitoro	SN1	1961	Son of FH1
	Juliano	SN2	1971	Son of FH1; b. August
	David	SN2	1972	Son of FH2; b. April
	Jorge	AM1	1960	Son of MHD and FH2 in household 3
12	Julio	MHD	1932	
	Juana	FHD	1937	
	Roberto	SN1	1955	
	Guillermo	SN2	1960	
	Elva	DA1	1964	
	Aurora	DA2	1972	b. May
	Estefania	AF1	1944	Sister of MHD; later moved to household 10
	Miguel	SN3	1972	Son of AF1
	Alicia	AF2	1960	Adopted by AF1
13	Karoroshi	MHD	1950	
	Virima	FHD	1945	
	Micaela	DA1	1962	Daughter of FHD (previous husband)
	Martin	SN1	1969	
14	Mariano	MHD	1950	
	Rosa	FHD	1955	
	Elias	SN1	1971	b. April
15	Camila	FHD	1912	
	Beatriz	DA1	1942	Daughter of FHD
	Maria Rosa	DD1	1956	Daughter of DA1
	Bertina	AF1	1968	Daughter of DD1
16	Geronimo	MHD	?	
	Shasharo	FH1	?	
	Maritina	FH2	?	
	Juanito	SN1	?	
	(Libia)	DA1	1965	Living in household 6
	?	DA2	?	
17	Italiano	MHD	1943	
	Maria	FHD	?	
	Rosa	DA1	1961	
	Hugo	SN1	1960	

TABLE 25. *(continued)*

Household	Name	ID[a]	Birth Year	Comment
	?	SN3?	?	
	Peruviano	AM1	?	Married to AF1
	Salomia	AF1	?	Married to AM1
18	Torres	MHD	1944	
	Almania	FHD	?	
	?	SN1	?	
	?	DA1	?	
19	Evaristo	MHD	1935	
	Teodora	FHD	1953	
	Ramona	DA1	1971	b. May
20	Tito	MHD	1948	
	Estella	FH1	1938	
	Juanito	AM1	1962	Son of ?
	(Viviana)	FH2	1947	Also in household 3
	(Armando)	SN1	1966	Son of FH2
	(Jorge)	SN2	1969	Son of FH2
	Maria	AF1	1959	Daughter of ?
	Ricardo	AM2	1952	Son of Omenko, household 2
	Rokania	AF3	1932?	
	Elvira	AF2	1944	
	Jaime	?	1971	b. April
21	Mario	MHD	?	
	Rea	FHD	?	
	Angel	SN1	1959	
	Americo	SN2	1960	
	?	SN3	?	
	?	DA1	?	

[a]The ID codes were unique identifiers assigned early in the research for the time-allocation study. Although some roughly identify roles in the family (e.g., FHD means "female head," etc.), they are included here primarily as a guide to researchers wishing to coordinate with the time-allocation data (Johnson and Johnson 1988).

goods, medicines, and a general sense of security, comes into conflict with many of their most basic preferences about where and how to live best. This conflict is the reason so many families refuse to settle in school communities. In addition, school communities, with their relatively dense settlement and more frequent contact with the outside, are vulnerable to epidemics of flu and other contagious diseases like colds and conjunctivitis; as a result, people often flee these communities for several months at a time. And although wild resources, both foods and raw materials, are equally scarce everywhere, they become quickly depleted when local population density rises. This is certainly one of the main reasons the Matsigenka live at a family level in the first place and why they are reluctant to settle in a school community or near any other hamlets.

A house site must ideally be near a good source of water and fertile soil. The Kompiroshiato overflight showed each house built close to a year-round river. For two reasons, however, it is rare to find a Matsigenka house on the river bank. First, fluctuations in water level from wet to dry seasons bring the danger of flooding, as happened in 1971, when Felipe's house along the banks of the Río Kompiroshiato was swept away. Second, strangers, who in the not so distant past captured children for sale and as slaves for the rubber trade and now bring dangerous illnesses, can more easily find houses that are along a river than those set back from it. Although land for gardens is abundant, certain kinds of soils are preferred, and they may make one site more attractive than another.

Because families consider many factors when thinking of moving to a new location, it is understandable that ideal residential sites are scarce. When a choice has been made, preferably a year in advance of the planned move, the married couple advertises their plans in order to learn whether competing claims exist. They want to avoid a dispute that might cause anger. Only when no one objects and the property in a sense "clears title" does a family make the move.

A Matsigenka household is often in some form of dual residence. Most regularly, whenever a household moves, it builds a house at the new site while continuing to inhabit the old house and harvest from its gardens. For example, when Javier (household 10) moved his family away from the downstream hamlet in 1972, his original plan was to continue to inhabit both old and new houses and tend both sets of gardens, but he eventually abandoned the old location. Also, often households maintain a secondary residence that acts like a vacation home. And, in low-water season, families commonly move down to the river and live on the exposed beach in caña brava houses, enjoying easy access to water and foraging areas.

Spatial Use in the House.   The traditional Matsigenka house is oval, about ten meters long and five meters wide, with a palm-leaf roof that peaks about four and a half meters off the ground, palm-wood or cane walls, and a single doorway (chapter 2). On first entering from bright sunshine, one finds a house quite dim and often smoky inside. Unless there is a separate kitchen structure (usually the same size as a house but without walls), a house has one or two hearths. A single hearth is located roughly in the center of the house, perhaps somewhat to the left or right of the doorway. Two hearths are located at opposite ends of the house, one or two meters from the wall. The number of hearths is determined by the number of women with children. When there are two wives with children, each has her own hearth; when an unmarried woman with children is present, she too has her own hearth. In Aradino's household in late 1972 there were three hearths in a separate kitchen: two for his two co-wives and a third for a co-wife's daughter and her two young children.

Two-thirds of the households we visited had a raised platform bed made of palm wood. The platform is the sleeping area for the man of the house and his primary wife. Their young children usually join them there, older children sleeping apart. The secondary wife usually sleeps off the platform, surrounded by her own children. As sexual intercourse does not usually take place in houses where co-wives or grown children are living, this arrangement does not indicate any unevenness in the distribution of sexual favors. On cold nights, however, the whole family sleeps near the fire because they do not use blankets. The family curls up in the circle of the fire, and members who would ordinarily sleep apart huddle together. Someone periodically tends the fire during the night.

Fieldnote 08–08–75—At dusk (about 5:30 P.M.) the teen-age son sets up his space, placing his mat close to the fire opposite his mother, telling his younger brother to set his mat next to him on the side away from the fire. On the other side of the fire is his mother, then his father. Their youngest daughter is right next to mother; their older daughter is near the fire to mother's left and teen-age son's right. Mother's married daughter, visiting, was sitting in teen son's space until he decided to put his mat down, then she moved and settled down again after he was settled. The second (and maligned) wife, when in the house, occupies the direction opposite older sister, but against the wall (almost "hunched" against it), as far as possible from the fire and next to the water jugs—also close to the door (sometimes giving the appearance of being ready to flee).

Older children and other members of the household sleep on mats on the ground in their own area near the wall. They keep their personal possessions in the rafters or hung from the walls where they sleep, and this is regarded as their own space. In the morning, members may remain on their mats while eating or doing indoor tasks, but as they leave they roll up their mats and store them overhead. A wife or older daughter sweeps the floor, and the house comes to appear quite clean and empty. Still, family members crossing the house do not walk through another person's sleeping area but walk around it as if it were actually a little room with walls.

HOUSE AND GARDEN

The Matsigenka house is a secure haven in an often-dangerous world. The dirt floor, the uneven wall slats that let in light and air, and the palm-leaf roof alive with the sounds of mice and insects may raise some doubts in the newly arrived visitor as to both the quality of construction and hygiene. But the Matsigenka build sturdy houses that remain completely dry inside even in drenching thunderstorms, and they proudly explain that their walls keep out the jaguars.

Walking outside the house, we find ourselves in a clearing that extends in a rough circle about fifteen meters around the house. Beyond this radius are garden land and perhaps a ravine or other uncultivable land. The clearing is swept every day and is weeded every week or two as a precaution against snakes entering the house; on dry days the clearing is an expanse of baked earth that is momentarily dazzling when one leaves the dim interior of the house. This area is effectively part of the house, for it serves as a patio in which all household activities can take place. During the heat of the day, food processing and manufacturing take place outside on the shady side of the house; in the evening, meals and manufacturing can be enjoyed while leaning against the walls of the house; and at night when guests are visiting men sometimes lie outside on mats gazing at the stars and talking for hours.

To keep the clearing free of rubbish, all garbage is carried beyond the clearing and disposed of in an unused place. Households living near the river mound their garbage into a pile and, using an old cushma or mat, carry the trash to the river for dumping. Other households maintain a rubbish dump at the edge of the nearest garden.

Nearby strips of uncultivated land where brush or cane grow are preferred areas for urination and children's defecation. Adults are fastidious about defecation and prefer whenever possible to refrain until they are at the edge of an old garden or out foraging in the forest. One path to several gardens near the school at Shimaa wound through a weed patch that was the latrine for household 8, and my companion Roberto always wrinkled his nose and expressed disgust when we had to pass by. No feces were visible from the trail, but the smell was a reliable reminder of the regular use to which the area was put. I never noticed that smell when we were around the hamlets away from the school community.

While a man is clearing his first garden at a new location, he erects a temporary shelter where his family may visit him; they bring crops from the old homestead and enjoy the greater access to wild foods that a new, unexploited area always affords. As the garden matures during its first year and manioc begins to provide a reliable staple in the diet, a man can turn his attention to building a new house, most likely somewhere within the new garden. The house can take several months to complete, so, about a year after beginning the new garden, a family can take up residence in the new dwelling.

Because a new garden has to be cleared each year, a patchwork of gardens comes to surround the house over a period of several years, each in a different stage of evolution, and each producing different crops in differing proportions. The original garden surrounding the old house, partly abandoned, becomes a small house garden for herbs, condiments, and some fruit trees; the abandoned part serves as a source of firewood and a refuse area. During the first year or two at the new house the family continues to return to the old homestead, where fruit trees, barbasco, and some other crops remain attractive, but that house eventually decays, and the gardens revert to weeds. Eventually, the old homestead turns into secondary forest and begins the lengthy process of regeneration.

Considering the amount of labor that goes into clearing a new garden and building a new house, it is startling to find that the average Matsigenka household moves to a new homestead every four years. This figure is the exact average of the moves made by six of the men since their first marriages. The men ranged in age from twenty-two to forty-eight, with an average age of thirty-six, and they had moved a total of twenty-two times in their combined eighty-eight years of marriage. The average move covered a distance of fourteen kilometers, although half were within a kilometer or two of the previous homestead. Raising the average were a number of long-distance moves of between twenty and sixty kilometers, often to adjacent river valleys.

Men give different reasons for moving. In the old days, they moved to avoid slave raiders. Then, and now, they moved to avoid illness: when Omenko left his previous homestead because of *kamagantsini* (flu), he was in such a hurry he left his axe and machete behind. But most moves were unexplained (*kogapai,* "no reason"). As we learned in chapter 2, however, there is a measurable decline in overall quality of life over time that can be remedied by moving to an unused area.

PROPERTY, EXCHANGE, AND POWER IN THE HOUSEHOLD

The respect for personal living spaces within the household is part of a general pattern in which household resources are the possessions of their individual "owner," *shintaro.* Among the Matsigenka, ownership of possessions is created through labor and transferred through gifting and barter. Nobody owns nature itself: people appropriate nature by using it, spending time and energy to convert it to useful forms.

Personal Property.   Everything the Matsigenka make and use is owned by someone. I first sensed this early in fieldwork when a neighbor borrowed one of what I thought of as "our" books from Orna, then carefully returned it to her although he had to walk past me to do so. I wrote in my field notes: "The implication to be explored is that husband and wife do not hold property in common."

As often and as generously as the Matsigenka share their possessions with kinsmen and friends who ask for them, they are careful never to take generosity for granted. Once an attractive piece of land has been identified, men make sure no one else has a prior claim to the site. When I asked Javier who owned the old avocado tree he discovered while clearing his new garden, he replied, "It belongs to 'secondary forest' [*magashipogo*]." However, when Karoroshi wanted to reclear a plot abandoned by his brother-in-law Mariano, he asked him for it, and Mariano "gave it to him," *ipakeri.*

Acknowledging someone as *shintaro* is a form of respect. For example, when I left Shimaa in 1973, I left behind a number of banana trees in my garden near Aradino's house. There was no certainty that I would return, and Aradino saw no reason to let my investment go to waste. When I returned in 1975, he spontaneously led me to where he had been cultivating my banana trees as well as some new ones he had planted. He pointed out which ones were mine and described how he had cared for and harvested them during my absence. He wanted me to know that he had not stolen my banana trees and that they were waiting for me. Otherwise, there was a risk I might talk badly of him to others.

The Matsigenka keep track of and can tell which plants in a garden were planted by which family member. In this way, they can know and acknowledge individual contributions to the family food supply, including those of children. In general, clarity with regard to property is at the heart of Matsigenka social relations, both within and outside the household. The division of labor by sex, and to a lesser degree by age, brings about a need to obtain useful goods and services from other members of the household and hamlet. That the Matsigenka keep track of this process of mutual exchange means only that they do not undervalue the ties that bind them. To blur the boundaries of personal ownership, to pretend to some sort of communal ownership, would be to deny the specific contributions each member makes to the whole and would deprive them of one of their prime sources of pleasure.

Every act of borrowing is consciously, and usually explicitly, by permission. One does not carelessly borrow the possessions of another, even a wife or brother. People keep careful track of their possessions and become agitated when something is missing: losing an item inevitably occasions a thorough search, managed through asking an ever widening circle of neighbors whether they know what became of it. Should the item indeed be missing, the reaction to the loss is one of outrage and suspicion. Although they are no more covetous than other people and probably a good deal less than many, the Matsigenka see theft as an assault and violation. Therefore, everyone handles other people's possessions carefully.

Everything in the household is individually owned. The house belongs to the man who built it, and the bar he places in front of his door when away for any length of time is ample claim of possession to keep others from wandering in. Just as the interior floor space is specifically allocated to family members, so too above their spaces, on the walls and in the rafters, are mats, bundles, boxes, and other containers with personal possessions. If you ask a Matsigenka over the age of six to name his possessions, he can give you a complete list. If you wish to see any of them, he can go to the exact container, retrieve it, and show it to you. If he says he has three needles, he has three. He begins to lose count only as numbers mount above five; like all his neighbors, he tends to remember in increments of five or ten and he can indicate these increments by opening his fists and flashing his fingers the right number of times.

Manufactures contain small elements of individual style that indicate who made them. Men of a hamlet can easily identify the arrows of all the other men, just as women can identify cushmas by their weavers' designs. People always remember who gave them any item they possess, even if it has no distinctive markings. For items not manufactured locally, such as needles, knives, or mirrors, people could state exactly where and from whom they obtained it, whether as a gift or barter.

Careful reckoning of ownership begins young. It is common to give a chick to an infant, so that even before the child can speak, he or she owns a full-grown chicken. Should you try to buy or beg for that chicken, the parents inform you that the matter is out of their hands; the chicken belongs to the child. This may seem a convenient fiction—the parents will manage to make a meal out of that chicken sooner or later—but it is also part of the general attitude that children have autonomy and personhood from the time they are born.

In daily living, the Matsigenka household is full of acts of generosity. It almost seems as though the emphasis on individual property exists in order to make generosity possible. The giver, by being acknowledged as owner of the gift and therefore empowered to dispose of it at his or her will, is assured that the gift will be acknowledged and respected, not taken for granted.

A wife does not have to ask her husband's permission to go into his garden because it is her garden too (some of its "property-ness" was created by her labor). But children have to get a parent's permission before going into the garden to harvest food. I learned early to be careful to ask permission before measuring any gardens and never to help myself to food in anyone's garden but my own. Out hunting, men sometimes entered someone else's garden, even someone from another hamlet, to cut one or two lengths of sugar cane to slake thirst and hunger. But sugar cane is never in short supply and is an inexpensive convenience that can be taken without offense. I have seen a brother walk into his brother's empty house and take his axe to cut a tree. And I have seen a man borrow another's axe from his wife when the axe owner was not home. Yet I have also seen a wife refuse to loan her husband's axe, saying, "I don't know. He's not here." The rules concerning property and permission are strong.

Power.   If we take power in the social arena to be the ability to get others to do what you want, then everyone in a Matsigenka household has power over other household members. Naturally, what each person wants from the others varies with age and gender, as does the degree of success in getting it. In the Matsigenka household, a strong ethic of generosity and congeniality inhibits the use of threat or physical force in gaining compliance. Words like *authority* or *respect* better describe

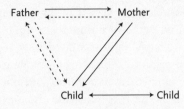

FIGURE 21. Pattern of actions directed toward family members (O. Johnson 1978: 230). Solid lines indicate the strongest (more frequent) actions; dotted lines indicate the weakest (less frequent) actions.

the mutual give-and-take than does the word *power*. But threat is also present: parents threaten corporal punishment, especially of toddlers, and husbands and wives know that, in the libertine excesses of a beer feast, they may exchange blows, sneak off for sexual liaisons, or, in the case of wives, run away somewhere until an apologetic husband comes begging forgiveness.

In her analysis of videotapes of domestic behavior, Orna Johnson (1978) was able to classify over five thousand individual actions taken by one household member (the "initiator") toward another (the "recipient"). Figure 21 summarizes the predominant direction in which actions were initiated. Solid lines represent the major direction in each case; dotted lines indicate the secondary direction. As discussed in chapter 3, male heads direct their actions predominantly toward their wives, whereas their wives direct their actions predominantly toward their children. Children evenly split their main actions between their mothers and other children. Secondarily, women direct a significant number of interactions toward their husbands, and men do likewise toward their children, but children direct only a small fraction of their actions toward their fathers.

Orna found that 2,161 of these actions could be unambiguously coded as either "supportive" (hugging, offering food, answering a question) or "unsupportive" (hitting, refusing to share, scolding). The rest of the actions were part of complex conversations that could not be readily coded in these terms. Of those actions that could be coded, four out of five were supportive, which "says a good deal about the tenor of life in the Matsigenka household" (O. Johnson 1978: 231).

Nowhere is this more clearly seen than during mealtime in a Matsigenka household. Most of the mealtime foods are provided initially by the mother from her hearth. Almost immediately, however, those who have been given food begin to share. Not everyone is seated next to the hearth, and not everyone is served at once. Those who are served first break off a portion and offer it to someone else, saying something like *nero pagiri,* "Look, grub." Those others in turn may break their piece into still smaller pieces and find someone to give them to. It is not uncommon for an ear of maize to be broken in two, then subdivided again and again until the piece being given has but a few kernels; the one who originally shared the maize may later receive a fragment of the very portion she gave away.

Other family members also prepare small amounts of food themselves, roasting a few caterpillars or slicing up a palm heart. They may take charge of distributing the food they brought into the household. In this way, new foods enter the circle of exchange at points other than the wife and mother. The result is a Brownian motion of bits and pieces of food moving among household members during mealtime.

Polygynous Households.   As we saw in chapter 3, children tend with high frequency to interact with their own biological mothers and with their full siblings within close range of the mother's hearth. They are far less likely to interact with their father's other wife and her children, although, being in the same household, they interact more with them than they do with members of other households. The husband frequently joins his primary wife at her hearth, but during mealtimes he may place his mat between the two hearths and act as a conduit through which food passes back and forth between the two hearth centers. Co-wives thus avoid each other's space and do not often share food directly, although food from each does reach the other eventually.

Among co-wives there are differences owing to age and levels of experience. The clearest pattern is between young wives without grown children and older wives who have the labor of their children at their disposal:

The younger wives, having fewer children, spend the most time engaged in the outdoor tasks that offer little opportunity to draw on assistance from others. And at home, they show the lowest relative authority. . . . The elder wives . . . spend relatively more time working at home, where they can take advantage of the children's labor. Consequently, among wives, the elders exercise the greatest relative authority, initiating the highest number of requests. (O. Johnson 1978: 251)

Time-allocation data according to the social setting in which activities take place also show that younger wives tend to spend more than three times as much time alone with their husbands as do older wives, who spend much more of their time socializing with adult kin than younger wives do (O. Johnson 1978: 252). Although younger wives receive more sexual attention from their husbands than older wives do, these behavioral differences contribute to a clearly higher overall social standing for senior wives.

Getting along with co-wives requires a husband to be sensitive and respectful.

Polygynous arrangements call for equality among co-wives in every respect. Co-wives have equal rights to household resources, and neither is subject to the authority of the other. A husband is expected to treat his wives equally, clearing garden space in which each can plant her own crops, providing each with meat and manufactured items, and exchanging food with each during meals.

That a man may have an emotional preference for one of his two wives is generally accepted. And such a preference need not provoke jealousy; all are aware that one of the two is the favored wife (the one the husband feels more desire for), but some men are said to favor both of their wives, for different reasons (e.g., one wife may be older and know how to weave well, the other may be younger and more physically attractive). However that may be, he must provide for his wives equally. . . .

Co-wife compatibility is also important in polygynous households. A man should not take in a second wife without the permission of the first, for it is important that they get along with one another. . . .

When questioned about their marital preferences, Matsigenka women express different opinions on whether monogamy is preferable to polygyny. Monogamous women feel monogamy is better, but polygynous women like having a co-wife because she contributes domestic help, especially as concerns obligations to the husband (e.g., weaving his clothes, making beer, or accompanying him on forest trips). It all comes down, as one monogamous woman said, to what kind of co-wife you have—whether she knows how to work hard, whether she would be generous and understand the sharing of things. (O. Johnson 1978: 204–6)

Many men would like to have a second wife. But it is a difficult matter to arrange. Mariano, whose young wife Rosa was considered lazy, tried on two different occasions to woo mature, productive women. One of them even entered into a trial marriage with him, but it did not last. A man must provide a respectable supply of meat, and co-wives must get along together for the marriage to work. Still, polygyny appeals even to men committed to monogamy: once, when Omenko and his wife, Victoria, dropped by to chat, I asked whether he would like a second wife. He answered, "No," but Victoria countered, "He wants more." Omenko was about fifty years old, and his monogamous marriage to Victoria had produced a successful extended family with many grown children, yet Victoria recognized his ambivalence.

In some cases there is a tension between co-wives. The division of the house into separate territories, each wife procuring and preparing food separately at her own hearth, sharing through her husband rather than directly with her co-wife, caring for her own children alone or with help from her own relatives—all these indicate that the polygynous household tends to operate as an aggregate of distinct nuclear families that happen to share a husband and father. Yet the division of labor between some wives creates interdependence, and when co-wives are also sisters, or mother and daughter, the already strong bond between them is reinforced.

There are many unmarried women of marriageable age in Shimaa who do not get absorbed into polygynous marriages but remain attached to other households. A woman does not enter lightly into a polygynous marriage. Especially in the zone of security provided by the school community, a woman can find alternative living arrangements with relatives. Although she does not have a husband, she can become a useful member of a household and can raise her children in reasonable safety and comfort. A few of the women in Shimaa seemed ready to live as single mothers, working hard at contributing to the households in which they lived. Yet they remain open to courtship by attractive men and ready to be convinced that even a polygynous marriage could be right for them.

Political Economy: The Hamlet

As applied to small-scale societies, political economy refers to the economic, social, and political relationships that tie subsistence-oriented households into larger collectivities (Johnson and Earle 2000: 24–27). Although the household participates in the political economy in order to achieve its own goals, its behavior and expectations in this outside sphere are different. Even in a family level society like the Matsigenka, the nuclear family is always embedded in a social matrix that includes not only portions of the extended families of both husband and wife but also an attenuated network of friends and relations throughout a large region, sporadic contacts with unknown Matsigenkas, and delimited interactions with non-Matsigenka Peruvians, missionary linguists, and anthropologists. Principles of kinship, patterns of marriage, gender segregation, political and economic dominance, and public events all have a tenor distinct from life in the household.

KINSHIP AND MARRIAGE

The Matsigenka social world is, conceptually, one of kinship. Their rare and curious deemphasis on personal names dramatically underscores the importance of kin: the Matsigenka of Shimaa are comfortable addressing or referring to someone only in the language of kinship. Their opening conversation with a stranger almost immediately turns to the question *ainyo piniro,* "Is there your mother?" and thence to other relatives and one's immediate social world. Conversation with one who has returned from a long absence in addition includes queries about any of the inquisitor's relatives who might have been encountered on the subject's travels. Even when I was reading *In the Shadow of Man* (Goodall 1971), people looking over my shoulder at the photographs of chimpanzees wanted to know who they were and whether they were relatives of anyone I knew.

Kin Terms.   Matsigenka kin terms make up a system of kin reckoning that is simple and elegant. It falls in the general class of systems based on the widespread "cross/parallel" distinction (Kay 1965). It is of the symmetrical-exchange type identified by Lévi-Strauss (1969: 119–33) as the most elementary of kinship structures, a view supported by comparative analysis of the complexity of kinship structures (Dole 1972: 154). The Matsigenka version has been well described by Snell (1964) and O. Johnson (1978). Because discussions of kinship terminology can quickly become esoteric and overly elaborate, I confine myself here to trying to convey the small number of principles necessary to see the Matsigenka kinship system from the inside out, as it appears to one living within it.

We can learn most of what we need to know from figure 22. From the vantage point of ego, looking directly up and to the side we find familiar concepts, differentiated only by gender: parent (*apa,* "father," and *ina,* "mother") and sibling (*ige* or *icha,* "brother," and *incho* or *pirento,* "sister"). Leaving aside for a moment the question of why there are two Matsigenka terms for brother and for sister, I begin this discussion using the English glosses, although I have put them in quotes to indicate that they need not mean to the Matsigenka what they mean to us.

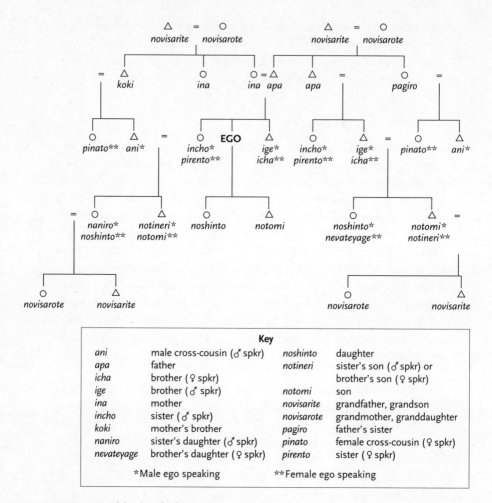

FIGURE 22. Matsigenka kin terms.

In the parents' (+1) generation father's brother is called "father," and mother's sister is called "mother." When a parent's sibling is of the opposite sex, he or she is designated by a different term: *koki*, "uncle," refers specifically to mother's brother, and "aunt" *(pagiro)* to father's sister, reflecting the cross/parallel distinction. That distinction is seen also in the children's (−1) generation: expectably, one's own children are called "son" *(notomi)* and "daughter" *(noshinto)*. A man calls his brother's children "son" and "daughter," just as they call him "father." And a man's children and his brother's children call each other "brother" and "sister" because they are related through parents of the parallel gender. A woman, however, calls her brother's children *notineri*, "nephew," and *naniro*, "niece," just as they call her *pagiro*, "aunt," and they call her children *ani*, "male cousin," or *pinato*, "female cousin," because they are cross-cousins (related through parents of cross-gender).

Although I was familiar with this kinship system in theory, I found in the field that I had no internal appreciation of it until I became incorporated into Matsigenka kinship relations. Then what had been theoretical knowledge became practical understanding. At its most basic level this kinship system creates a social world made up of two kinds of people: own family and affines. From a man's standpoint, all men of his generation are either brothers or brothers-in-law; all women are either sisters or potential spouses. The gender obverse is true for a woman. For both men and women, in the generation above are either parents or parents-in-law, and in the generation below are either sons and daughters or people one's sons and daughters can marry.

Why the existence of two terms for brother and for sister? The gender of the speaker determines which term is to be used. What is really being labeled is whether the sibling is the same gender (that is, the same kind of person) as the speaker. Thus, a woman calls her sister *pirento*, which might be rendered "my sister, like me (my gender)," and calls her children daughter and son. A man calls his sister *incho*, "my sister, unlike me (other gender)," and calls her children niece and nephew. Similarly, we may understand *ige* to mean "my brother, my gender," and *icha*, "my brother, other gender." Gender of speaker, therefore, owes its prominence in sibling kin terms to the cross/parallel distinction.

The other instance in which the speaker's gender is important is in relation to the cross-cousin. A man calls his male cross-cousin *ani*, but has no term for his female cross-cousin. His sister can call her female cross-cousin *pinato*, but, reciprocally, she has no term by which to call her male cross-cousin. The crucial relationship between potential spouses is marked by the absence of a term. When cross-cousins do marry, they refer to each other as *nohina*, "wife," or *nohime*, "husband." Otherwise these two delicately related people go through life without a kin designation for each other. Because a wife's "sisters" or a husband's "brothers" fall into this category, there are frequent situations in which one must talk to or about someone for whom no term exists. The neighboring Campa avoid this situation by use of a construct *nohinacori*, from *nohina*, "wife," + *cori*, "potential" (Snell 1964: 14). This term allows them to speak of "one who could be my wife." A Campa woman may similarly call her male cross-cousin *nohimecori*. But the Matsigenka allow the odd vacuum to exist. "Opposite-sex cross-cousins are defined as potential spouses, a relationship characterized by ambiguity and embarrassment. Unless involved in a conjugal relationship, classificatory spouses avoid one another and do not refer to one another as kinsmen" (O. Johnson 1978: 97–98).

Another notable feature of this terminological system is that all the work is being done in the three generations of ego, parents, and children. The system appears almost completely disinterested in grandparents and grandchildren, distinguishing them only by gender: *novisarite,* "grandfather" or "grandson," and *novisarote,* "grandmother" or "granddaughter." Because grandparents and grandchildren of the same sex are called by the same term, we must translate it with some strange gloss like "grandmale" for *novisarite* and "grandfemale" for *novisarote.* Owing to the hard reality that grandparents are not often still living when their grandchildren reach the age of reason, a merging of the worlds of kinfolk at these distant boundaries creates little confusion. Indeed, there is no incest taboo on marriage between grandrelatives. Realistically, such a marriage would almost always involve classificatory relatives rather than immediate family members, but Snell (1964: 7) reports a case of a woman who mistreated her granddaughter because she was jealously afraid her husband might marry the child when she reached puberty.

In a rather nice bit of symmetry, the kin-term system wraps around after the second generation up or down. That is, grandmother's mother is called "daughter" because, after all, grandmother = granddaughter, and daughter is the mother of granddaughter. Likewise, grandson's son is called "father." This situation occurs rarely, but Rosa, who was our "granddaughter," had a young son whom we called Apa, "Father."

The basic incest rule is "you shall not marry a parent, child, or sibling." This rule becomes immediately extended to "you shall not marry the sibling of a parent, or the child of a sibling." The elegant artifice that is introduced into this simple prohibition is to treat two sets of cousins as absolutely different. Because siblings of the same gender are merged into the same kin category, their children become—to one another—parallel cousins and by definition siblings whom it would be incestuous to marry, whereas the crucial gender difference between brother and sister turns their children into the opposite, cross-cousins who are the ideal marriage partners.

In daily life, and equally in folklore, seemingly different relationships

TABLE 26. Matsigenka Kin Terms Analyzed on Four Dimensions:
Gender, Generation, Cross/Parallel, and Gender of Speaker

Generation +/−	Male *novisarite*		Female *novisarote*	
	Parallel	*Cross*	*Parallel*	*Cross*
+1	*apa*	*koki*	*ina*	*pagiro*
0 (male speaker)	*ige*	*ani*	*incho*	*[nohina]*
0 (female speaker)	*icha*	*[nohime]*	*pirento*	*pinato*
−1 (male speaker)	*notomi*	*notineri*	*noshinto*	*naniro*
−1 (female speaker)	*notomi*	*notineri*	*noshinto*	*nevatyage*

are collapsed into a single category. Not only does father's brother become "father" or mother's sister's son "brother," but the person referred to as *ani* becomes simultaneously my mother's brother's son, my father's sister's son, my wife's brother, and my sister's husband—a family member and in-law at the same time. *Pagiro* is at once father's sister, mother's brother's wife, and mother-in-law. That each of these people is, at the conceptual level, all these things at once is no problem for the Matsigenka because all is implied directly by the terminological system. However, conflicting aspects of such kinsmen and kinswomen do arise from their being simultaneously kin and in-laws.

Matsigenka kinship terminology is created out of four dimensions of contrast: gender, generation, lineality, and gender of speaker. Lineality refers to the bifurcation created by the cross/parallel distinction, which as we have seen is rooted in a gender difference. So, we could say the kin terminology is ultimately based on only two dimensions of contrast: gender and generation. In table 26 we can see that Matsigenka kin terms are efficiently analyzed in terms of these four (two) dimensions.

Marriage.   We have gone as far as we need looking at the kinship system from the inside (ego's standpoint). If we turn to look at it from the outside, its most striking feature is that it tends to create a symmetrical exchange structure consisting of two families intermarrying endlessly across the generations (figure 23; cf. Chagnon 1987: 26). The pattern begins with two brother-sister pairs intermarrying. With the cross/parallel distinction, the offspring of each couple are cross-cousins of the offspring of the other couple, and hence ideal marriage partners. In principle, a very small group of people may stay together across the generations, without needing to leave the group in order to find a spouse.

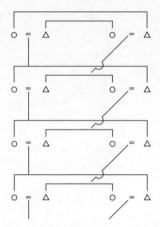

FIGURE 23. Two intermarrying
lines: the ideal hamlet.

This is the ideal form of a hamlet— both sets of newlyweds can stay close to their parents after marriage. Incest prohibitions do not require people to marry outside such a hamlet. In reality, children are often effectively betrothed to an appropriate cross-cousin in their hamlet. This arrangement should not be thought of so much as child marriage as of an understanding between married brothers and sisters that their offspring, when grown, would make an ideal match. That the children do not have to leave the hamlet upon marriage is seen as a blessing for all (cf. Kensinger 1995: 137).

The hamlet, while divided by the cross-parallel distinction and the implied split between two intermarrying families (an emic split between kin and in-laws), is at the same time a tightly knit kindred. In general, relatives traced bilaterally, through both father and mother, are equally weighted in Matsigenka reckoning. Although the Matsigenka may in some ways be described as having a matrilateral or matrilocal bias (Casevitz 1977; Rosengren 1987b: 335), their social organization is strictly bilateral, with flexibility as the key (O. Johnson 1978: 126; Löffler and Baer 1978). Indeed, the opposition created at one level by the prohibition on parallel-cousin marriage is counteracted at a higher level by bilateral descent reckoning, which ensures that "in-laws" are part and parcel of the individual's kindred, without regard to "male line" or "female line" (O. Johnson 1978: 93–96):

The Matsigenka also lack terms for social categories. For example, there are no terms for affine, agnate, or family. Bodley (1970: 65) suggests that the Campa word *noshaninka* corresponds to "my family." For the Matsigenka, *noshaninka* corresponds to "my people," those who live in ego's general locality; *nomagi-moigirira* ("those who sleep with me") designates the people living in ego's immediate settlement cluster. Both terms reflect physical proximity rather than social standing. For ego's kin . . . there is the term *nohitane*, "the people I treat as kinsmen," which constitutes an egocentric kindred. The only relationship denoted by a categorical term is blood sibling. *Notovainka* (literally "my others") refers to both male and female siblings who have at least one parent in common. The Matsigenka also distinguish between "real" kin and people who are simply regarded as kinsmen. For example, *apa sanorira* is a true or biological father (also *itomintakenarira*, meaning "the one who fathered me"). When kin terms are extended to incorporate new relationships, the Matsigenka say, *nopegakeri (apa)*, literally "I changed him into [a father]."

Outside of the general category of being a Matsigenka, which is primarily a linguistic distinction, the Matsigenka do not classify people according to membership groups, as the lack of linguistic terms for social categories implies. Emphasis is placed on the genealogical core of male and female kin, which extends outward through marriage. The ordering principle is kindred unity through incorporation rather than exclusion. And because the kindred is ego-centered, its boundaries vary with the perspective of each individual, never establishing a defined sociocentric group. (O. Johnson 1978: 114–15)

Of course, the ideal hamlet of the right proportions of marriage partners does not often occur. For example, in the downstream hamlet the children of the classificatory brothers Felipe, Mariano, and Julio included seven boys and four girls (all "brothers" and "sisters" to each other), whereas the children of their cross-cousins Karoroshi and Javier included seven girls (including 12-AF2) and two boys (all cross-cousins to the other set of children). Even if they were all matched off to their cross-cousins, there would still be two girls from Felipe's group without mates.

When a man and woman court, their households are most interested in the event and carefully cross-examine their potential in-laws. If the marriage is bringing together a man and woman from different hamlets, the usual pattern is for the man to move into his bride's home and work for her father for a year or two. This bride service seems primarily to provide a period for a trial marriage, when the newlyweds discover whether they truly like each other and can make a marriage. As Matteson (1954: 79) describes for the Piro, "There is usually matrilocal residence for an indefinite period. It seems to be a matter of protection of the bride and of mutual help, rather than of actual bride service. The son-in-law does the hunting and more active work, and the families have fields adjoining if possible. The wife seems to consider herself bound more to her parents than to her husband." Marriages frequently fail during this period. In such cases, the ex-husband simply packs up his belongings and leaves to effect a divorce. Because he has been working for his father-in-law during this period, no disputes arise over the ownership of garden lands he cultivated.

If the couple remains together, once the period of bride service is past, typically marked by the birth of a child, the young couple has freedom to decide where to live. They may remain with the wife's family, move to the husband's hamlet, or strike out on their own for some period of time. They may form a close bond with one of their siblings and branch off to form a new hamlet within easy visiting distance of one of their original hamlets. Judging from our migration histories, they will move in and out of residential proximity to their other kin on both husband's and wife's sides more than once in the years to come.

It should be clear, therefore, that the social structure provided by the kinship system is limited to a kind of conceptual ordering that prohibits nuclear-family incest and tends toward a pattern of intermarrying families over the generations. This is not "sister exchange" (O. Johnson 1978: 104), although it may work out that way some of the time; it is just as often "brother exchange," perhaps even more so because of the matrilocal bias created by the custom of bride service. And often it is marriage between cousins so distantly related that the genealogical details are unknown. There is no evidence that in the general region around Shimaa the system of asymmetrical alliance postulated by Casevitz (1977: 129–37), including local exogamy, preferential patrilateral cross-cousin marriage, and matrilocal residence, can be found (cf. Löffler and Baer 1978).

And this is not in any way a system of two lineages intermarrying. A lineage system regulates not only marriage but generally residence as well, and is most likely to occur where land or other productive property is controlled by descent groups. The Matsigenka hardly impede the access of other Matsigenka to agricultural land, which is generally abundant, and certainly do not use kinship and marriage to determine who can farm where. The freedom they have to move from one place to another, from one living arrangement to another, means that they are much more likely to decide how to apply the kinship system to their own advantage than to sacrifice their freedom of choice to social-structural imperatives.

This freedom is especially clear in the frequent, occasionally blatant, manipulation of the kin terminology to suit individuals (cf. Chagnon 1987). We learned about this firsthand when, after perhaps six weeks in

Shimaa, Felipe approached us and asked us to be kinsmen. I said that would be pleasing and asked how we should be related. He suggested that I could be his father *(apa)*. I suggested being brothers *(ige)*, but this idea seemed to disconcert him.

I had suggested *ige* because of the egalitarian implications, but Felipe had other considerations in mind. A father-son relationship would minimize any ambiguity about sexual relationships between us and them, by bringing virtually every adult member of Felipe's hamlet under the incest prohibition, as either our sons, daughters, nephews, or nieces. Later, when we told this to Wayne and Betty Snell, they smiled knowingly and said, "Also, as your sons, it is appropriate for Felipe and his brothers to ask you for things. Brothers do not feel as free to ask favors from each other." So we had been neatly positioned in a kin relationship that maximized Felipe's self-interest. Very quickly thereafter everyone in his hamlet was calling us by the kin terms that made sense in view of their relationship to Felipe (that is, his children called me "grandfather," his cross-cousins called me "uncle," etc.). A less common, but still satisfactory, strategy was for men to ask me to treat them as *ani* (cross-cousin/brother-in-law). This had the advantage of making my wife their sister and their wives my sisters, eliminating any possible sexual involvements.

In the same way, Matsigenkas beyond the confines of the hamlet reserve the right to choose how to refer to other Matsigenkas. It is common to find that a person simply does not treat *(tera nohuteri)* another as kin at all, even though they encounter each other on public occasions. It is also common for them not to use the usual kin terms but to choose alternatives such as *nocharinantsi*, "my rival/friend" or "my friendly adversary," or *notsipatarira*, "my friend of same sex" (O. Johnson 1978: 118). These terms leave the kinship relationship unspecified and future marriage possibilities ambiguous.

If this terminology is not possible—if, for example, a man finds himself in a hamlet where all the women of his generation are classified as sisters—"he will want to reexamine the existing relationships in order to establish marriageability. Likely there are alternatives in the reckoning of his own kin" (O. Johnson 1978: 122). In one case, a man who wished to marry his stepmother, widowed when his father died, refrained from calling her *ina*, "mother," while he emphasized that her sister was married to his own parallel cousin (i.e., his "brother"): thus, his "mother" became the sister of his brother's wife, moving her into the marriageable category (see also Casevitz 1977: 125–26).

Finally, if such delicate restructuring does not work, a man can simply redefine a relationship and dare the world to object. Snell (1964: 33, quoted in O. Johnson 1978: 99) offers an example of a man who stood in marriageable relation to a woman he did not want. When she persisted in trying to marry him, he stopped her in a public place and said, "From now on you are my niece." In chapter 3 we learned of Aradino, who changed Erena from daughter to wife in a few months. It was a public scandal, but he simply put up with the condemnation and had soon fathered children by her.

In all these cases, the manipulation is possible because the true kinship relationship is ambiguous. No such ambiguity exists about nuclear-family members who have grown up together or members of a hamlet who can trace their relationships to known ancestors. Where the relationship is close—siblings, first cousins, children of siblings—these manipulations are much more difficult to pull off. This varying ease or difficulty of manipulation also is evidence for the absence of clearly bounded kin groups: kin relations are egocentric and the more distant a kin relationship is, the more room the Matsigenka have to redefine it in a form that suits their individual interests. Throughout the process they remain opposed to incest in principle, while being more flexible the greater the genealogical distance.

KINSHIP AND GROUP IDENTITY

The Matsigenka lack a sense of belonging to any group larger than the hamlet. In quantitative terms, they spend only a tiny fraction of their time in group settings like barbasco fishing and beer feasting—in fact, less than 4 percent of adult daylight time. Qualitatively, these short periods of group interaction are intense and of undeniable importance, but Matsigenka days are lived out mainly in solitary work and nuclear-family intimacy.

The Hamlet as an Enduring Group.   We have seen that economically the hamlet is held together in part by collaboration in critical activities like house building and obtaining and sharing wild foods. Despite the advantages of this collaboration, households do leave hamlets and isolate themselves for shorter or longer periods of time. However, migration histories document that households tend to remain in the general vicinity of a group of families that is fairly stable over time. These families comprise people who grew up together as siblings or cross-cousins and remain closely linked through intermarriage, just as the structural model of the ideal hamlet (figure 23) suggests.

The social closeness of hamlet members is evident in behavior. Just as members of a household interact far more frequently with one another than with nonhousehold members, so too members of a hamlet interact more with each other than with members of other hamlets. For example, the members of the downstream hamlet visited one another about five times as often as they did households in the school community (O. Johnson 1978: 109). Although this contrast in visiting patterns is a function of distance in Shimaa, Rosengren (1983: 57) reports a similar pattern in a "Communidad Nativa" of the upper Urubamba. And Baksh (1984: 416–28) shows how the sharp drop-off in visiting patterns between hamlet-sized kin groups persists even after they have been brought into close proximity in a school community. Like stones in a mosaic, hamlets retain their shape even when combined into a large village.

Four of the men of the downstream hamlet used to live upriver in the vicinity of what is now the school community of Shimentaato, where they knew one another as children. When Maestro invited them to come to Shimaa in 1968 they did so as a group. Felipe and Mariano were full brothers, and Julio treated them as brothers although he could not trace an exact relationship to them. Javier stood in relation to them as cross-cousin/brother-in-law *(ani)*. The fifth household in the hamlet was headed by Karoroshi, who had recently married the sister of the two brothers, so he also was their *ani*, although he had come from a different tributary of the Kompiroshiato and was not closely linked to the other four. During our research, Mariano entered a trial marriage with the widowed sister of Javier. Although it failed to take hold, it was natural to try. The members of these five households were very close to one another—they cleared gardens near one another, helped each other build houses, shared meat, constituted a beer-feasting group—and had evidently been so since their parents' generation.

When living together in a hamlet, households are subject to certain intimacies. Members of one's own hamlet may walk in through a closed door unannounced and expect to share valuable items like meat or steel tools; this practice reflects a long, close association that includes friendship as well as strong biological ties. In partial response to this intimacy, they take certain steps to maintain privacy. They often position their houses so that they are not visible from one another, allowing a stretch of forest or a knoll to separate them. They maintain separate paths to their houses, so that people walking on the main trail need not pass any given house unless they have specific business there. Even when Mariano and his cross-cousin, Karoroshi, lived side by side in the same clearing, they placed their doors in opposite walls—Mariano's facing the river and Karoroshi's facing the mountain—so that their comings and goings were not directly visible to each other.

To a degree men view their brothers-in-law *(ani)* as interlopers into the family. This was evident in the way Felipe and Mariano treated Aradino, who married their sister Rosa and lived outside their hamlet. They visited Rosa and were courteous to Aradino, but in private they made fun of him. Once they accused him of beating Rosa, and on another occasion they angrily accused him of stealing Felipe's machete. Aradino may have been more vulnerable to such open disrespect because he had no relatives of his own and was an uncooperative loner who spent as much time in an isolated house far up the Río Shimaa as he did in the school neighborhood.

The ambivalence in the brother-in-law relationship is seen in the tale of Shintori (Peccary). It tells of a man who went hunting for fresh peccary meat even while he still had meat smoking over his fire from a previous hunt. A shaman had specifically prohibited such greedy behavior, but the man ignored the ban and was captured by peccaries. Rather than kill him, they took him with them to have him climb trees for the fruits they could not reach because their hooves kept them from climbing. After a while, the man became friends with the peccary leader and married two of his sisters, becoming his brother-in-law. When his peccary troop once again visited the gardens near his old home, they, being animals, were shot by his human relatives, who captured him. But, from eating caña brava he had lost his voice (making him more animal-like), which was restored only when humans gave him sugar cane to eat. Then he could walk mournfully among the dead peccaries saying, "There's *ani*," "There's *ige*," and so on. The story plays on the ambivalent sense that in-laws are alien (like animals), yet are kin (like humans).

Many joking interactions between men at beer feasts reflect underlying tensions, whether between in-laws or others. It is not always clear whether someone is joking or fooling ("taking advantage," *yamitavinatakena*). For example, if your sister's new husband joked about abandoning her, then actually did so, you would feel betrayed and angry. And "jokes" at a beer feast may actually be insults *(ininatakeri)*. When Maestro jokingly told Aradino, "If you don't want to work for me, then get out of my house," Aradino took it as an insult and left the beer feast Maestro was hosting. But other guests accused Aradino of not taking the joke.

Gender Segregation in Public.   Matsigenka is not a society strongly polarized by sexual antagonism. Within the privacy of the household, hus-

TABLE 27. Food Exchanges during Meals
(*n = 111*)

Exchange Category	Observed Exchanges (%)	Expected Exchanges (%)
Opposite-Sex Exchanges		
Married	33%	11%
Nonmarriageable	21	31
Marriageable	0	13
Same-Sex Exchanges		
Female	29	21
Male	17	24
TOTAL	100%	100%

SOURCE: O. Johnson 1978: 218.

band and wife are generally respectful and frequently affectionate. Despite the emotional ambivalence between men and women explored in chapter 3, the division of labor by sex ensures that husband and wife need each other and appreciate the many everyday services they provide.

Outside the household, however, interaction between men and women is uncommon. We have seen how, at a fishing expedition, the men and women segregate into separate work groups that then break down into nuclear families when the actual fishing begins. A similar situation occurs when men and women come together to share a meal when meat or fish is available. O. Johnson (1978: 212–19) ties gender separation at communal meals to the general pattern of avoidance between men and women who could marry but have not—that is, between opposite-sex cross-cousins who are not married and have no kin term for each other. The tension arises because sexual liaisons between them are permitted by the kinship system but would be socially disruptive, especially if one or both of them are already married. The problems that could follow from intimate exchanges are thus avoided by gender segregation in groups. Behavioral interactions during meals, as seen on videotapes, show extreme avoidance between people who could marry each other (table 27). In fact, of 111 observations of food exchanges between a man and a woman during meals, 37 (33 percent) are between husband and wife, although only 11 percent would be expected by chance. In sharp contrast, none of the food exchanges were between marriageables

FIGURE 24. Women and girls straining manioc beer at Maestro's house.

not married to each other, although 13 percent would be expected by chance. In short, husbands and wives share food disproportionately often, unmarriageable pairs share food often, although less than would occur by chance, and marriageables never share food.

In addition, both men and women have their own networks of same-sex friends and relatives, and so it is natural for them to socialize in same-sex groups when several households are together. In fact, the larger the group, the more formal the segregation appears to become. In large beer feasts hosted by Maestro, for example, the men gathered on the veranda, whereas the women met in the kitchen, a separate structure next to the house. Women and children moved back and forth between the two groups delivering beer to the men and retrieving their empty bowls.

When segregated groups of men and women occur at work, mealtime, or leisure, the interactions among the women involve more mutuality than those among the men (O. Johnson 1978: 52, 136, 219). Men tend to work alone, whereas women tend to work in the company of others; women say they do not like to work alone because they fear attack by demons more than men do. At communal meals, women exchange food with other women more than men exchange with other men (table 27). And in the dances at beer feasts, the general pattern is for men to dance ahead of the women, individualistically drumming and darting and twirling so that their cushmas billow out like full skirts. The women, by contrast, follow the men in a group, holding hands and singing in unison.

Socializing in Groups.   Even group work, as in the hand mowing of the airstrip under Maestro's direction, appears to have social rewards. Strung along a line that moves slowly forward down the airstrip, men fire off jokes that provoke hearty laughter. Despite the extreme drudgery of the task (mowing thick, unpleasant weeds from a crouch, using a machete), the men seem to enjoy themselves socially. As one man from Camaná told me in 1980, after working in a group weeding project, "You don't get tired—finish quickly! My own garden takes five days to weed. But with the group, you finish in less than one day." Baksh (1984), however, found that men accomplished less on the whole in such groups than their rates of work in individual projects would have predicted; some labor efficiency may thus be sacrificed for a more playful sociability.

The Matsigenka clearly enjoy recreational gatherings and prepare for them with enthusiasm. We noticed again and again how the level of excitement rose as the day for an expedition or feast approached. The Matsigenka are normally quiet and calm, moving gracefully and without hurry. But as the participants begin to gather for the event, the area becomes animated with laughter and movement. If there is work to be done on a fishing dam, no beer is served, but people work quickly and much is accomplished. Jokes fly back and forth, and when work offers the opportunity to play, as when the men rode logs downriver as though they were bucking broncos, they give themselves over to the fun of the moment. Everyone is friendly; all the old animosities seemingly evaporate. Such a mood may persist through one or two days and into the feasting and beer drinking.

These are common occasions for individuals to engage in trade. In the generosity of the moment, people give away possessions or beg them from another. Because these events rarely involve visitors from distant communities, people do not come to the feast with a pack of items to barter. But as a natural outcome of the gathering individuals compare possessions and may swap them or give them away in the interest of building friendships.

Here is a description of a beer feast I attended fortuitously during the second month of fieldwork:

Fieldnote 09–17–72—Omenko had told me that he was going to his garden to plant today, so I went to Oscar and told him I wanted to go, too. We left at

7:20 A.M., walking up the Shimaa and crossing it after about 15 minutes, and arriving at Tito's at 7:45. A large crowd was gathered, sitting in the shade of Evaristo's kitchen drinking manioc beer. Those present were Ricardo, Angel, Evaristo, Juanito, Tito, Eduardo, Omenko, Oscar, Alicia, Victoria, Rokania, and some other women unfamiliar to me. When I arrived, Evaristo said *pokakempi . . . kameti* ["You have arrived—good"], making me feel at home, and I was offered yuca, a small catfish-like fish *(etari)* and manioc beer. The men were drumming and dancing (except Omenko), but stopped while I was there. At 8:00 I went with Omenko and Oscar to view Omenko's garden, and I thought to work in it, but after a few minutes we returned to the party.

Those drumming were Evaristo, Tito, Juanito, Angel, Eduardo, and Ricardo. The drum is a wooden cylinder about one foot in diameter and 18 inches long, with a monkey-skin cover on each end and a snare at one end made of fine cotton string, taut, with small beads strung along it.

The men drum and dance, the women walking along behind hand-in-hand and singing. The dance steps include a snake-like forward motion in between the houses and around the yard, with various turns around to the left and the right while moving forward. All the drinking and socializing take place in what appears to be a kitchen rather than in two other structures that appear to be sleeping areas.

The men and women sit at opposite ends of the kitchen (women upstream, except for Victoria, who sits next to Omenko). One woman, possibly Evaristo's wife, serves the manioc beer to everyone else and the women continue to work on making more manioc beer while everyone gets drunk—the manioc beer is pretty strong, probably three days old.

After a while I brought out my cameras and started taking pictures. At first, everyone seemed a little tense, but I handed around the cameras and let everyone handle them and look through them, and pretty soon things were relaxed enough for me to film the event.

The men wanted to know how much everything cost. Ricardo said he wanted my machete. My knife passed around and Angel cut himself on it (thumb), which occasioned mirth. He played with the blood and even smeared some on Juanito's foot, finally tying the thumb with string.

All ages of both sexes drink the manioc beer, so the inebriation and lassitude are general. One dance by Tito, Angel and Ricardo, however, lasted from 9:10 to 9:45 and represents no mean physical exertion, since the pace is fast and consistent. My presence by now seemed to be accepted, although occasionally all attention would center on me.

Ricardo gave me a feather headdress, offered me some plantains which I refused (probably shouldn't have), and blew his nose on his cushma. Everyone seemed to be pretty drunk by 10:00 A.M., although the older members and the very young children seemed to drink less. At one point (10:20) Victoria asked Rokash to pick out the one remaining little fish from the ashes, and Tito, seeing this, stood up and got about a dozen more from a pot.

Between the drinking, eating, dancing, and conversation the time was pretty much spent. Oscar asked me if I wanted to leave around 11:00, and I said yes.

FIGURE 25. Drumming, dancing, and singing at a beer feast.

The day was very hot and dry as we returned by balsa raft (a roller-coaster of a ride which we all enjoyed like schoolboys).

Drinking beer at first intensifies the social high. Men take turns working on a drum or other project, begin to drum, play flutes, and sing. Dancers rise, drumming and singing (figure 25). In the separate circles of men and women, friends hug one another and protest their abiding love. The shouts and laughter and the rhythmic drumming can be heard far away above the background noise of the river.

The high is complex however. Whereas at first it is a genuine feeling of good will and fellowship, the jokes often have a sharp edge of ridicule in them. As the party wears on, the slow but steady supply of beer has the intended effect. Men and women slur their words and stumble about. Children begin to appear more mature and capable than the adults; they cook, serve, and clean up for their incapacitated parents. Individuals liberated by drink from their usual courteous restraint reveal a harsh, aggressive side. They begin to tease those they view as transgressors. People who have broken taboos are called to task and harshly ridiculed, to great roars of laughter. If one man suspects another of stealing his fishing tackle or his wife, he confronts him with a detailed cross-examination concerning his movements. Long-suppressed angers flare up and sometimes result in violence. More often than not, the aggressors later apologize through a haze of tears and become friends again, but not inevitably: resentments aired at a beer feast can lead to broken marriages and disintegrated hamlets.

On the whole, however, the gathering of many families is a public forum in which to express feelings that would not be appropriate under other circumstances. In a society without institutional procedures for police investigation, judgment, and punishment, the gathering is an opportunity for airing grievances and seeking justice, and in many cases it leads to a resolution of suspicions and disputes.

The Division of Labor in the Hamlet.   Although the division of labor by sex makes it possible for a husband and wife to have between them a complete set of skills necessary for the maintenance and reproduction of the household, sometimes certain skills are deemphasized in one household but emphasized in another to create a division of labor and mutual dependence between households within a hamlet. Rosa, who lived next to her mother, could not weave but did spin cotton and continued to help her mother as a daughter should, although she had the reputation for being lazy. Her mother was an outstanding weaver who made cloth for both households. In a way, Rosa's continued dependence on her mother allowed her to postpone becoming a fully skilled woman.

Another example of specialization concerns Julio, whose large, productive gardens became the breadbasket for his hamlet (and for some relatives outside the hamlet) during the scarce period in 1972 before new crops became ripe. Julio, who was crippled by polio, could no longer hunt effectively, but he had a grown son and a nearly grown one, and the three of them maintained high levels of garden productivity. In turn, Julio shared in the meat brought in by his healthy relatives in the hamlet.

The hamlet, or the circle of kin who have lived together as a hamlet in the past and probably will again, is the common unit of participation in beer feasts. The event is planned well in advance. Women of the group collaborate in beer making while the men go hunting or fishing. The person extending the invitation always includes the phrase *aityo shitea,* "There will be beer," and excitement and interest peak as the time for the feast approaches.

Maestro was a social center for several hamlets. The division of labor he organized may hold some clues to what might have existed in the neighborhood of a respected shaman in the past. We have already seen how certain men and women, orphaned, not well integrated into enduring hamlets, attach themselves to a strong household as if to find protection and community where little or none exists. They are willing to subordinate their autonomy to serve the political needs of the powerful household, which, because of its large labor pool, becomes a center of unusually high levels of food production, manufacture, and feasting. In Shimaa, Maestro's household commanded a remarkable amount of labor. The gathering of a half dozen or more women boiling, grinding, and straining the ingredients for beer for a feast had, by local standards, the feel of a cottage industry. Meanwhile, their husbands were out hunting to provide meat for the feast. The same kind of joint labor was used to cultivate the schoolteacher's huge gardens, which were many times larger than those of the average household. Although the schoolteacher had modern goods to offer as rewards, rather than spiritual healing, he was seen as protective in dealing with the outside world, which was the leader's function to some degree in the past.

Hierarchy in the Hamlet.   The Matsigenka are certainly "egalitarian" in any typology of comparative political systems. When disputes arise between households, they are difficult to resolve because household members are basically independent of and equal to members of other households, an equality that ultimately rests on their freedom either to resort to violence or (more commonly) to move away.

But individuals differ in the intrinsic respect they evoke. For example, once during a fishing expedition, the low-status adult Evaristo and the preadolescent youth Pepe were catching stunned fish in the same pool.

Pepe's eyes lit with pleasure when he caught a *segori,* one of the finest-tasting fish in the river. But Evaristo immediately confronted him: "Where did you catch that?"

"Right here," said Pepe, indicating the place.

"That's mine, then." Evaristo reached for the fish. "I was chasing it earlier right in that spot and it got away from me." Pepe held the fish out of Evaristo's reach, obviously upset. His older cross-cousin, Oscar, who was highly respected, inquired as to the problem. Listening to the explanations, he told Pepe he would have to give up the fish. This was the only acceptable choice: Evaristo was older than Pepe and, as a fellow hamlet member, Oscar had to think about long term relations with Evaristo's household.

The story had a happy ending. Pepe soon caught another *segori* and was allowed to keep it, his delight undiminished by the earlier incident. But the lesson here is that a senior and prestigious member of the hamlet imposed his judgment to resolve one of those sour little incidents that are bound to arise between neighbors, and this kind of involvement in disputes entails leadership.

And just as careful analysis of patterns of command and compliance demonstrated the hierarchy within the household, so also analysis revealed asymmetries of behavior between members of different households within a hamlet. Visiting patterns from the time-allocation study showed asymmetries between even closely related households (A. W. Johnson 1978: 106–10; cf. Rosengren 1983). Some households received many more visits than they paid, while others paid more than they received. Further analysis (O. Johnson 1978: 263–69) showed that those who paid the most visits were of lower status than those who received the most. Perhaps the most noticeable pattern in the data on visiting was the predominance of visits paid to Maestro's house, especially from two of the dependent households (Santiago's and Aretoro's), a flow of visits that reflects the status differential of a patron-client relationship (A. W. Johnson 1978: 109).

This pattern was reproduced in frequencies of exchanges of food or labor between households. Maestro was very much central to this process, exchanging with eleven other households. The next most involved household exchanged only with four other households, others with as few as one or two other households. Maestro was equally involved in both giving and receiving, although there was an asymmetry: whereas he gave either meat or trade goods to others, he tended to receive garden produce, firewood, and labor from them in return.

Such asymmetries in small-scale societies often signal the existence of local leaders (Henry 1951; Stearman 1989). Maestro was a local leader. Apart from his role in holding together the multihamlet school community, as examined in the next section, he was also a patron to many individuals. He hired men and women to grow, harvest, and process food in exchange for trade goods. On shopping trips to Kiteni, he took men who would not have the confidence to go without him. He encouraged the inhabitants of the hamlet to grow coffee and marketed it for them. He heard complaints and tried to resolve disputes. He asked after people's health and sought outside medical advice for them.

A different situation existed in the more traditional downstream cluster. As we have seen, this hamlet consisted of intermarrying families that went back several generations, decades before linguists from the SIL arrived and launched the formation of modern communities. The hamlet was essentially egalitarian, but only in the sense that social status freely rose and fell with the life cycles and dispositions of its members. At any point in time, however, it was likely to be hierarchically ordered.

In the downstream cluster household 11 was the favored recipient of visits from households 13 and 14. The head of 11 was Felipe, the older brother of Mariano, head of 14. Felipe's senior wife, Eva, was the mother of Mariano's wife, Rosa. These differences in seniority affected relationships between the two households. Of special importance was that Eva was a major producer of beer and manufactured goods, as she was somewhat freed of other duties by her co-wife, Amaria. The extra members of Felipe's household, as contrasted with the three people in Mariano's house, made it the social center of the cluster, the host of periodic beer feasts. Although the male heads of houses 11 and 14 were equally skilled and hard-working, the female head of 11 was far more productive than her daughter, head of household 14.

The male head of household 13, Karoroshi, was married to Virima, the sister of Felipe and Mariano. Karoroshi had no family in the vicinity apart from his in-laws. Virima had, of course, her brothers, as well as a "sister" (parallel cousin) in household 10 who was her co-wife during a previous marriage. But this small household did not host beer feasts, and Karoroshi had only recently completed his bride-service obligations not only to Felipe and Mariano but also to their parallel cousin Julio, head of household 12. Karoroshi's household paid a total of seventy-six visits to households 11 and 14, yet received only eight in return.

For the most part, households 10 and 12 kept to themselves more so than the other households of the hamlet. Julio in household 12 lived only a few minutes away, although this house was separated from the others by a patch of secondary growth and a small garden. His abundance of manioc during a time of general shortage had made his household the second most frequently involved in exchanges between households in Shimaa. His productive gardening did not make him a leader, but it contributed to his overall high standing, as did his intelligence, sharp wit, and knowledge of lore. Household 10, headed by Javier, was an outrider of this hamlet, having moved forty-five minutes deep into the forest after finding the hamlet too crowded. Later, when Javier's sister formed a trial marriage with Mariano in household 14, members of household 10 stopped by 14 frequently on their way to the river or upstream. During this period, the status of household 14 rose sharply as the new wife produced large quantities of beer and enabled the household to host a beer feast.

These examples show that both male and female heads of household take an active role in determining their household's status. The number of visits a household receives depends on kinship ties and economic status. Both the husband's kin and the wife's kin become integral parts of their social network. To attract visitors, both spouses must be hard workers; they must have an active household and plenty of food. The Matsigenka criterion for hard work is more than mere time and effort; it also entails initiative. There is always a clear "owner" of any communal enterprise, someone who assumes the responsibility and takes the credit. As the examples of households 11 and 14 show, it is not enough for one of the spouses to be hard-working—both must contribute if their household is to attract visitors. (O. Johnson 1978: 268)

Some individuals clearly feel stronger and more effective than others. Some men and women are not very bright or are fearful or have low energy levels. They are objects of lower esteem but generally have a pleasant manner and are accepted as marriage partners. They are likely to come into the orbit of a strong and active person who, in a sense, takes charge of them. These relationships are inherently hierarchical, with the lower-status partner taking orders from the higher-status one. Both parties seem to derive satisfaction from the relationship.

One avenue to low status is to be without close kin. Orphans are often adopted into families as second-class citizens, *nampiriantsi* (literally "the person by one's side," but translated into Spanish as *empleado/empleada,* "employee") (O. Johnson 1978: 163). Adopted children appear conditioned to a lifetime of shyness and dependence on more confident people who have grown up in and continue to be surrounded by a supportive extended family.

BEYOND THE HAMLET

As a rule, Matsigenkas from separate hamlets regard one another with considerable suspicion. When someone marries out, people frequently complain about the poor treatment their out-marrying relative has received in the other hamlet. In short, people outside the hamlet are portrayed as scoundrels lacking the virtues of members of one's own hamlet.

The School Community.   The school community is a modern creation, only four years old when our research began in Shimaa in 1972 (figure 26). It exists because the school, and Maestro, created opportunities for integration and leadership that would not otherwise have occurred, although comparable opportunities might have arisen in the past to deal with slave raids and other outside intrusions. But school communities in general are rather fragile. Members of one hamlet visit others occasionally, but beneath the surface friendliness and even fascination lie suspicion and denigration. Following such a visit, rumors abound

FIGURE 26. Students at school in Shimaa.

that the visitors stole something, that their true motive for the visit was to look for a spouse, or that they brought a virus with them that is now infecting the host hamlet. On the trail men sometimes warned me that the trails in the vicinity of another hamlet were dangerous places where one could meet *koveenkaripage* (man killers), powerful animals like jaguar or anteater whose danger is partly spiritual. In 1976, when I asked the schoolteacher at Camaná why a quarter of the people who had lived with him at Mantaro Chico had stayed behind when he moved the community to Camaná, he replied "Because it is our culture to live apart— we are not united."

Once, for example, I asked Julio in the downstream hamlet whether his bamboo-point arrow was for peccary *(ashi shintori)*; he said yes, and then there was a silence until his son Roberto said, "It's for Evaristo" *(ashi Evaristo)*. This remark provoked a roar of laughter from those present. Evaristo was a member of the upstream hamlet, a man who appeared weak and ingratiating and was generally looked down on by others. This mean joke not only implied that Evaristo deserved to be shot but also placed him in the category of peccary, as in the folktale described earlier.

Only two men, Maestro and Italiano, tended to move freely between hamlets. Italiano's role was as trader and culture broker because his family lived the farthest downstream. His was the last Matsigenka household before *ponyarona* immigrant households began to appear near the mouth of the Río Kompiroshiato. He had evidently played this role near Shimaa before the school was established. He was not afraid of *ponyaronas* and used his access to trade goods as well as his hunting success (based on shotgun ownership) to play a minor "big man" role by making gifts of meat to several hamlets around Shimaa. But, though generous, he was not particularly integrative in the sense that his activities did not bring the hamlets together in larger political relations.

Maestro was similar to Italiano in parleying generosity into higher status, but Maestro played a deliberately integrative role. The work crews he mobilized to cut the grass of the airstrip, which needed to be done several times a year when a bush plane was expected, included men from all the nearby hamlets, and these were the same people he invited to his house for the only multihamlet beer feasts in the vicinity. When he called meetings to celebrate important holidays, the schoolhouse was packed, men on one side, women on the other, with a standing-room-only crowd. By 1974 he had begun inviting *ponyaronas* to these events, hosting a soccer game and a beer feast after the meeting. These were true political events, bringing househeads together in separate men's and women's groups to know one another better, to be united by collaboration and sport, and to hear political messages about the status of their community in relation to the Peruvian nation-state.

But in Shimaa these efforts by Maestro were only partially successful. The integrating events were few and far between and did not erase the fundamental distance between hamlets. Often, men from different hamlets attended his beer feasts, but their wives stayed home, uncomfortable in the company of so many strangers. And although other communities like Kamisea and Camaná had more numerous households more closely spaced, households that appeared more friendly and that seemed to visit one another more frequently than those in Shima, even there the underlying pattern of hamlet separateness could be discovered (Baksh 1984: 416–28). Indeed, most Matsigenka school communities have undergone periodic crises that have threatened to result in fission and dissolution of the community, and it is a reasonable assumption that the lines of factionalism in those cases reflect the same familistic divisions that kept Shimaa disunited.

Regional Integration.   Overall, Matsigenkas spend rather little time visiting others. Even full siblings, if they live in separate hamlets, visit one another rarely. A common kind of visit is a brief stop en route to another destination. Host and visitor exchange greetings, and then the visitor stands outside the house, exchanges a few words with someone inside about his destination, his state of health and that of his family, and goes on his way. If he stays more than a minute or so, his host rises and offers him a mat to sit on. He enters the house and then must stay a while in order not to insult his host. Conversation about fairly mundane matters continues for a while. If the guest has a particular reason for visiting, he mentions it eventually, and when his business is concluded, he rises abruptly, without further ado, and leaves with the parting *noate,* "I am going."

Longer visits, which may occur only once a year or less, keep people informed about deaths; they also inform others of divorces and of which young people have reached maturity, topics that indicate the availability of potential mates. And they convey general information about the social and economic environment. Such a visit is a high-intensity talkfest. A spirit of good will moves guest and host alike to stay up late into the night swapping stories and information. Others, even non-kin of the guest, come by for various lengths of time to enjoy the news and festive atmosphere. Even if some residents of the hamlet do not show up to see the guest personally, they hear all the news as the visit is dissected after the guest departs.

By such means the Matsigenka of one hamlet have a rather detailed knowledge of many other hamlets and individual households in their region. The members of the downstream hamlet at Shimaa, for example, had virtually complete knowledge of all the households along the Shimaa River and of those along the Kompiroshiato from Shimaa to the Urubamba River. They had less complete knowledge of the households of the school community of Shimentaato, several hours' walk upriver, but they knew many of them well. They also knew at least something about a number of households far up the Kompiroshiato watershed, unattached to a school community but still engaged in the old pattern of visiting.

Today, the centers of such regional networks of acquaintance are the school communities. In the past, shamans *(seripigari)* or charismatic political leaders *(itinkame)* played a similar role. Although settlement was scattered along available streams, as it is today, people in the vicinity of a local leader looked to his household as a social center. For his part, the leader furthered this process by marrying many women, who helped maintain his prestige by their industrious food production and manufactures. We have heard of at least two cases in which leaders acquired as many as twelve wives, although it is not certain they all lived in his household at the same time. I assume that this opportunity for differential reproductive success was one of the motivations for men to take on a position that "had few special rights but several demanding duties" (Rosengren 1987a: 171).

We can get some idea of traditional interaction at the regional level by how the Matsigenka interacted with the school community at Shimaa in 1972–73. Beyond the several hamlets that sent children to the school, many other hamlets and single households lived at a distance. They might come for a beer feast when Maestro invited them, and they came to request trade items and medicines. During these visits they looked around them, curious about any new people or material goods, and gossiped. But they seemed reluctant visitors, eager to get back to their homesteads.

Strangers and Enemies.   The degree of integration made possible by local leaders created regions of relative peace and security where everybody knew everyone else at least casually. Beyond this orbit, security was increasingly at risk. Until after World War II, slavers roamed the montaña, delivering whole families to serve as cheap labor in various Peruvian enterprises. These were not always intolerable circumstances, and some families stayed voluntarily attached to their "owners" even into the 1970s, when they could no longer be compelled to do so. But people did not want to be captured and forced to work for someone else, and they looked on strangers with fear, fleeing when they approached; many were terrified of any member of the Pereira family (Rosengren 1987a: 166).

The Matsigenka of Shimaa believe that the only witches now practicing are in the outside world and that some of the tribes downriver eat demons and snakes. Whenever outsiders come upriver, even today, they are spotted from far off, and word rushes around to all the households, where the anxiety is palpable. Viruses *(merentsi)* come from the outside, just as slave traders did in the historic past, and who knows what kind of enemies came in the distant past, with Inkas on the west and powerful warrior tribes downstream to the east?

Our first visit to a Matsigenka household was at a small settlement on the Urubamba, where there is constant boat traffic up and down the river. But when we walked to a house set back in the hills, accompanied by an acculturated Matsigenka, no one came out to greet us; a hand ap-

peared through a crack in the door to offer us mats to sit on. This encounter is reminiscent of Marcoy's (1872: 1:446) experience a century
earlier when the Matsigenkas who were camped with his party along the
Urubamba would not let them inside their shelter, even when a terrific
storm broke out. The house is the secure bastion of the family; strangers are intrinsically dangerous and must not be permitted inside.

During my first two months in Shimaa, I came to feel that the Matsigenka saw me as a source of valuable goods whom they could take advantage of to get as much and give as little back as possible. They seemed
to regard me without "sympathy," like a supply depot rather than a person seeking friendship. I didn't realize it then, but I was on a learning
curve: I had to become clear and explicit with the Matsigenka about
what I wanted, for they would not anticipate my wants or be eager to
supply them. I later read with amused familiarity a passage from Gulliver (1951: 9), whose work with the familistic Turkana of Kenya raised
similar issues:

One of my better informants came to us one day and asked what I was going to
give him for his help in the past (he had had several small gifts) since, he explained, he knew that I had given a blanket to an earlier informant. My wife told
him that he must wait and see, for in our country one did not ask for presents,
but if one was a friend one was given them in due course. "Oh, we do not do
that," he replied immediately, "we ask for what we want or we do not get anything." "But," said my wife, "No-one ever gives us presents in return for those
we give out." "Well, you should ask for them," was his answer.

In this early period of fieldwork I formed a transitional friendship
with the assistant schoolteacher, Antonio, who was a Campa Indian
married to a Matsigenka woman. In part, we were drawn to each other
as mutual outsiders. Before long, he left to return to his family in Picha,
but by then the downstream hamlet had incorporated us into their extended family, where we were no longer treated as strangers.

But the Matsigenka notion of stranger begins even closer to home.
They refuse to consider some people as kin *(tera nohuteri)* even though
they may encounter them frequently through events arranged by the
schoolteacher. They do not treat them the same as they would treat
a stranger, but the cleft between kin and non-kin is obvious. The palpable mistrust between members of even neighboring hamlets is a sign
that they are seen as partial strangers at best, people who must interact
with care.

On one occasion, two Matsigenka men arrived in Shimaa to gather caterpillars they had heard were abundant nearby. They were careful to appear first at Maestro's house and at our house and explained that they had been sent by the schoolteacher at Shimentaato. Thus, no one could suspect them of acting improperly because a man of high status and power had told them to come. By this time, our house had also become a sort of public place, where speeches were sometimes made and inter-hamlet disputes aired, and strangers usually made a point of stopping by to see and to be seen.

The difficult terrain and poverty of resources in the montaña have kept population density low and minimized competition from outside. These circumstances may historically have protected the Matsigenka to some degree: they had nothing to steal, and little could be gained from trying to control them politically. Aside from occasional trips to trad-ing zones, the Matsigenka of the Kompiroshiato watershed have had limited contact with the outside. They tell vivid stories about their few contacts, especially those that resulted in the death, enslavement, or sale of Matsigenkas. But the stories about events at a distance, say along the Río Urubamba upriver past Kiteni or downriver past the Pongo de Mainique, become vague: they are not based on personal experience and blend into the realms of myth and the supernatural. Their belief in *kogapakori,* "wild men far off" (cf. d'Ans 1974: 342), also has this fan-tastic quality.

CHAPTER 5

Cosmos

Matsigenka religion may at least partly be understood as the
attempt to reduce or completely eliminate the influence of the
death spirits *(kama'garini):* wicked and evil is everything that
threatens life in any way, that brings sickness and death; it
must be opposed.

Baer 1984: 187

For the Matsigenka of Shimaa, *kameti,* "good," and *tera onkametite,*
"not good," are pervasive components of everyday conversation. In the
semantic space generated by our "colors of emotion" experiment
(Johnson, Johnson, and Baksh 1986: 677), the Matsigenka clustered
"good" with "happy" at one pole and "not good" with "sad" at the opposite pole, as if the pleasure principle were operating in its most elemental form: "What makes me happy is good; what makes me sad is not
good." In much of their world this dimension has a pragmatic, utilitarian aspect: black soil is good, yellow soil is no good; sugar cane is good
to eat, caña brava is not. As we move toward the human sphere, however, from inert matter to personhood, the good-versus-not-good dimension takes on an increasingly moral tone, becoming good-versus-
evil as transgressions against persons are seen as bringing on cosmic and
spiritual ruin.

We can see both the impersonal and the personal aspects of the
good/not good dimension in the story of how two mythical figures,
Tasorintsi and Kentivakori, helped create the world.

Tasorintsi said, "I will give you an example of my power." And saying this, and casting upon the waters a kind of dust he carried in his right hand, after blowing on it, he caused the greater part of the watery element to form land: the original or archetypal soils of highest quality that still exist today. In these soils manioc, and many other plants of great usefulness to humans, produce abundantly.

Then, turning to Kentivakori, he said, "Let's see if you can create anything to equal or surpass what I have just done." Then Kentivakori, following almost exactly the same procedure as his divine rival, also caused a great portion of the watery element to become land, or at least something like it. Such is the origin of those clay soils we find today where no cultivated plants will grow; of swamplands; of that ferruginous mud that causes ulcers on the feet of those who walk upon it; of soils that support the growth of the arco iris plant, believed to be an evil spirit; of pits of gravel and sharp stones; and of the gloomy crags and rockpiles where evil spirits dwell. (Alegre 1979: 42)

Some have been tempted to identify Tasorintsi, or Blowing Spirit (Shepard 1998: 322), with God, and in some Matsigenka narratives he is referred to as Dioshi (< Spanish, *Dios,* God; Pereira 1952; Alegre 1979: 40). By implication, Kentivakori is the devil. But the analogy is weak (Baer 1984: 166–75). Tasorintsi and Kentivakori have more in common with Trickster than with the great deities of any world religion (cf. Baer 1979: 106). They act willfully and selfishly, exercising the powers they possess without regard for their impact on human welfare. Baer (1979: 107) regards Tasorintsi as a cover term for a host of deities, including Sun and also Moon, a most dangerous being, responsible for the deaths of countless human souls.

Although this story of the origins of good and bad aspects of the world has a mechanistic, "just so" quality, when we get to the origins of people a moralistic thread emerges that proves to be of fundamental importance. This characteristic is especially clear in the origins of *ponyarona,* "Quechuas," and *virakocha,* "whites" (Euro-Americans). Here we begin to see the moral side, as careless humans unleash bad people onto this plane of existence:

The First People

The origin of man.—The Matsigenkas are the first people that existed in the world. *Tasorintsi* made them, in large numbers and already adult, by blowing upon the balsa tree.

The *Chonchoite,* tribes of cannibalistic savages, were created by the demon *Kentivakori.* They live far away, three months travel. They kill people and eat them roasted. Long ago, a Matsigenka *seripigari* went there and was unable to free himself from them; they killed, roasted, and ate him.

The *Kogapakori,* a tribe of savage bowmen, are the work of Kentivakori. He made them by blowing upon the violent ants of the *Kanae* tree (palosanto), and for this reason they are so fierce that they shoot and kill anyone who comes along.

The *Puñarunas* [*ponyaronas*], or Indians of the puna, were created by Kentivakori below in *Gamaironi* [Underground]. In ancient times there were no Puñarunas here on Earth. A child was digging in the earth for amusement, as was the custom, when the Puñarunas poked their heads through the hole he had made. Startled, the child ran to give warning, saying, "What has reared its head?" He ran right back, but he could not block the hole, for they were coming out in a mad rush. Tasorintsi did not wish that there should be Puñarunas.

Virakochas (civilized people or whites) were also created by Kentivakori in Gamaironi. Originally there were none on Earth. The spirits called *Inkakuna* were excavating for the brilliant ore of the metal *kori* (gold, silver, or other precious metal). One day, while they were busy at work, the Virakochas poked their heads through an opening in the excavation. Aghast, the Inkakunas shoveled dirt furiously to stop up the hole and keep them from coming up; but they pushed with such force from below that they were unable to contain them, and they came up in vast numbers. Then Tasorintsi, who did not wish there to be Virakochas, blew from above and out of the air fell a cloud of arrows, that killed almost all Virakochas. The shafts of those arrows were of Tasorintsipi, a species of caña brava. Tasorintsi told the Inkakunas not to dig there any more, so that no more Virakochas would get out, and they obeyed. Still, many more Virakochas climbed and climbed up out of that same hole.

The Puñarunas and Virakochas that escaped to this world are only a fraction; the greater number remained below in Gamaironi and are Kamagarini or demons. Those who escaped and live here on Earth were also once Kamagarini, but since they began to eat manioc they have become, though still evil, no longer demons. (Garcia 1939: 229–30)

The version of this story I was told in Shimaa is even clearer on the moral issue. A shaman told the people, "Don't fish, the whites will come." But they disobeyed him (a moral lapse), and once one white caught hold of the hook, the others began to follow him out of the water in great numbers.

The Natural World

The Matsigenka have extensive and detailed knowledge of their world. I found that a few simple questions could elicit a wealth of information. *Tatoita oka* ("What is that?") generally elicited the name of an object, as did *tiara opaita* ("What is it called?"). From the Matsigenkas' standpoint, these were entirely natural questions. The drawback to such queries was that they too often opened the floodgates: my male companion often began to name everything in sight far more quickly than I could write. Then, a few days or weeks later, I might ask the name of another object and be told, "Don't you remember? I told you the name of that before!" Once they recovered from their surprise at my ignorance, many Matsigenkas genuinely enjoyed naming things as a way to teach me about their world.

As powerful as this simple eliciting technique is for acquiring lists of words for things, it teaches little about how the Matsigenka order their universe and give it meaning. As I tried to move from the exuberant naming of diversity to some order of groupings and relations, however, the Matsigenka found my efforts perplexing, often boring. If their enthusiasm for supplying names ultimately exceeded mine, their enthusiasm for discovering pattern and organization—a typology or structure of the world—was much less. And the problem was not an absence of pattern but rather too many patterns, each generated by separate organizing principles. Just as a complex geometric sculpture appears to change form as it is viewed from different angles, the Matsigenka may be said to rotate the world and view it from different perspectives according to the conditions and purposes of the moment.

In describing their world, the Matsigenka value honesty and accuracy. The distinction between what is true *(arisano)* and false *(tsoenti)* is important to them. Although telling a lie is, in the right setting, considered a good joke, the joker will ultimately admit *inti notsoenti,* "That's my lie." Someone who, like Aretoro, lies frequently and not in a joking manner is said to be characteristically false *(inti tsoenti)*. When people recount stories and histories, they distinguish reports based on their own personal experience *(kenkiagantsi)* from hearsay *(kenkitsarintsi)*. People vouch for *kenkiagantsi* because they themselves witnessed the events being reported, but they do not take responsibility for *kenkitsarintsi,* saying—when pressed for the truth—"I don't know; it's what I heard." As a corollary, the Matsigenka take for granted that knowledge is incomplete and that differences in specifics of belief are common. For people who live so close to nature and are keenly observant, individuals showed a surprising number of gaps in knowledge, from not knowing what lemons were to never having seen the house of someone who lived a fifteen-minute walk away.

The Matsigenka world is charged with supernatural significance, but everyday conversation is dominated by pragmatic, one might say materialistic, descriptions. The material world is described primarily in terms

TABLE 28. Basic Matsigenka Color Terms

potsitari	black
kutari	white
kiraari	red
kiteri	yellow
kaniari	green
kamachonkari	blue

SOURCE: Johnson, Johnson, and Baksh 1986.

TABLE 29. Modifications of Color Terms

Modifier	Example
Color term + *kipatsi* (soil)	*kitepatsari* = color of yellow soil
Color term + *-tuma-* (little)	*okiraatumatake* = pale red
maani (little) + color expression	*maani okiteritake* = a little yellow
panike (almost) + color expression	*panike ompotsitatake* = almost black

of sight and smell and, to a lesser degree, taste. Although hearing is extremely important to the Matsigenka, especially in the forest, they are less likely to describe a sound than to imitate it, often with conventions like *tsein!* for the sound of an arrow flying, *tin!* for a footstep, and *jiririririririri!* for the wind. For sight, smell, and taste they use a small number of basic terms to label broad qualities of the world. Then an ample supply of modifiers, including words made up by referring to particular species, is available to provide rich and evocative descriptions.

A good example is the domain of color. In the comparative typology of color-terminology systems (Berlin and Kay 1969; see also Berlin and Berlin 1975), the Matsigenka have a Stage V system with six basic color terms (table 28). The Matsigenka use the term *sanori*, "true" or "real," to refer to the focal colors in each range: focal yellow *(kiteri sanorira,* or *okitetasanotake)* centers on lemon yellow, focal red *(kiraari sanorira)* on a fully saturated fire-engine red, and so on. The basic terms can be modified in a variety of ways to express gradations of color. In addition to *sanori*, the most common modifier is *choeni*, a distance term meaning close or near. So, "it's almost blue." *(choeni okamachongatake)* can refer to a greenish-blue, a bluish-gray, and so on. Other common ways of modifying basic color terms are described in table 29. The flexibility of color naming is also expanded by referring to particular species, such as *choeni onarankatumatake,* "almost the color of a pale orange" (< Spanish, *naranja,* orange). Matsigenkas use modifiers and references to particular species to expand on the limited basic terms for describing other domains as well. Hence their capacity to describe a world rich in detail is fully developed.

The Living World

As I discussed in chapter 1, the Matsigenka draw a fundamental distinction between living and nonliving, based on whether something "has breath." Earth, water, fire, and air, in all their diverse forms, are mere matter: *terira ontime aniane,* "not exist its-breath." Even though they may be occupied by indwelling spirits, the elements themselves are inert and without spiritual qualities. Rock is just rock, and only a shaman can discern which rocks are inhabited by spirit helpers *(inetsane).* Fire is simply a property of burning wood. Wind is just wind, although some sudden gusts may indicate the passage of an unseen one *(terira ineenkani).*

Living things have another quality as important as breath: they feel pain *(-katsi-).* As Roberto put it, including plants in the generalization, "When you cut them, they hurt." At this point moral issues (good versus evil) begin to join the pleasure principle (good versus not good) in Matsigenka psychology and cosmology. Because animals and even plants can feel pain, it is wrong to hurt them unnecessarily. True, my self-interest (pleasure) compels me to cut plants and shoot animals in order to eat them, but I recognize that I am hurting creatures that do not want to be hurt and eaten and who could be expected to be angry and vengeful. Even though some cases of sadism toward animals seem to contradict this rule, the Matsigenka clearly believe that breathing, feeling pain, and having an intimate connection to the spirit world are defining characteristics of living things.

In the living world, the grammatical distinction between inanimate and animate marks the boundary between plants and animals, respectively: *ogagani* (edible plant) versus *yogagani* (edible animal); *inkenishikutirira* (forest plants) versus *inkenishikunirira* (forest animals). Therefore, although the Matsigenka have no cover terms equivalent to *plant* or *animal,* the distinction is built into their world-view at a fundamental linguistic level. The ability to move around, or willful locomotion, "appears to be the basis of the distinction made between animate and inanimate objects" (Shepard 1995: 13).

PLANTS

Nowhere was I more overwhelmed by the richness and detail of Matsigenka lore than in trying to learn about their plant world. The complexity has several aspects:

1. a large number of specific names for plants (a kind of "species-level" lexicon)

2. a general absence of higher categories for grouping (no genera, families, etc.)

3. a large number of varietal names within certain specific categories (such as *ivenkiki*, to be examined below)

4. a certain degree of idiosyncrasy, such that different informants gave me different names for the same plant

5. a certain amount of unevenly distributed ignorance (*tera nogote*, "I don't know")

As I worked in field and forest with various companions, however, a broad distinction among three categories of plants took shape that I was later able to validate in systematic interviewing. These are the categories of *pankirintsi*, "crop," *tovaseri*, "weed," and *inchato*, "tree." Implicit in the three-part scheme is a dichotomy between wild and domestic, a reflection of a nature-versus-culture contrast present in many areas of Matsigenka culture. *Pankirintsi* (< *-panki-*, "to plant") are crops purposely planted in prepared garden sites. *Tovaseri*, which may or may not grow into *inchato*, are intruders into this constructed garden space, enemies that threaten the garden and require the single largest input of energy of all garden tasks. Many have thorns, thistles, burrs, and other unpleasant attributes that annoy and cause pain. Tasorintsi created many *pankirintsi*, while Kentivakori created *tovaseri*.

The Matsigenka, however, draw the boundary between cultigens and wild plants differently than I had expected. For example, in the forest we often came across plants that I assumed were remnant crops from abandoned gardens: avocados, oranges, pineapples, lemons, sweet potatoes, and plantains, among others. Though my instinct would have been to call them all *pankirintsi*, I was wrong: the Matsigenka invariably called them *inchato* (or *tovaseri*, in the case of pineapple and sweet potato). In their view, these were not straggling survivors of some old garden but wild plants that "just grew," *ogantaka otimake* ("it-is-

[habitually] it-exists"). What distinguishes a wild plant from a cultigen is, therefore, that "no one planted it," *tera impankitero,* not (as I had learned to think) a genetic breeding of domesticated species out of distinct wild ancestors.

Another blending of wild and domesticated plants occurs when a man spares certain species of trees during garden clearing. A good example is the palm *kuri (Bactris ciliata),* whose hard outer wood is used in making arrowheads and other artifacts. Because the tree is rather scarce in the forest, it is not felled during clearing and becomes part of the garden. "Wild" avocados or orange trees may also be left standing during garden clearing. Yet, when asked "Is that a crop?" a respondent replies, "No, it was already there." It is not a cultigen unless created through human activity, a crop that a known person actually planted with his or her own hands. When the Matsigenka let go of a garden, they say it is "peccary's" *(ashi shintori):* by turning it over to a wild animal, they release it from human responsibility and, one might say, allow it to revert to nature.

Beyond the *pankirintsi/tovaseri/inchato* typology, there are few cover terms. Each species is like an individual being: it has its own character, which distinguishes it from other such beings. But a few important species are finely subdivided. Names for key crops like maize *(shinki)* and manioc *(sekatsi)* act as cover terms for all their varietals. A good example of how the plant categories of the Matsigenka work can be seen in the way they classify the group of herbs known as *ivenkiki* (sedge), including *Dichromena ciliata* and *Cyperus* sp. (cf. Taylor 1983), a class of medicinal herbs known widely throughout the Peruvian Amazon as *piripiri* (Rutter 1990: 184–86). Most Matsigenka house gardens contain *ivenkiki* plants that have a range of specific benefits. Each individual plant has a history that is known and discussed. One is for headache, a nearly identical neighbor is for nausea, and a third is to improve hunting success. What differentiates one *ivenkiki* plant from another, in the Matsigenka view, is not its physical appearance but its lineage: each plant has been obtained from someone else, and its history includes use, provenience, and method of preparation.

Possibly, distinct pharmacological effects will be found among sedges (Shepard 1998), but it is unlikely that such effects determine in every case the use to which *ivenkiki* is put. Whatever powers it possesses are not evident from direct inspection. It is of no value to take some *ivenkiki* encountered along the trail home to plant: unless someone can tell you what it is for, it would be foolish, and dangerous, to use it. The individualism inherent in the classification of *ivenkiki* characterizes the Matsigenka approach to plants and, indeed, to all living things: they see each individual as unique and potentially surprising. This is why they enjoy so much exchanging seeds and cuttings to be planted experimentally in their house gardens. This practice is at once evidence of their particularistic view of individual organisms and a method of preserving genetic diversity among the plants of most utilitarian value to them.

ANIMALS

As with plants, the Matsigenka do not divide the animal world into intermediate categories like fish, birds, insects. The most general division of the animal world—comparable to the pragmatic crop-weed-tree distinction among plants—is between *piratsi,* "game," and *tera iron-kenkani,* "inedible animals." Although this division does not cover the whole animal world—neither fish nor caterpillars are piratsi, but they are edible—it does apply widely. *Piratsi* share the attribute that they are obtained through hunting. Rosengren (1987a: 65) and Baer (1984: 130) report that the distinguishing feature of *piratsi* is that, unlike other animals, they have been domesticated by *saankarite* (the unseen ones; see below) and are thus ritually clean.

As with plants, the general tendency is to name animals distinctively at the species level. Each species has its own spirit ruler *(itinkame)* and a unique history and personal characteristics—for example, the violent *osheto* (spider monkey) and the lazy *yaniri* (howler monkey). Generic categories like these may then be grouped ad hoc according to context—for example, *inkenishikunirira,* forest animals, in contrast to *oakunirira,* river animals. These classifications do not come up often in ordinary conversation but can be readily elicited.

This system of classification conveys useful information about resource zones. For example, some birds walk on the forest floor *(saaviku),* meaning they can be caught in certain kinds of traps, whereas others live among the branches *(enoku,* "up," or *oshiku,* "in the leaves") and thus require different traps. Such a classificatory system groups animals according to the spaces they occupy in a local ecosystem, a kind of de facto recognition of plant and animal associations (Wilbert 1992: 71). As Wilbert interprets this aspect of cosmology, it is not the descent of species that matters but their "balanced complementary diversity" within the natural (and spiritual) world. Such a classification groups biotic communities rather than a Linnaean tree of genetic relatives.

The only domesticated animals the Matsigenka are familiar with are dogs, cats, chickens, guinea fowl, and Muscovy ducks. Except for dogs and cats (inedible), these fall in the nongame but edible category along with fish and insects. Chickens and ducks are never treated as pets, but many people in Shimaa begged us to bring them dogs and cats. However, when we did, they all died from one cause or another. They did not die of neglect—pets are treated well—but of environmental hazards. Birds and monkeys are often captured and treated as pets.

People

Matsigenka means "person, people." The standard opening for many folktales is *Ainyo matsigenka itimi parikoti,* "There was a man, he lived far away." The term applies to a person essentially like the speaker, who lives in a similar setting, with a familiar style of house, clothing, gardens, and so forth. So, the most nearly or fully human sort of person is, of course, the speaker and other people indistinguishable from the speaker in any way that matters. By implication, the more different a person is from this standard, the less fully human that person is.

NON-MATSIGENKA HUMANS

The Matsigenka view many other humans as cannibalistic, uncontrollably violent, or demonic. In the story Ineantavageigira (A Distant Journey), a group of Matsigenkas travel to other lands and encounter humans who eat snakes they claim are fish and demons they claim are agoutis (Davis and Snell 1984: 36–44). To eat snakes or demons is horrifying beyond words. Because the people of Shimaa have little knowledge of outsiders, we may connect their belief in such disgusting and terrible humans to a larger process (explored below): they deny the possibility of forbidden desires in themselves and project them onto other creatures, usually outside the family group.

As has no doubt been true for centuries past, their main contact with outsiders is with *ponyaronas*, who in 1972 were beginning to colonize the region from the mouth of the Río Kompiroshiato upstream to within a few kilometers of Shimaa. Toward these new immigrants their attitude was courteous but somewhat fearful. They saw them as more or less good people and attempted to converse in broken Spanish on the few occasions when *ponyaronas* passed by, but only a few families downstream along the Río Kompiroshiato included them in their visiting and exchange networks, a continuation of the ancient pattern of minimal blending between Amazon Indians and Andean Indians.

Salient too were *virakocha*s, mainly middle-class Peruvians and North Americans. Occasionally, government officials and survey teams passed through, socializing briefly. These visits had great significance because Maestro was encouraging the Matsigenka of Shimaa to think of themselves as Peruvians. He viewed these outsiders as powerful models to emulate. Other Matsigenkas, however, remained ambivalent: they were attracted by the *virakocha*s' wealth and the opportunities they offered for trade, yet were still frightened by the old stories linking them to danger and disease.

Although the North American linguists and anthropologists were of less importance to the Matsigenka as models than the Peruvians they encountered, the linguists Harold and Patricia Davis spent much time in the vicinity of the school community in Shimaa before and after it was started in 1968 (Davis 1994). They were greatly admired for their honesty and generosity, as well as their linguistic and cultural mastery. Many men spontaneously and with great pleasure told me of Harold Davis's physical skill and endurance in negotiating even the most treacherous mountain trails and of his profound knowledge of their language. My household inventories in 1972 showed that many of the trade items people owned had been gifts from the Davises.

In general, despite the representations of non-Matsigenkas in their folktales, the Matsigenka of Shimaa have a cautiously positive view of these outsiders. Although extremely shy on first meeting, most made a distinction between the current situation and the fearful abuses of the past. As the Matsigenka are generally trusting by nature, once they learned that neither the *virakocha*s nor most of the *ponyarona*s wanted to cheat or abuse them, they were curious, warm, and almost naively trusting. Many of them made sincere efforts to adopt the lessons in religion taught by the linguists and in Peruvian nationalism and civic responsibility taught by Maestro.

In Shimaa, awareness of other Amazon groups, such as the Piros and Shipibos, was slight. In the tributaries of the upper Urubamba, the only other Amerindian group besides the *ponyarona*s was the Campas, whom the Matsigenka call *ashaninka*. The two languages are not mutually intelligible for the ordinary person (perhaps roughly equivalent to the difference between Spanish and Portuguese), and in some villages, like Picha, Matsigenkas and Campas lived together and intermarried to some degree. But in Shimaa the only *ashaninka*, a schoolteacher, left in late 1972. In the larger region around Shimaa, including the communities of Shimentaato, Pogentimari, and Mantaro Chico, there were none. *Ashaninkas* do not appear in any of the life histories or folktales I recorded and are not a salient part of the Matsigenka world-view in this region.

MATSIGENKA

In the division between Matsigenka and other humans the split between good and evil is fully present. It is not just that Matsigenkas are good and others are bad but that the badness of others is linked to demonic behavior like cannibalism and unrestrained violence. In chapter 3 we saw how raising a Matsigenka to adulthood is a constant balancing act between encouraging strong, self-centered agency, on the one hand, and limiting impulsive behavior that could damage the family group on the other. As true as it may have been in the past that outsiders really were violent cannibals, they now provide a convenient place in which to "locate" feelings the Matsigenka are intensely uncomfortable with in themselves. This projection amounts to a kind of defensive splitting of the world into good people like us, who are self-controlled, and bad people like them, who are out of control, like the always-distant Kogapakori. This demonizing of others even begins, as we have seen, with in-laws and the people in the neighboring hamlet.

That feelings of hostility within the household, especially between spouses, are not absent but are rather carefully controlled is revealed in the occurrence of spousal hostility in folktales and in fears of spiritual attack by spouses. The interdependence of the married couple and the close ties of dependence between offspring and their same-sex parents help keep the ambivalence within the household under wraps, but even within the hamlet the option of going off and living in isolation is frequently exercised.

The pull of security, sharing, and sociability, countered by the push of social friction, contagion, and competition, results in the dialectic of aggregation and dispersion characteristic of all family level societies (Johnson and Earle 2000: 50). Put as simply as possible, the Matsigenka want to be with others (enjoy the benefits) and at the same time do not want to be with others (avoid the costs). As we saw, folktales generally begin with a problem created by the conflicting desires of two willful individuals, and they depict the danger created by the resulting anger. As frightening as anger is, it does not always lead Matsigenkas to placate angry people, especially beyond the walls of the household. An egalitarian political ethic limits the ability of members of one household to control members of other households. This is not so much a political contract to respect each other's independence as a recognition that intervention is fruitless and possibly dangerous.

Spirits

The idea that some plants and most animals have spirit rulers or protectors who can do harm or good to humans is usually referred to as *animism,* but in the Matsigenka case it might as well be known as *personism.* It projects human qualities onto nonhumans. The content of the projection is not only that other organisms feel pain but also that they can know who harmed them and plot revenge. In taking ritual steps to appease angry and vengeful spirits, the Matsigenka evidence a kind of internalization of responsibility or blame that, in its anticipation of punishment, shares something in common with the complex emotional state we call guilt.

If humans are continual sources of danger because of the inevitable conflicts, so too are animals and spirit beings potentially dangerous individuals dominated by self-interest. At home, in the garden, or in the forest, the Matsigenka continually adjust their behavior as they receive cues about the possible presence and activity of spirit beings. They assume that each human, animal, and spirit being has a soul or spirit, *isure/osure,* which has an existence apart from the material, this-worldly substance of his or her body. As is common in animistic, shamanic religious systems, the Matsigenka believe in the full coexistence of two worlds, a material world and an "other," invisible world (Lévy-Bruhl 1923; cf. Kensinger 1995: 207, Roe 1982: 17). The spirit, which exists essentially in the other world, is not formless: it can appear just like the body it normally inhabits, or it can take on a new form—that of an animal or some other human. Many of the spirits are invisible and can pass through walls "like the wind." All souls or spirits have goals and purposes that have consequences for the humans who come into contact with them.

Most of these consequences are bad. The Matsigenka world is full of harmful spirits close at hand, whereas beneficial spirits are distant and hard to reach. Many illnesses and deaths are traced ultimately to spirit action. Matsigenka loved ones, when they die, are thought to lose human generosity and respect. They become remorseless in sating their appetites, which nearly always involve either food or sex. For this reason, the Matsigenka have traditionally placed the corpse of the deceased in the river; the soul is then carried so far away it is unable to find its way back home and importune its grieving family. As a further precaution, the house of the deceased is usually burned so that the soul will become disoriented and finally abandon its effort to capture the soul of a living kinsman for companionship in the next world.

Spiritual Beliefs

In order to avoid the ethnocentric implications of the concepts of good and evil, Rosengren (1987a: 33) has suggested that the basic distinction for the Matsigenka is between perfect (Tasorintsi) and imperfect (Kentivakori). There are two difficulties with this approach however. First, although Tasorintsi is extremely powerful and brought great good to humankind, he can also be irritable and cause bad things to happen, as when he withdrew the gift of immortality humankind once enjoyed (cf. Reynard-Casevitz 1984: 5). Second, too much evidence links suffering to transgression and punishment in Matsigenka belief to justify leaving good and evil out of our description altogether. Matsigenka stories portray many sinlike behaviors (rage, greed, lust, envy), the bad consequences of which cause human suffering. If the suffering is not unambiguously punishment for sin, it is at least the price of indulgence. In this sense, most Matsigenka folktales are morality tales.

Early in fieldwork this moralistic side to Matsigenka character and culture largely escaped me. I wondered whether I had come to a place where people had no concern with sin or spirituality. When I tried to explore the mystical underpinnings of everyday reality, my informants preferred to give me this-worldly (as opposed to other-worldly) explanations. In part they were reluctant to be open about spiritual beliefs, having been criticized for them by other *virakochas*. But in part also their preference for this-worldly explanations reflects a substrate of practical materialism in Matsigenka outlook: many things just happen—a branch falls and breaks a man's arm, a raft overturns in the river and a woman drowns, a child is bitten by a maiini ant—and there is no suspicion of spiritual causation.

Farabee (1909: 128–29) long ago noted the absence of ritual and ceremony among the Matsigenka. Because of their lack of ceremony with the dead—their simply throwing the corpse in the river—he came to the conclusion that they have no fear of the dead, indeed, "no belief in ghosts or in the return of the soul," a startlingly erroneous conclusion. That he completely missed the richness of Matsigenka spiritual beliefs discounts his value as an ethnographic resource, but I have to sympathize. In this aspect of their lives, as in many others, they do not wear their hearts (or their souls) on their sleeves.

In time I learned to appreciate how filled their world is with spiritual forces and beings. Despite the absence of public spectacle, the spiritual is potentially lurking almost anywhere and can be activated suddenly and without warning. Most prominent and dramatic are spirit beings that are, in effect, humans with exaggerated attributes and life-and-death powers. But there are also less personified powers or processes, intermediate between the materialistic world of mere matter and the personalized world of spirit beings.

TABOOS

The first encounter I had with Matsigenka spiritual belief was when I tried to measure Javier's garden and he refused to let me, standing arms akimbo at his garden entrance, bow and arrows in hand. Simply by setting foot in his garden while the maize was in its vulnerable stage, I would have, without wanting or intending to, endangered his whole maize crop. Anyone who ate certain kinds of meat (especially howler monkey, *shito* monkey, deer, anteater, and *charava* fish) after helping him plant his maize would also bring harm, but only to the maize plants the meat eater had planted.

This is typical of a host of consequences that automatically happen when someone breaks a taboo deliberately or even innocently by accident. Although no willful spirit is blamed for the harm, punishment has occurred, and the implication is that disobedience or carelessness is at fault. Hunting is a major focus of taboos, and loss of hunting skill (failure to bag game over a series of hunts) is sure evidence that some taboo has been broken. Practices such as avoiding contact with women and applying protective potions can correct the problem:

Do Machiguenga men develop the aim and skill required to hunt monkeys through years of daily training with bows and arrows since boyhood? Or do some men inherit natural talents from a father with exceptional vision or athletic abilities? If you ask a Machiguenga, the answer is no. There is no such thing as good practice, or good luck, or good genes. There are only good hunting medicines. (Shepard 1997: 6)

LOVE MAGIC

Closer to personalized spirits are spiritual acts practiced deliberately by one person at the expense of another. In chapter 3 I discussed love magic, which is feared as the cause of weakness and the result of control by another. Beliefs in such attacks are rooted in the assumption that the thwarted or disappointed desires of others motivate them to use magic either to achieve their desires or to exact revenge. The Matsigenka also believe that if a man kills an animal he should not have killed, the animal *ipugatakeri,* "takes revenge," by making the man's baby sick (Shepard 1999: 102–3). Although the Matsigenka of Shimaa in 1972 practiced relatively little witchcraft, we can see the seeds of witchcraft beliefs in such personal magic. (I examine beliefs in good and evil shamans below.)

The Spirit World

The Matsigenka believe in a profusion of evil spirits, against which are arrayed only the protective powers of the *terira ineenkani* (unseen ones) and *seripigari* (shamans). Because both can turn against humans under certain circumstances, the Matsigenka world is indeed fraught with spiritual peril. What is primarily in peril is the human soul or spirit, *isure* (m.), *osure* (f.). For the Matsigenka the soul is the ineffable essence of the self, the part or aspect that goes where a person goes during a dream or in the trance induced by ayahuasca. Animals, humans, shamans, demons, and the unseen ones—all animate beings—have active souls—that is to say, selves—that move in and around this world and are capable of bringing about great harm or great good.

In a certain sense, the soul is separate from the body. When a woman, for example, meets her lover in the forest, they may play together, run and laugh, make love and share wild fruits. She returns home with the memory of an afternoon's pleasure. She does not know that it was a demon who had adopted her lover's form, who raped her soul with his huge penis, "breaking her up." That night she sickens, and, within a day or two, she dies. The experience of her soul in that other reality was entirely different from, though in a sense parallel to, the experience of her body in this one.

Yet, although her soul broke up and her body died, she did not die. She, or some version of her, became the spouse of the demon who took her. But her humanity has been stripped; she is now evil and dangerous to humans. Still, she has a (demon) body with desires, and she uses craft, deceit, and force to satisfy them. She has become in some sense immortal—at least, her complete annihilation has not yet taken place.

To be sure, her tryst in the forest may not have been with a demon, and she may live to a ripe old age. With the help of good spirits, she could go on to live a happy afterlife. In that afterlife, she will have a body much like her living body. It will be free from pain and aging, a fine body to enjoy. Then she may also be able to change her body, to become an ant or an anteater, without changing her soul.

In this sense the Matsigenka soul is both embodied and disembodied. Shepard (1990: 18) notes that his informants sometimes contrasted soul and body, but on other occasions spoke of a "spirit-body": "Terms like 'soul' and 'body' are not simple to translate since they involve complex cultural concepts. The Matsigenka soul is a concrete 'body' (ibatsa) or life-giving 'core' (isuire) whose interactions with other such beings in the other half of reality determine matters of life and death in our everyday half of reality." The soul is capable of leaving its mortal body (through the crown of the head) but is not generally without a body; it has either its own familiar body or the body of a bird or other creature that it becomes while traveling in a spiritual dimension (cf. Shepard 1998, 2002). It may become temporarily as ephemeral as a breeze, but even the breeze is a tangible signal that a spirit is passing by.

We must avoid trying to be too precise in understanding the Matsigenka conception of the self. Intuitively, viewed subjectively, my self is the essential me I experience in my daily life, with all my skills, knowledge, and aspirations. But my self also has an otherness that I experience only tangentially. For example, when the Matsigenka tell their dreams, they routinely use the expression "I dreamt I saw . . . ," as in Andrea's dream that began,

maika inkara nokisanivagetake nonei noatake oaku notentanaka ina

Now earlier I dreamt. I saw I went to the river with Mother.

nonei nokogake koriti

I saw I wanted snails.

In this manner of description, Andrea is both the dreamer ("I dreamt I saw") and the one who goes to the river and wants snails. This inherent ambiguity of subjectivity is also evident in the standard ending of many dreams. This is from one of Casiano's dreams:

noneake kañotasanomatakatyo kutagiteri impogini nokireanake ontityo

I saw it was just like day! Then I woke up. It was

nokisanivagetake teratyo arisano.

I was dreaming! It was not true!

The exclamatory suffix, -*tyo,* indicating emphasis or surprise, appears three times in this statement, as if to underline the strangeness of an experience he both had and did not have.

The realism of dreams has an eerie or uncanny quality for the Matsigenka, but they do not for the most part regard dreams as real events in the world. The ending comment essentially says, "It was only a dream!" The dream can be frightening but not have real-world consequences, as in Emelio's dream of a terrifying encounter with a jaguar:

maika nokisanivagetake inkaara kañotaka kutagiteniku impogini noatake
Now, I dreamt before. It was like daytime. Then I went

anta nonkenavagetera impogini noatanake noneapaakeri matsontsori
there to hunt. Then I went on, I saw on arriving jaguar

vataitaka avotsiku
seated in the path.

yovataitaka enoku timashitake avotsiku impogini imitaanake tera iragena
He sat up high guarding the path. Then he jumped, not he bit me.

impogini nokentakeri kañomatakanirika kutagitenirikatyo onake
Then I shot him. Like real daytime it was!

kantankicha ontityo nokisanivagetake impogini nokireavetanaka aiñona aka
But it was I was dreaming! Then I woke up, I was there

nonake nomagakera tsarogamatakena kantakena shigeshige teratyo ontityo
I was in my bed. I was scared to death, shaking. Nothing! It was

nokisanivagetake
I was dreaming!

Even in telling this dream, which is remembered from before, Emelio seems to want to reassure himself that it did not really happen.

But some dreams do have real-world consequences—usually negative (Shepard 2002)—such as a dream of seeing a deer or of being perfumed *(okasanka-)* like sweet-smelling herbs all over. In a fragment of a tale involving Moon, a character repeatedly avoids being burned by his garden fires until he has a dream; the next day he is roasted by his garden fire, and Moon eats him. In the tale of Jaguar, below, the shaman dreams that Jaguar takes him deep underground, and after he wakes, he falls ill and dies. These stories tell of dreams where a real encounter with a spirit has taken place.

The Matsigenka imagine all sorts of possibilities for themselves beyond the physical limitations of this ordinary world, but they almost always imagine it happening to them, their essential selves, in a definite embodied form, whether animal, human, or spirit.

ANIMAL SPIRITS

Many animals and some plants have immortal spirit rulers *(itinkame)* or spirit mothers *(inato;* cf. Baer 1984: 153), who in folk literature are the founders of the species. In keeping with the ambivalence and splitting that dominate the Matsigenka view of the world, these spirit rulers sometimes appear to be good spirits *(terira ineenkani)* and sometimes evil ones (often labeled by the suffix *-niro,* "mother," as in *oshetoniro,* the foul and vicious spirit ruler of spider monkeys; Baer 1979: 110–11). *Itinkame* look out for the well-being of their species and to that end may exercise spiritual force for or against humans.

In stories (see chapter 3), the spirit rulers of *yaniri,* "howler monkey," and *osheto,* "spider monkey," threatened other protagonists with violence. *Tsiroenti,* "hummingbird," is the spirit ruler of *yairi,* "paper wasp," whose spirit form is a huge wasp that shoots arrows into people, causing pneumonia *(ikentakena yairi,* "he-shot-me wasp"). Like many demons, Yairi can take either male or female form. For example, a married couple, Aradino and Rosa, returned from a foraging trip convinced they had been shot by wasp; yet Aradino said, *"He* shot me" *(ikentakena),* whereas Rosa said, *"She* shot me" *(okentakena).* Both were pale and terrified.

The way that Matsigenkas, in both folktales and interviews, go back and forth between referring to individual animals (such as a peccary shot that morning) and the spirit ruler (Peccary, who allows or prevents peccaries from being available to hunters) indicates that they see all individuals of a species as manifestations of a single spirit ruler. When the hunter encounters a male howler monkey in the forest, he is encountering the powerful spirit ruler, the *seripigari* (shaman) of the origin folktale, made manifest in the body of this particular animal. This is one example of how close the Matsigenka find themselves to spiritual encounters in their everyday lives.

Many animals can take human form in seeking mates. Most prevalent of these is *maniro,* "deer," who can cause one to have perfumed dreams that lead to encounters and death. The story of Narani in chapter 3 is another example.

Matsontsori *(Jaguar).*   The category *matsontsori* includes the jaguar, puma, and ocelot. These are the largest predators in the forest, besides people, and they are the main threat to domesticated animals. But the primary danger is spiritual. Long ago, people and animals metamorphosed *(ipeganaka)* freely into *matsontsori,* but in the present only a limited number of animals are capable of converting into jaguar, including armadillo, squirrel, woodpecker, frog, turtle, and several monkeys and birds. These animals are potentially dangerous, therefore, and must be hunted and killed with respect. In particular, if the hunter laughs at them or takes their eggs or their young, they are likely to convert right then and there into *matsontsori.*

Matsontsori can take human form or become an insubstantial spirit that can move through walls. In the story Matsontsori (Jaguar), a young woman trapped a *tsonkivinti* bird *(Phlegopsis barringeri)* and kept him at home until he escaped. He reappeared to her in the forest as a man, criticized her for trapping him, and then asked her to marry him. She refused and returned home, but when a shaman heard of the incident, he immediately warned people that Jaguar would be coming and they should make sure the walls of their houses were secure. Not all men believed him, but by nightfall all houses were secure. The shaman spread herbs on the trail so that Jaguar could not come like the wind but would have to be in physical form. Jaguar came in the night and began eating chickens. The shaman shot him but did not kill him. The next night, the shaman had a bad dream in which Jaguar came to him and said, "Why did you shoot me? Now I will take you under the earth." He took him deep underground. When the shaman awoke, his head was all stuffed up, like a bad cold. He said, "I am going to die." And he did.

Maranke *(Snake).*   All snakes are objects of terror and loathing. They are the most feared of all animal spirits (possibly along with jaguar) and for this reason are attacked and killed at every opportunity. For the Matsigenka there is no such thing as a harmless snake because snakes as a group are seen as the arrows of their spirit ruler, who hunts human souls the way humans hunt peccaries. Not mere arrows in the mechanical sense, snakes are intelligent beings (persons) who themselves stalk humans and, when they wound one, call their kin to come and help them finish off their prize (just as human hunters do when they wound a peccary). *Maranke* spirit eats human souls with the same relish that

FIGURE 27. Taking a killed snake to be thrown in the river.

humans eat the flesh of peccaries. For this reason, when a man kills a snake, he carries it off and disposes of it in the river, so its soul will be carried so far away it will be unable to mobilize its kin to take revenge on its killer (figure 27). The Matsigenka expend much physical energy keeping the clearings around their houses weeded and swept so that they will be free of snakes.

If bitten, the victim must get home as quickly as possible and make noise to ward off another—spiritual—attack that would be lethal. To bang a metal object on stone makes a sound that seems like thunder to the snake, scaring it away. Poultices and teas may be administered to reduce the pain and swelling of the physical bite, but the real danger is further spirit attack. In fact, it is possible to be attacked by a snake without ever being physically bitten. To hallucinate a snake *(okepigatanake maranke)* is a bad sign, portending the possibility of death. The snake spirit bites the soul just as a physical snake bites the flesh.

To eat snake is inconceivable. When I asked people whether they ate such tabooed meats as jaguar or otter, they simply said, "No." But when I asked whether they ate snake, they were startled and laughed out loud, the idea was so outrageous. This kind of response was otherwise most rare and completely out of character for the Matsigenka, who were usually extremely patient and respectful of even my oddest questions.

Exposure to snake carries a serious danger of spiritual contamination.

Because of the danger of further stalking by *maranke* kin, a snakebite victim should be carried to an empty house and kept isolated from all who have ever been snake-bitten. Otherwise, through a kind of contagion, these previous victims will be bitten again. The victim must be bathed in hot water and remain awake all night making noise. In one treatment, food is forbidden, especially fish and meat, for five days (manioc is allowed). When the swelling has abated, the person goes to the river after midnight and eats red pepper in large quantities, then bathes. The pepper is to prevent another snake bite: snakes are said to be afraid of the burning of red pepper.

DEMONS (*KAMAGARINI*)

Beyond (though sometimes including) the spirit rulers of animal species, the Matsigenka world is populated by a host of horrible, lethal demons, who, being generally invisible, could be almost anywhere. Demons tend to be exaggerated versions of humans or animals, usually deformed, defective, and disgusting in some way. The vast majority of them (including the females) possess huge penises that penetrate a person's soul and cause it to break up. The motivation of the demon is to possess a human soul, either to eat it or, more commonly, for companionship, just as lonely humans seek a spouse for companionship in this life.

Perhaps the most prominent demonic spirit is Moon (Kashiri). Actually, Moon has some of the qualities of a culture-hero deity (Baer 1984): he came down to earth from the next higher plane of existence, first brought manioc to humans, taught them how to chew their food, and fathered the Sun, bringing daylight to a cool and dimly lit world. But when he left this plane, he also took with him the best and largest manioc. Now he has a weir *(shimperetsa)* to trap the souls of dead people trying to reach the afterlife on the plane above. Only those souls with spirit helpers to guide them escape; Moon catches the rest and eats them, ending their existence.

In the folktale Kashiri, Moon comes down to earth and asks a young woman what is it that she is eating. She tells him it is manioc, but he says it is not manioc but a species of earth, and he gives her real manioc. She and her family much prefer this manioc to the earth they had been eating, and Moon also teaches them how to chew their food, whereas before they gulped it down like chickens. She and Moon are married, but she dies giving birth to Sun. Moon tells her mother what she must do to restore her daughter to life. But the mother is so angry with Moon that she tells him he may as well eat her daughter, which he does. Then he returns to the sky, taking Sun and all the best manioc with him. A key moment in the story is when the mother becomes angry: "Matsigenkas, remembering these episodes, criticize that bad mother-in-law, for, had she not offended her son-in-law Kashiri, the miracle of resurrection he would have performed on his wife's body would have been extended for all time to all women. That is to say, he would have had the power or custom of reviving women who died in childbirth" (F. Pereira 1942: 243).

Moon is not an ordinary demon. Unlike many demons, he does not kill with a huge penis, although he does bring huge manioc tubers with him and, as father of the Sun, Poreatsiri, he is certainly a powerful masculine figure. In the version of this tale collected by Shepard (1989), his wife's belly swells with a great many snakes, much like the episode in the tale of Narani (see chapter 3) where the woman's belly swells with hundreds of baby birds. That Moon is a godlike creator figure, an inhabitant of the heavens *(enoku)* who is also dangerous to humans, illustrates that Matsigenka cosmology is not based on any simple heaven-and-hell dichotomy.

Kamagarini, "death-cause-ones" (also known as "rotten," *ivegaga, ovegaga*), are in a way the negations of the unseen ones (discussed below). Many illnesses are personalized as demons who hunt humans like game or seek them as spouses (Bennett 1996). A *kamagarini* killed Serafina (see chapter 3). The term *kamagarini* is often treated in the literature as a cover term for evil spirits (Baer 1984: 175–87), and it was often used this way in Shimaa.

Kamagarini are said to be numerous around Shimaa. Felipe pointed out to me a large *nearometiki* tree in which lived an *ivegaga* who was hairless and possessed a huge penis. Felipe cut down the tree, and Mariano removed a tubular piece from the center, called *otinkame,* "ruler" of the tree. It had a rotten smell but did not seem to have any special aura about it. Mariano gave it to his son to play with. Men say that if they were to see a *kamagarini,* they would shoot and kill it.

The danger from *kamagarini* is in not knowing when you are dealing with one. Any illness may be a sign that *kamagarini* have been at work, and even relatives of the victim practice some avoidance (figure 28). In the story of Narani we saw how a man, simply by talking to his wife, who had become *ovegaga* in the course of the story, was fatally damaged. As is common in such stories, the man did not die immedi-

FIGURE 28. Pororinta lies alone, sick with flu *(kamagantsi);* a plate of manioc is to her left.

ately but sickened and was dead by the next day. After the soul has been broken by the powerful demon penis, the body may live on for a day or two, growing progressively weaker.

The demons Segamairini, Maniti, and Matsiti are variations on a theme: Segamairini is said to resemble tapir, Maniti jaguar, and Matsiti fox: all are similar in being four-legged, having long snouts and tails, and possessing large, deadly penises. The penis is likened to the pod *(segapa)* of the *sega* palm *(Jessenia batava),* a very hard, pointed pod more than a meter in length and fifteen centimeters in diameter. It may be used to beat or impale the victims in the chest and stomach, the cause of their "very rapidly breaking up."

The demon Sevatatsirira lives in rock piles *(imperitaseku)* like those caused by landslides, typically taking the form of the bird *tsimpimpini* (heron, *Tigrisoma fasciatum*). It can also appear as a midget, either male or female, with a large penis. But it is fond of occupying abandoned houses and of assuming a human shape, indistinguishable from one's lover or spouse. Sevatatsirira seduces a person, who becomes entranced and unable to resist. Having sex with Sevatatsirira pulverizes or softens a person's bones. The victim falls ill with fever and nausea, followed by death. Sevatatsirira removes the soul *(inoshikapitsatakero osure),* taking it away *(yagapitsatakero)*. Just seeing Sevatatsirira may or may not be fatal (it is worse for women), but having sex is inevitably fatal. Although there is no remedy, a kind of *ivenkiki* can be crushed and spread along the trail to kill Sevatatsirira.

Beyond these demons, which I heard about over and over again, there are many, many other dangerous spirits. In addition to the animal spirits discussed above, a great many animals, perhaps all, are capable of converting *(ipeganaka)* into demons. As I have explained, there is a kind of shared identity or interchangeability between a physical animal and its spirit ruler and thus always the possibility that any encounter with an animal can turn spiritual. Because animal spirit rulers are often identified with the good spirits, the unseen ones, this is an area of ambiguity, where good and evil spirits blend into one another.

A smaller number of animals, but still amounting to dozens of different species, are capable of taking human form *(ipeganaka matsigenka)*. Typically, a human encounters one of these metamorphosed creatures in the forest and, taking him or her for a lover, has sex. In addition to deer, *kemari*, "tapir," and *tontokoti*, "screech owl" (*Otus* sp.), may take human form. *Tontokoti* can fly in addition to having the usual ability to take human form and to kill with a huge penis. All these animals were once human beings: some were told to turn into animals by the unseen ones; others became animals through events in the past, like the transformation of howler monkey *(yaniri)* into a shaman (see chapter 3).

The idea of multiple transformations of animals, humans, and spirits is completely natural to the Matsigenka. Children, when playing games, say, "I have become anteater" *(nopegakero shiani)*, using a similar construction to the phrase "Anteater becomes human" *(shiani ipeganaka matsigenka)*. What seems natural to the Matsigenka here is that any being that had the power would—like a child at play—use that power to become whatever it wanted to be at any given moment. If it is necessary for a spirit to become human in order to obtain souls to eat or to marry, then of course that can be easily done, as easily as a child becomes anteater or jaguar.

In light of the previous discussion of Matsigenka views toward other people, the demon Kogapakori is of particular interest. According to one story, Kogapakori decided that *ponyaronas* and *virakochas* had become such a nuisance that he would kill them all. He ordered his assistant to wake him at a certain time so that he could do so. But his assistant neglected to wake him, and so he failed. Otherwise, he would have killed them all, and the Matsigenka would not be bothered with them today. Today, if a man drinks ayahuasca and is visited by Kogapakori, he turns inherently evil. If one prepares yuca and it turns red, it is a sign one will be visited by such an evil man.

THE UNSEEN ONES

Countering to some degree the dangerous world of animal spirits, lost human souls, and demons are the good spirits, the unseen ones (*terira ineenkani*, "not he-is-seen-ones"). They are also known as the pure ones (*saankarite* < *-saanka-*, "pure," "clean"), although the people of Shimaa rarely used this name when discussing them with me. These good and powerful beings reside at a distance and must be invoked by a shaman *(seripigari),* usually in a hallucinogen-induced trance. The unseen ones are immortal, beyond pain and death. A shaman can enter into a personal relationship with an unseen one, who then becomes a guide and protector, curing the ills of this world and accompanying one's soul on the perilous journey into the afterlife. A powerful shaman can obtain the help of unseen ones for his family and loyal followers.

In the story Terira Ineenkani (Unseen Ones), men from another hamlet come seeking the daughters of a shaman, who refuses them. Angry, they decide to wait until the shaman is dead; they plan then to kill his sons and marry their sisters. But the shaman divines their plan and takes his sons on a journey to show them the path to the land of the unseen ones. On the way, the sons must learn how to tell which path is theirs to take (not the path of the unseen ones) and which game is theirs to kill (not the pets of the unseen ones). They learn not to eat all the game they catch but to save some to bring home. Eventually, the shaman dies, and the brothers and sisters set off for the land of the unseen ones. On the way, they encounter the demon Maniti (Jaguar), but they learn it is their father's spirit and their terror is abated. In the land of the unseen ones, their gardens come quickly to fruition, and the sisters meet unseen ones who at first look like their brothers (setting up some episodes of incestuous sexual romping). But then the unseen ones reveal themselves, and the children meet their father's spirit. The only unhappy people at the end of the story are the men from the other hamlet, who cannot figure out where the girls have gone.

The father in the story is a shaman whose soul flies regularly to the land of the unseen ones, where he changes places with his counterpart there, who comes to occupy his body in this world. In the story, it is impossible to tell from the text whether he is himself or his counterpart at any given moment. The man who takes the sons on the journey behaves like an unseen one. For example, he only eats a little meat off the back of the fish, just as the unseen ones are said to do. Yet he is always addressed as "Father." The two are the same or are aspects of each other (cf. Baer 1979: 118). And, too, the brothers in the story have their spirit counterparts, who look just like them. These spirits seduce their sisters, but the incestuous implication is moderated at the end of the story when the unseen ones become brothers-in-law and marry the sisters. The mother, who is a minor character in this story, also has her unseen counterpart in "that-one-like-your-mother," frequently mentioned in the tale.

The unseen ones are idealized humans who lead lives without suffering. They are perfect in the sense Rosengren was referring to (Baer 1984: 155; cf. Rosengren 1987a: 33). However, their place in the scheme of good and evil is complex. They are clearly good, but they are also judgmental and punitive, and they refuse to help people in the afterlife if they have been bad in this one (Ross 1947: 46). In this respect the unseen ones are linked to other harmful spirits. For example, jaguars are the pet dogs of the unseen ones (Baer 1984: 156). In some tales, like Peccary, the link between an animal spirit ruler and the unseen ones is explicit. (Baer [1984: 160] suggests that all spirit rulers are unseen ones.)

In other tales the link to the unseen ones is implicit. For example, in the story Piitiro (Cricket) (Ross 1947: 37–38), a man encounters Cricket (in human form), who promises to take him to Meshiarineku, "the River of Skin" (the Milky Way), where he can renew his skin and become immortal. However, he must agree never to reveal this secret to any other human. But he thoughtlessly tells his neighbors, who, desiring immortality for themselves, rush to find Cricket. The man dies, and his wife laments, "In vain he told you not to tell. Now, you see, you have lost your chance at immortality. You've chosen to die!" This story turns crucially on the man's disobedience. As so often happens in Matsigenka stories, failure to respect and comply with a powerful being has dire consequences (Shepard 1998: 323–24).

In contrast, in the story of the Unseen Ones, a main theme is the sons' obedience to their father. This father is a kind, protective, and expert parent whose task is to instruct his sons in life-saving knowledge before he dies and "is no more." Terira Ineenkani, then, is a story about how good children go to heaven. The parents are represented as a united pair—the father is the central figure, and the mother is his helpmate.

Both parents are linked to their spirit counterparts, who already live in the land of the unseen ones. Their sons are represented as dutiful, respectful, and eager to learn. They never protest or rebel. They are feisty only when they do not want to give their sisters to the threatening men who want to take them by force, and even here it is their father who expresses their objections and provides them with the wherewithal to defend themselves. The sisters go along with the program, which includes representations of guiltless incest, and everyone ends up happy.

In this sense, then, the unseen ones are idealized parent figures who know what is right and amply reward good behavior. And the expected ambivalence is not far to seek. In several episodes of Terira Ineenkani the father is represented as the terrible demon Maniti, one of those hyperphallic monsters of long snout and penis who kill by raping human souls. The sons and daughters reveal their terror by building a tree house where the four-legged creature cannot get at them. Yet they discover him to be their father in disguise and gradually overcome their fear. So father appears here split in two: he is both the terrible phallic demon who kills and the pure wise spirit who protects. If the good child deserves the good father, by implication the bad child deserves the demon.

THE SHAMAN (*SERIPIGARI;* ALSO, *SHINKITACHARIRA*) AND THE WITCH (*MATSIKANARI*)

The most common term for shaman is *seripigari,* from the roots *seri-,* "tobacco," and *-piga-,* "hallucinate" or "inebriate." Shepard (1990: 31–32) also finds a semantic connection to the root *-pega-,* "to transform." So the seripigari is "one who inebriates himself with tobacco and transforms himself." As is common with tobacco shamans in South America (Wilbert 1973: 452), the shaman's breath is believed to be charged with sacred energy that is enhanced through the use of tobacco smoke—hence, the healing practice of blowing tobacco smoke over an afflicted person. As Matteson (1954: 84) notes among the Piro, "Whenever a death or serious illness is mentioned the question is quickly asked, 'Who blew?'"

Beyond his healing breath, however, the shaman's power depends on his ability to connect with good spirits. In the story Terira Ineenkani the link between the childlike, vulnerable brothers and the unseen ones was provided by their father, the shaman. The unseen ones become visible to the shaman by virtue of his mastery of hallucinogens (Shepard 1998). Over time, the shaman builds a set of relationships with unseen ones, or *inetsane* (visitors; Baer 1981: 49–50), whom he calls "Brother," "Brother-in-law," "Aunt," and so on (like humans, unseen ones do not have personal names). He may activate this network of spirit-friends to improve hunting, combat illness, and acquire guides for the journey to higher planes of existence after death.

In Shimaa people made occasional reference to the *shinkitacharira,* a more powerful shaman than the *seripigari.* The distinction is between the *seripigari* as a "tobacco shaman" and the *shinkitacharira* (< -*shinki-,* "inebriate") as an "ayahuasca shaman." The *shinkitacharira* is more powerful because ayahuasca gives more powerful visions than tobacco and is a more reliable means of travel to the land of the unseen ones. But, in daily conversation, people used the term *seripigari* most often and meant it to indicate the user of ayahuasca, which is by far the main hallucinogen they recognize. *Seripigari* is thus the best general term to translate our concept of shaman, and in Shimaa it sometimes acts as a cover term for the various kinds of shaman. Although it is said that some women in the past drank ayahuasca, my data refer only to male *seripigari.* Rosengren (1987a: 342) reports that the "separation of the genders is legitimized by reference to the greater pollution of women, and men's consequently closer relation with the *sáangarite.*"

A *seripigari* works by changing places with his spirit helper (or counterpart, or double) among the unseen ones. Working only at night, the *seripigari* drinks ayahuasca and climbs a ladder or notched pole to his platform *(menkotsi)* in the roof beams of his house. According to Shepard (1990: 32), the *seripigari*'s counterpart simultaneously drinks ayahuasca, and the two trade places, occupying each other's bodies. The spirit is now present in this world to help treat those who need his powers.

Let us say, for example, that Wasp shot me *(ikentakena yairi,* "pneumonia"). One way of describing this experience would be to say that Wasp, being an invisible spirit, has shot an (invisible) arrow into my (invisible) spirit. But, perhaps better, I could say that, in addition to this world, there is an equivalent, co-existing world where a real, gigantic wasp has shot a real arrow into my real tangible spirit. Being only of this world, I can see nothing of that. I only know that something feels wrong, and I know without doubt that this other world exists and that I will die if the attack on my soul is not treated. Therefore, I seek the *seripigari*'s help with urgency and dependency. The *seripigari,* like me, occupies both worlds, but unlike me he does so with full awareness and with power to act in both. He (his spirit counterpart) sees the arrow embedded in the body of my spirit and sucks it out. The real wound to my spirit has been treated, and I am on the mend.

His work done, the shaman's spirit counterpart flies back to the land of the unseen ones (*nopigarora,* "from where I return"), and the shaman returns to his mortal body. Although the two in many ways act like aspects of each other, they are conceptually distinct. In fact, it is most important for a shaman who has traveled to the land of the unseen ones to return to his own body before dawn, or he will become so attached there that he will stay and his mortal body here will die. The Matsigenka conceive that land to lie at a great distance, not like a parallel universe that is right here in some other dimension all the time.

In the folktale Shintori, an aspect not summarized in chapter 4 is that the *seripigari* is able to command the peccaries because he changes places with the peccary spirit ruler, who is an unseen one. Out of respect for the spirit ruler or because he becomes the spirit ruler, the *seripigari* must abstain from the hunt—he may only command the peccaries to come and direct the hunters to their quarry. Once the peccaries have been killed, the *seripigari* warns the men not to be greedy, to finish the meat they have before hunting for more peccaries. He returns the souls of the dead peccaries by offering their teeth to the peccary spirit, who removes the souls from the teeth. Only then may the women use the teeth to make necklaces. Of course, it is because of his gluttonous disobedience of the *seripigari* that the hero of the story is captured and enslaved by the peccary band.

The shaman's spirit can fly to the land of the unseen ones because ayahuasca enables him to take a form such as that of a *kimaro,* a game bird. To be successful, he needs the help of spirit guides *(iserepito)* who reside in sorcerer's stones *(yogevuroki)* that were given to him by unseen ones. He must sing *(imarentaka)* to call the guides, whose owner *(shintaririra)* he is: they help him find his way, keep him from falling in flight, and protect him from the traps Moon sets to catch human souls. Only years of drinking ayahuasca and practicing to sing enable the *seripigari* to obtain spirit guides and to make use of them.

Ayahuasca *(kamarampi)* is a beverage prepared by boiling the fibrous bark of the vine *Banisteriopsis* sp. Unlike dreams or visions, the experiences a *seripigari* has with ayahuasca are believed to be real events. You really fly, you see the unseen ones, you visit their homes in Mamoriku or inside the mountain Tasorinkamairorini. Julio's father, Yokari, had actually visited Mamoriku, although Julio had not. Experienced *seripigari* achieve levels of intoxication from tobacco and manioc beer that allow them to see their spirit allies, but ayahuasca is the royal road to their land. With ayahuasca, you meet only good spirits on your spirit journeys.

It is tempting to translate *kamarampi* as "death medicine" (< *-kama-*, "death," and *-ampi*, "medicine"). Shepard (1991: 6), however, finds the more natural root to be *-kamara-*, "to vomit." *Kamarampi* would then be "vomiting medicine," accurately referring to an inevitable and much desired consequence of drinking ayahuasca: the Matsigenka associate vomiting with cleansing and seek it as a property in many medicines (Shepard 1991: 8).

The Matsigenka also include datura *(saaro)* in their pharmacopoeia. Datura grows along trails and in house gardens, but the people I spoke to were nervous about datura and used it in carefully controlled ways because they consider it too powerful for regular use. They prepare datura by boiling the leaves into a thick syrup *(seri*, "tobacco"). They soak cotton balls in it, and when the balls are dry, they store them. When they are ready, they chew and swallow many of the cotton balls (perhaps fifteen to twenty). Most men I spoke to had tried it but once or not at all *(nopinkake*, "I am afraid"). Their usual description of datura was *pogemparora pishiganaka*, "You take it, you run away." Many men told me about how they took datura and lost control, running disoriented in the forest for several days until they came out of it or were found and guided back home by relatives. They regard datura as a poison *(okepigate)* and described two cases in which people used it to commit suicide *(irogamagakempara ikiro)*. For this reason, datura is most likely to be used in milder preparations. Leaves may be boiled and the steam allowed to bathe the eyes of a sufferer of conjunctivitis. A single seed of datura may be chewed for headache. Preparations of leaves are used for fever and for rubbing on body sores.

A *seripigari* is seen as a powerful force for good in this life. The tale Terira Ineenkani and many others portray the shaman as a loving but authoritarian guide who, like a father, must be obeyed. The ambivalence toward powerful beings, however, attaches to the *seripigari* as well. One who has power to do good certainly has power to do evil, just as parents (and others) not only satisfy, but frustrate and punish.

The dark side of the *seripigari* is the *matsikanari* (= Man-Guan?: < *matsi*, "human," and *kanari*, "guan"), a witch who serves only himself or herself and causes the suffering and death of others. In Matsigenka belief, a *seripigari* can never be a *matsikanari*, and vice versa. The problem is that ordinary people cannot tell which is which. A *matsika-*

nari has one or more sorcerer's stones *(serepitontsi)*, with spirit guides in them, obtained not from the unseen ones but by drinking ayahuasca and searching the beach looking for stones that have spirits. The *matsikanari*'s stones look the same as the *seripigari*'s: three to fifteen centimeters in diameter, smooth and black, with flecks of white. But the spirits that dwell within, although also known as *serepitontsi*, are evil, whereas the helper spirits given by the unseen ones are incapable of evil. As owners of the stones in which they dwell, the *matsikanari*s command them to do their bidding. The spirits are their arrows.

Men and women who become very old without getting sick are suspected of being *matsikanari*s. They cannot cure others, but their wisdom and spirit helpers may be used to cure themselves. And they can direct their spirits to kill others. Their spirit arrows seek out the intended victims and eat their heads (that is, the heads of their souls). In this world, the bodies of their victims sicken and die within a few days. To kill *matsikanari*s you must go to their houses and steal their sorcerer's stones and throw them into the river. Then their urine will dry up, and they will grow cold and die.

Whereas the *seripigari* labors in love, the *matsikanari* labors in rage:

yo'viigaka igamaran'pite ine'akero o'sure 'yoinato
he-drinks his-ayahuasca it-converts his-soul [plant]

ipega'naka matsika'nari ikisae'gakeri to'vaiti
he-converts-into witch he-enrages plenty

yogama'gakeri matsigenka
he-kills people (Baer 1979: 131)

That is to say, "He drinks ayahuasca. His soul converts into the *yoinato* plant. He becomes a witch. Full of rage, he kills people."

Just as the shaman in Terira Ineenkani was split into a kind, protective father and a potentially lethal demon, so the shamans of today are split into *seripigari* and *matsikanari* (cf. Baer 1984: 221). Although the splitting does construct the *seripigari* as a pure, selfless, all-loving and all-powerful father, even *seripigari*s who are not *matsikanari*s raise doubts. In the Yaniri story, the lazy and gluttonous howler monkey becomes a *seripigari* by the violent action of his cross-cousin. His presence in the forest is far from comforting: his howler roar is called by the same name as a shaman's singing *(imarentaka)*, and hunters fearfully ask whether the monkey they have wounded is a *seripigari*. Furthermore, in a fragment of a folktale I never identified, Seripigari was a culture hero who brought maize to humans from the land of the unseen ones, but when angered he took back the biggest and best varieties, leaving only inferior seed for humans, just as Moon took back the superior varieties of manioc. Even today, when a *seripigari* dies, all his manioc withers because he has taken it (that is, its soul) with him to the other world.

Casiano, however, remembers being cured by a *seripigari* in his childhood, when *seripigari*s used to drink ayahuasca. Casiano's illness—chest pains—went right away, and he was well. Memories like this are the basis for a deep faith in the power and benevolence of *seripigari*s. The image of the *seripigari* blowing tobacco smoke, sucking out deadly spirit arrows, and passing bamboo fronds back and forth over a patient is strong even today, when the disapproval of the missionaries and exposure to Western medicine have thrown doubt on the old practices. But, by virtue of this profound dependence on the curative power of the *seripigari*, there persists an ambivalence, a basic skepticism about the goodness of others, even one's own family. The ambivalence is not often openly expressed, but it finds its way into the core religious beliefs of the community.

From Not Good to Evil

The Matsigenka recognize that self-centered impulsiveness represents a threat not just to the larger group but to the family itself. For all their everyday freedom, they cannot escape the human dilemma of having to discipline their desires to conform to cultural rules. From the nettles hanging on the wall, to the gentle but implacable pressure of commands continuously issued by parents and older siblings, to the warnings and injunctions in folktales against impulsive sex, eating, and aggression, Matsigenka children encounter an environment that persistently channels character development toward culturally constructed ideals.

A system of ideals always implies positive and negative evaluations, notions of good and bad. In the amoral sense, good and bad are attributes of the world, according to the test "Does it please me?" A system of ideals becomes a moral system only when the focus shifts from the environment to the self: "Am I/Are you a good or evil person?" We begin to see this shift in the Matsigenka belief that much of what is bad resulted from the wrong behavior of primordial humans. Had Moon's mother-in-law not become wrongly enraged, women today would not die in childbirth; had Spider Monkey's mother cooled her rage, the demon Oshetoniro would never have existed; had Woolly Monkey shared his beans with Howler Monkey, there would not be the dangerous *seripigari* Yaniri. According to Baer (1984: 188), even sickness and death originated in the disrespectful behavior of the first humans toward Tasorintsi. The clear message regarding these transgressors is "Had they controlled their impulses, today we would not suffer."

We can see these morality tales as culturally constructed warning signs posted to help people make decisions that will protect their families from being torn apart, but is there any evidence that these ideals have been internalized in the form of a conscience (Spiro 1987; D'Andrade 1992: 36; Strauss 1992: 4)? In a sense, this question asks to what degree the Matsigenka may experience guilt. Before working through the ethnographic material for this book, I was inclined to say that the Matsigenka do not experience guilt. Although shame (shyness, embarrassment) is both named *(pashiventagantsi)* and readily observable among them, guilt is neither. Compared with people in my own culture and in peasant communities in Latin America, where guilt is easy to spot, the Matsigenka, I concluded, were too self-assured and impervious to blame to feel guilty about anything.

Although guilt is less evident among the Matsigenka than in the more complex societies of my experience, and therefore perhaps less effective as social control (or, obversely, less debilitating to individuals), something like it is nonetheless active and influential in their lives. The primary evidence for this conclusion is the psychological mechanism of splitting, whereby the Matsigenka disavow unacceptable impulses, wishes, or parts of themselves and project them onto others. Splitting occurs only when it is too painful for individuals to admit to themselves that they harbor this or that desire. This pain, a consequence of the belief that only evil people harbor such wishes, is a component of the complex process we call guilt, according to the syllogism "I wish to do X; only evil people wish to do X; therefore, I am evil (and evil people are punished)."

Fearing the consequences of my evil—especially illness—I must repudiate it and (as humans are wont to do) locate it somewhere outside myself. And, lo!, the world around me is filled with demons. Dramatic evidence of the firmness of this split among the Matsigenka is their belief that spiritually powerful humans may be either good *(seripigari)* or evil *(matsikanari)*, but never both at the same time. The tragedy (or irony) is that it is usually impossible for ordinary people to tell which is which.

Matsigenka religion is based on splitting: "the *kama'garini* are the reverse of the *saanka'rite*" (Baer 1984: 176). As we see in the folktales, the primary characteristics of demons are their aggressive and self-centered desires for sex, companionship, and food (although, just as often, the evil done in folktales flows from humans). Of the seven deadly sins, the ones most prominent in Matsigenka stories are anger first and foremost, followed by lust, gluttony, and sloth (all of which can cause anger). Greed and envy make occasional appearances, as perhaps does pride if we count willful disobedience. We know these impulses are treated as sins in the tales because the protagonists who act on them are punished, almost always by death, loss, or metamorphosis into animals or demons (Baer 1984: 187). And we know that individuals are afraid that their own transgressions will result in spiritual attack.

On the other side of the split are the unseen ones. Their living is easy; they eat little, and yet all their wants are satisfied. They are pure, imperturbable, immortal. The shaman who seeks their help must avoid sexual intercourse before drinking ayahuasca and must live an exemplary life (Baer 1979: 115). Yet into this happy image comes an unwelcome intrusion: even the unseen ones are not unambiguously good to us. They can be offended by our bad behavior, and so we must be careful lest they withhold the benefits we seek from them. Like the ambiguity surrounding animal spirits, who can either help us or harm us, the ambiguity of the unseen ones signals the reservoir of ambivalence, originally felt toward parents and other loved ones, in which the splitting originates.

Humans occupy, or are caught in, the middle of this split, which implies a nature-versus-culture dichotomy: the negative idealization is animal-like (cf. Baer and Snell 1974: 67), while the positive idealization epitomizes cultural values. Demons have animal characteristics like four-leggedness, long snouts, large penises, hairy bodies, filth, unrestrained sexuality and violence, whereas good spirits are beautiful, clean, modest, and refined. The demons inhabit the lower plane (*savipatsa*, "underground"), humans the surface (*kipatsi*, "earth"), and the good spirits the elevated and exalted plane above (*enoku*; Baer 1983: 2; Roe 1982: 132). In body imagery, this dichotomy splits off the purity of mind from the defilements of the flesh. A major class of demons are *ivegaga, ovegaga,* "rotten," and Andean Indians and Euro-Americans, coming from underground, bear this demonic stigma (Baer 1984: 124–25).

Many Matsigenka folktales end on a plaintive note: "Had you not done that, this evil would not have happened." They attribute blame on the one hand and warn the audience on the other: "Do not act thus or the same will happen to you." Some tales are also instructional: the girl who becomes Moon's wife is cautioned to eat only a fraction of the fish she has been given, or she will grow up to be one of those wives who is stingy with her husband; the sons of the shaman are taught to kill only as many birds as they need and to set a share aside to take home to their mother. In this sense a Matsigenka folktale has a moral message that is intended to promote the internalization of proper values and to reinforce that internalization by providing concrete examples of the consequences.

That adult men and women project evil tendencies onto others, particularly in-laws and nonkin in other hamlets, reflects the same splitting found in folktales: individuals try to ally their essential selves with goodness while locating evil in others. Something similar appears to be happening in Casiano's poignant dream about his son's death (see chapter 3): when his son says, "Father, you got angry at me, you abandoned me," Casiano replies, "You died. If you hadn't died, I wouldn't have abandoned you." The dreamer has constructed an accusation leveled at himself (projected as coming from his dead son) and then has defended himself from the accusation; the implication is that he feels some sense of guilt or responsibility for the separation from his son. He might also blame his dead son for abandoning him in anger—the two contradictory accusations are not incompatible in one dream. In either case, the air is full of hurt and blame, the same evil air that causes people to abandon their homes when a loved one dies, for fear of the angry, hurt, lonely spirit left behind when the physical body is gone.

CONCLUSION

A Family Level Society

Family level societies similar in their general characteristics to the Matsigenka are a basic form of human society (Johnson and Earle 2000: 41–53). They were the predominant form of human society for much of prehistory, but they have long been overshadowed in the eyes of anthropologists and historians alike by the larger, more complex societies that came to dominate the world landscape dramatically after the end of the Pleistocene. Certainly nineteenth-century social theorists had an unabashed enthusiasm for the rise of social complexity as evidence of "progress" (Johnson and Earle 2000: 2–3) or at least as a sign of an intrinsic human movement toward elaborate division of labor, intercommunication, and increased size and social integration. The anthropological discovery of tribal society, with its rich elaborations of kinship and ceremony, helped defend "primitive society" from the charge of being not just simple but simple-minded and less than fully human. Regrettably, this formulation left family level societies out. The criticisms of Steward's concept of the family level society discussed in the introduction carry the strong implicit message that family level societies do not exist (at least in any recent epoch) except as shattered remnants of something bigger, more complex, and (by implication) more interesting.

It is the case that ethnographically known family level societies, like such foragers of desert and tundra as the Nunamiut of Alaska (Gubser 1965) and the Kalahari !Kung (Lee 1979), tend to be found in marginal environments. The reason for a family level of sociocultural integration in such environments is obvious: a low density of key resources and few real advantages to cooperative work lead people to scatter "competitively" to avoid getting in each other's way. Such environments allow few opportunities to intensify production, which would enable the larger and more sedentary populations that accompany local and regional social integration.

The absence of such technology as domesticated crops or animals is not what matters: many well-known foraging societies achieved high levels of sociocultural integration, even chiefdoms (Arnold 1996), and well-documented family level societies had domesticated crops and livestock (Johnson and Earle 2000: 90–120). Rather, a set of on-the-ground conditions makes it advantageous for people to live in small family units and makes it difficult for them to form larger cooperative communities even should they want to.

I hope it is clear from the preceding chapters that the Matsigenka live in an extraordinarily complex, culturally constructed world that differs from tribal societies primarily in the flexibility allowed within its social structure and cultural beliefs for family autonomy in response to changing opportunities. To judge this society simple or reduced would be an outsider view based on superficial comparisons to larger-scale societies, a failure to appreciate the beauty and effectiveness of Matsigenka technology, social structure, and cosmology as they are experienced by the people themselves.

At the time of the European Conquest, many family level societies existed in both North and South America. In addition to the obvious foraging peoples in the Arctic, the Great Basin, and Tierra del Fuego, some mixed forager/horticultural people may have qualified as well, including such groups on the western Amazon fringe as the Jivaro (Harner 1973), the Siriono (Holmberg 1969), and the Campa/Matsigenka. Despite their potential for horticulture, these are marginal environments by Amazon standards, and in fact in the lower elevations along the richly endowed large tributaries of the Amazon, much larger communities, with such familiar complexities as unilineal kin reckoning, endemic warfare, calendrical ceremonies, and leadership (even chiefs), predominated. Unfortunately, those societies did not survive the brutal early phases of the Conquest and the devastation of Western diseases. Our knowledge of how they lived and of the extent of political development they accomplished is limited to such documentation as was left behind by ethnocentric intruders who wanted mainly to destroy, exploit, or convert them.

The Matsigenka escaped destruction because they live in the remotest reaches of interior South America, where travel is extremely difficult and where the removal of the few marketable resources is prohibitively costly. Although in the past, under the Inka, the total human population of the region was likely higher than it was in the ethnographic present of the 1970s, Matsigenka social and political organization was probably not significantly different. There are no hints of a more complex past in their stories, no remnants of a possibly more complex social structure, and no archaeological evidence of larger and denser Matsigenka settlements. More complex societies were definitely present in the region, including both the Inka and the robust warrior tribes from downriver who made their way to the upper Urubamba region seasonally. But the Matsigenka shied away from contact with such groups, except for reasonably controlled trading opportunities at specified times and locations.

In theory, a family level society is a form of adaptation to low and scattered resources. Although such a society is often described by what it lacks, it is important to stress that the absence of social-structural constraints at the family level is an advantage: people are free to move opportunistically as local resources become depleted, to move in and out of association with other families according to the conditions of the moment, and to avoid violence and domination by bullies. Although the resulting isolated existence places a premium on individual (family-based) self-reliance, the Matsigenka accept the challenge of an autonomous existence and in fact prefer it. Their way of life is predicated on the freedom of the family, and every aspect of their lives is shaped by this reality.

Of prime importance is their capacity to sustain the family economically with little or no outside assistance. Except for their dependence on steel tools, which have been available via trade (albeit at great hardship) for hundreds of years, and to a lesser degree on aluminum pots, the Matsigenka of Shimaa can meet all their needs for food, shelter, clothing, and tools, as well as toys, decorations, and entertainment, employing only the skills and labor of family members. Quantitative data summarized in this book show beyond a doubt that household labor produces enough of everything to sustain the family. Unless a husband or wife becomes too ill to work, families are not threatened with starvation or exposure to the elements. Households vary in their degree of comfort only because some individuals work harder and with more skill than others.

Individual households do form into hamlets, and into the very loose neighborhoods of which the school community is a modern form. Free to leave the hamlet whenever they want, they stay because certain advantages of cooperation outweigh the real costs of hamlet living. Cooperating in barbasco fishing, sharing meat (sharing the risk of hunting failure), and dividing some labor in manufacture are reasons for living in a hamlet. But the costs of disease transmission, conflicts around sharing, and suspicions of theft and adultery come to a head during a beer feast and may shatter the hamlet group for months or years at a time, although eventually its members will probably give it another try.

The Matsigenka style of raising children helps prepare them for independent living. In behavior as in folktales, they acknowledge that very young children are impulsive and selfish. The parents' task is to rear children into adults who understand their role in the division of labor by sex and are self-motivated to undertake hard, often lonely, work. They must be capable of considerable marital loyalty and a strong emotional attachment to their immediate family, yet also be comparatively indifferent to the needs and wishes of distant kin and nonkin. The Matsigenka instill independence in children by balancing intimacy and autonomy. In early life they encourage deep attachments in the family through constant holding and touching and through the pervasive reinforcement of generosity through food sharing at mealtime. The expressed needs of young children are usually met quickly and willingly. At the same time, a balancing act is underway: let the child express desires freely, but do not satisfy them immediately. As children grow, let these little frustrations grow also by testing and encouraging the children's ability to do without or to satisfy their own needs.

The crisis of weaning, which occurs when mother becomes pregnant again and which sets off the dramatic excesses of the temper-tantrum phase, marks the point at which the balance finally shifts away from childhood dependence toward adult responsibility. Thereafter, the older child is expected to be more and more like an adult in ability to work and to be alone without supervision. Still intimately bound in the nexus of the family, the child now acquires the attributes that will be emphasized in puberty seclusion and in folktales: generosity, diligence, reliability, and self-control.

Behaviorally, the Matsigenka show much restraint. Within the home, they speak softly, smile often, and try to be agreeable. They are unrestrainedly affectionate with infants and toddlers, and in groups the men hold hands or put their arms around one another, as do the women. But, except at the beer feast, grand displays of emotion are avoided: the sick person lies alone, perhaps weeping quietly; the injured child is left to cry alone; the injured man limps painfully off to his garden; mournful widows do not wail and tear their hair but flee the frightening location where the soul of the departed lurks dangerously.

In this society, the greatest fear is of impulsive outbursts, especially of anger, sexual desire, and food hoarding. Virtually all Matsigenka stories, instructions to children, and jokes and teasing address these dangers. Their dilemma is to raise strong-willed children who are self-reliant yet without a degree of willfulness that threatens the ability of family members to work for and nurture one another. The one at home alone who is tempted to snack on the meat smoking over the fire recalls stories in which such gluttony brought evil into the world; the spouse tempted to be unfaithful knows of other lovers who were seduced and killed by demons.

Their kinship system is of a variety that can be elaborated into complex social structures. The cross-parallel distinction is employed in some Dravidian kin systems to create lineages, moieties, and still more complex ways of grouping people in villages and clan territories. Among the Matsigenka, however, kinship remains a symmetrical exchange system with the ideal world a hamlet of two intermarrying families that can reproduce itself indefinitely down the generations. Although this system theoretically places each person in a definite kin relation to everyone else in the hamlet, it is not a highly constraining system. On the contrary, the freedom of individuals within the system is maximized by their ability to redefine kin (except for immediate family members) or even to refuse to acknowledge that a kinship relation exists. As is characteristic of family level societies, the kinship system provides connections to others that can be actualized or not according to the needs of the moment. It does not create definite obligations within groups, such as territorial defense or marriage payments.

Outside the extended-family hamlet, Matsigenka social relations are tenuous at best. They may enjoy the occasional visit between hamlets to share gossip and to stay informed about the availability of spouses or good residential sites, but such events are short-lived. A general sense of discomfort seems to hover in the air: members of other hamlets may be thieves or worse, and the zones around their hamlets are likely to contain more spiritual danger than areas close to home. It is difficult to convince a Matsigenka that sacrifices for the good of a larger, multi-hamlet community are justified, hence the almost universal disappointment of priests, schoolteachers, and others who would realize the ambitions of an outside world for the greater social and political integration of the region.

In the Matsigenkas' world-view, all living things, including plants, have a kind of individuality or willfulness that explains their behavior;

they thus attribute to other beings the same kind of strong individual willfulness that they expect in human children. Only some seeds grow (have the strength and will to grow), absent fish are hiding, evil spirits seek to satisfy their desires with human victims. Much of a human's nature is inherited directly from the same-gender parent. This view is generalized to plants and animals. The true nature of an individual *ivenkiki* plant, for example, can be known only by knowing where its parent plant came from. The nature of individual animals is a reflection of the spirit ruler who created the species. In general, the emphasis is on individuality at the expense of larger groupings or orderings

As with the kinship system, there is nothing inherently "familistic" about a shamanic religious system. Indeed, shamans, and the animistic beliefs that underpin their religious practice, are found in societies at all levels of complexity. But the particular form of shamanism practiced by the Matsigenka reflects their family level existence. The emphasis is on a basic, even simple, problem: What causes sickness and death? And the answer is equally simple: the impulsive actions of selfish individuals.

In this world, the actions of the individual or someone close bring about suffering. Although the Matsigenka populate their spirit world with a wide array of beings, these beings all fall within three major categories: the human souls, who occupy this earth; the hateful demons, who populate the underground; and the happy and powerful helper spirits, who live in the sky. Demons are hungry for sex or companionship or souls to eat, and they take advantage of opportunities that arise when humans are careless, self-indulgent, or heedless of the shaman's advice. Even though the world of demons is largely invisible, humans suspect they have behaved improperly when they become sick. The shaman, a benevolent authority figure, can draw on his relationship with invisible good spirits to counter the evil supernatural attack. The shaman also provides general advice to other members of the family to help them avoid the mistakes that demons exploit.

The detective work to discover where the fault lies when sickness strikes focuses on the behavior of the patient or someone close, like a spouse or co-wife. Rarely is witchcraft invoked—the emphasis is not on other vindictive Matsigenka but on someone's misdeeds. The belief system seems geared to support the individual in efforts at impulse control: if I behave myself, the logic goes, I am less vulnerable to spirit attack. People beyond the immediate family do not come into the picture unless they happen to live nearby and interact regularly. As in so many aspects of life, others beyond the family group are largely irrelevant to the central concerns of everyday life.

Glossary

Matsigenka	English Gloss
aniane, iraniane	breath
inchato	tree
inkenishiku	in the forest
intaati	across the river
isure, osure	soul
ivegaga, ovegaga	rotten; also, type of demon
ivenkiki	sedge (Spanish *piripiri*)
kamagarini	demon
kamatikya	downstream
kameti	good
kashiri	moon
katonko	upstream
Kentivakori	original creator of bad things
kimoariniku	high-water season (literally "grown water")
kipatsi	earth, soil
kogapai	no reason
koraka	leader, patron
kuri	palm wood (*Bactris ciliata*)
kutagiteri	day
maestro	schoolteacher
maiini	poisonous ant (*Grandiponera* sp.)
maranke	snake

matsigenka	human being
matsikanari	witch
matsontsori	jaguar, wildcat
nampiria	servant, adopted child
oaku	at the river
oani	water
osheto	spider monkey
oshintsiatanaira	high-water season (literally "rushing water")
pankirintsi	cultigen
peranti	lazy
piratsi	game
ponyarona	Quechua Indian
poreatsiri	sun
potogo	abortifacient (Spanish *ojé*)
saankarite	pure ones (also, *terira ineenkani*)
sekatsi	manioc (literally "what is eaten")
seripigari	shaman
shima	boquichico fish *(Pruchilodus nigricans)*
shintaririra, shintaro	owner
shintori	peccary
shiriagariniku	low-water season
shitea	manioc beer
Tasorintsi	original creator of good things
terira ineenkani	unseen ones (also, *saankarite*)
timatsi	what exists
tovaseri	weed, bush
tsamairintsi	garden
virakocha	Euro-American
yaniri	howler monkey

References Cited

Agenbrod, L. D. 1988. Clovis People: The Human Factor in the Pleistocene Megafauna Extinction Equation. In R. C. Carlisle, ed., *America before Columbus,* pp. 63–74. Ethnology Monographs 12. Pittsburgh: University of Pittsburgh Press.

Alarco, Eugenio. 1971. *El hombre Peruano en su historia.* Lima: Ausonia Talleres Graficos.

Alegre, P. 1979. Tashorintsi: Tradición oral Matsigenka. In *Ensayos,* vol. 1. Lima: Centro Amazónico de Antropología y Aplicación Práctica.

Anderson, E. 1952. *Plants, Man and Life.* Boston: Little, Brown.

Arnold, J. 1996. The Archaeology of Complex Hunter-Gatherers. *Journal of Archaeological Method and Theory* 3: 77–126.

Baekeland, G. B. 1964. By Parachute into Peru's Lost World. *National Geographic* 126: 268–96.

Baer, G. 1979. Religión y chamanismo de los Matsigenka. *Amazonia Peruano* 2: 101–38.

———. 1981. Religion and Symbols: A Case in Point from Eastern Peru. The Matsigenka View of the Religious Dimension of Light. *Scripta Ethnologica* 6: 49–52.

———. 1983. The Beauty of the Shaman's Song on the Upper Amazon. Paper presented at the International Congress of Anthropological and Ethnological Sciences, Vancouver.

———. 1984. *Die Religion der Matsigenka/Ost-Peru.* Basel: Wepf.

Baer, G., and W. W. Snell. 1974. An Ayahuasca Ceremony among the Matsigenka (Eastern Peru). *Zeitschrift für Ethnologie* 99: 64–80.

Bailey, R. C., G. Head, M. Jenike, B. Owen, R. Rechtman, and E. Zechenter. 1989. Hunting and Gathering in Tropical Rain Forest: Is It Possible? *American Anthropologist* 91: 59–82.

Baksh, M. 1984. Cultural Ecology and Change of the Machiguenga Indians of the Peruvian Amazon. Ph.D. diss., University of California, Los Angeles.

———. 1995. Changes in Machiguenga Quality of Life. In L. E. Sponsel, ed., *Indigenous Peoples and the Future of Amazonia,* pp. 187–205. Tucson: University of Arizona Press.

Balée, W. 1988. Indigenous Adaptation to Amazonian Palm Forests. *Principes* 32: 47–54.

Barriales, J. 1977. *Matsigenka.* Madrid: Secretariado de Misiones Dominicanas Claudio Coello.

Bennett, B. 1996. La traida y el destierro de Inaenka: Transformaciones en la salud y la medicina entre los Machiguenga. In F. S. Granero, ed., *Globalización y cambio en la Amazonia indígena,* vol. 1. Quito: Ediciones Abya-Yala.

Berlin, B., and E. A. Berlin. 1975. Aguaruna Color Categories. *American Ethnologist* 2: 61–87.

Berlin, B., and P. Kay. 1969. *Basic Color Terms.* Berkeley: University of California Press.

Bodley, J. 1970. Campa Socio-economic Organization. Ph.D. diss., University of Oregon, Eugene.

Brown, M. F. 1994. Beyond Resistance: Comparative Study of Utopian Renewal in Amazonia. In A. Roosevelt, ed., *Amazonian Indians from Prehistory to the Present: Anthropological Perspectives.* Tucson: University of Arizona Press.

Brown, M. F., and E. Fernández. 1991. *War of the Shadows: The Struggle for Utopia in the Peruvian Amazon.* Berkeley: University of California Press.

Bruhns, K. E. 1994. *Ancient South America.* Cambridge: Cambridge University Press.

Bryan, A. L. 1983. South America. In R. Shutler Jr., ed., *Early Man in the New World,* pp. 137–46. Beverly Hills, Calif.: Sage.

Butts, Y., and D. J. Bogue. 1989. *International Amazonia: Its Human Side.* Chicago: Social Development Center.

Camino, A. 1977. Trueque, correrias e intercambios entre los Quechuas Andinos y los Piro y Machiguenga de la montaña Peruana. *Amazonia Peruana* 1 (2): 123–40.

Carneiro, R. L. 1964. Shifting Cultivation among the Amahuaca of Eastern Peru. *Volkerkundliche Abhandlung* 1: 9–18.

———. 1995. The History of Ecological Interpretations of Amazonia: Does Roosevelt Have It Right? In L. E. Sponsel, ed., *Indigenous Peoples and the Future of Amazonia,* pp. 45–70. Tucson: University of Arizona Press.

Cartagena, N., and H. Cartagena. 1981. *Paititi: Dernier refuge des Incas.* Paris: Editions Robert Laffont.

Casevitz, F.-M. 1977. Du proche au loin: Étude du fonctionnement des systèmes de la parenté et de l'alliance Matsiguenga. In *Actes du XLII Congrès International des Américanistes,* vol. 2, pp. 121–40. Paris: Société des Américanistes.

Chagnon, Napoleon. 1987. Male Yanomamö Manipulations of Kinship Classifications of Female Kin for Reproductive Advantage. In L. L. Betzig, M. Morgerhoff Mulder, and P. W. Turke, eds., *Human Reproductive Behaviour: A Darwinian Perspective,* pp. 23–48. Cambridge: Cambridge University Press.

Chesser, R. T., and S. J. Hackett. 1992. Mammalian Diversity in South America. *Science* 256: 1502–4.

D'Andrade, R. G. 1992. Schemas and Motivation. In R. G. D'Andrade and C. Strauss, eds., *Human Motives and Cultural Models,* pp. 23–44. Cambridge: Cambridge University Press.

d'Ans, A.-M. 1974. Estructura semantica del parentesco Machiguenga (Arawak). *Revista del Museo Nacional* 40: 341–61.

Davis, H., and B. Snell. 1984. *Kenkitsatagantsi Matsigenka: Cuentos folkloricos de los Machiguenga.* Comunidades y Culturas Peruanas 5. Lima: Instituto Lingüístico de Verano.

Davis, P. M. 1994. Literacy Acquisition, Retention, and Usage: A Case Study of the Machiguenga of the Peruvian Amazon. Ph.D. diss., University of Texas, Austin.

Denevan, W. M. 1974. Campa Subsistence in the Gran Pajonal, Eastern Peru. In P. J. Lyon, ed., *Native South Americans,* pp. 92–110. Boston: Little, Brown.

———. 1980. La población aborigen de la Amazonía en 1492. *Amazonia Peruana* 3 (5): 3–41.

Descola, P. 1994. *In the Society of Nature: A Native Ecology in Amazonia.* Cambridge: Cambridge University Press.

Dole, G. E. 1972. Developmental Sequences of Kinship Patterns. In *Kinship Studies of the Morgan Centennial Year,* pp. 134–66. Washington, D.C.: Anthropological Society of Washington.

Drewes, W. U., and A. T. Drewes. 1957. *Climate and Related Phenomena of the Eastern Andean Slopes of Central Peru.* Syracuse, N.Y.: Syracuse University Research Institute.

Dundes, A. 1985. The Psychoanalytic Study of Folklore. *Annals of Scholarship* 3: 1–42.

Eisenberg, J. F. 1989. *Mammals of the Neotropics: The Northern Neotropics,* vol. 1. Chicago: University of Chicago Press.

Farabee, W. C. 1909. Some Customs of the Macheyengas. *Proceedings of the American Antiquarian Society* 20: 127–31 (n.s.).

———. 1922. Indian Tribes of Eastern Peru. *Papers of the Peabody Museum of American Archeology and Ethnology,* vol. 10. Cambridge: Harvard University Press.

Ferrero, A. 1966. *Los Machiguengas.* Villava-Pamplona, Spain: Editorial OPE.

Ferreyra, R. 1970. *Flora invasora de los cultivos de Pucallpa y Tingo Maria.* Lima, Peru: R. Ferreyra.

Fraiberg, S. H. 1959. *The Magic Years: Understanding and Handling the Problems of Early Childhood.* New York: Scribner.

Gade, D. W. 1967. Plant Use and Folk Agriculture in the Vilcanota Valley of Peru: A Cultural Historical Geography of Plant Resources. Ph.D. diss., University of Wisconsin.

———. 1972. Comercio y colonización en la zona de contacto entre la sierra y las tierras bajas del Valle del Urubamba, Peru. *Historia, etnohistoria y etnología de la selva Sudamericana* 4: 207–21. XXXIX Congreso Internacional de Americanistas. Lima: Instituto de Estudios Peruanos.

Garcia, S. 1939. Mitología de los salvajes Machiguengas. *International Congress of Americanists* 27: 229–37.

Gentry, A. H. 1988. Tree Species of Upper Amazonian Forests. *Proceedings of the National Academy of Science* (U.S.A.) 85: 156.

Gibbons, A. 1995. First Americans: Not Mammoth Hunters, but Forest Dwellers? *Science* 272: 346–47.

———. 1996. The Peopling of the Americas. *Science* 274: 31–33.

Goldschmidt, W. 1959. *Man's Way: A Preface to the Understanding of Human Society.* New York: Holt, Rinehart and Winston.

Goodall, J. 1971. *In the Shadow of Man.* Boston: Houghton Mifflin.

Goodspeed, T. H. 1961. *Plant Hunters in the Andes.* Berkeley: University of California Press.

Grain, J. 1939. Pueblos primitivos—Los Machiguengas. *Proceedings* 2: 239–44. Lima: International Congress of Americanists.

Gray, A. 1987. Perspectives on Amarakaeri History. In H. O. Sklar and F. Salomon, eds., *Natives and Neighbors in South America: Anthropological Essays,* pp. 299–328. Göteborg, Sweden: Göteborgs Etnografiska Museum.

Gubser, N. 1965. *The Nunamiut Eskimos.* New Haven, Conn.: Yale University Press.

Guinness, G. 1909. *Peru: Its Story, People, and Religion.* London: Morgan & Scott.

Gulliver, P. 1951. *A Preliminary Survey of the Turkana.* Communications from the School of African Studies, n.s. 26. Rondebosch, South Africa: University of Cape Town.

———. 1955. *The Family Herds.* London: Routledge.

Hames, R. 1983. Monoculture, Polyculture and Polyvariety in Tropical Forest Swidden Cultivation. *Human Ecology* 11: 13–34.

———. 1988. Time, Efficiency, and Fitness in the Amazonia Protein Quest. *Research in Economic Anthropology* 11: 43–85.

Haney, E. B. 1968. The Nature of Shifting Cultivation in Latin America. *LTC* 45. Madison: Land Tenure Center, University of Wisconsin.

Harner, M. J. 1973. *The Jívaro: People of the Sacred Waterfalls.* Garden City, N.Y.: Anchor Books.

Haskins, C. P. 1943. *The Amazon: The Life History of a Mighty River.* Garden City, N.Y.: Doubleday, Doran.

Hastings, C. M. 1987. Implications of Andean Verticality in the Evolution of Political Complexity: A View from the Margins. In J. Haas, S. Pozorski, and T. Pozorski, eds., *The Origins and Development of the Andean State,* pp. 145–57. Cambridge: Cambridge University Press.

Henderson, A. 1995. *The Palms of the Amazon.* New York: Oxford University Press.

Henry, J. 1951. The Economics of Pilaga Food Distribution. *American Anthropologist* 53: 187–219.

Holmberg, A. R. 1969. *Nomads of the Long Bow: The Siriono of Eastern Bolivia.* Garden City, N.Y.: Natural History Press.

Hornborg, A. 1988. *Dualism and Hierarchy in Lowland South America.* Stockholm: Almqvist and Wiksell.

Hsu, F.L.K. 1972. American Core Value and National Character. In F.L.K. Hsu, ed., *Psychological Anthropology*, pp. 241–66. Cambridge, Mass.: Schenkman Books.

Hyslop, J. 1984. *The Inka Road System*. New York: Academic Press.

Isbell, W. H. 1968. New Discoveries in the Montaña of Southeastern Peru. *Archaeology* 21: 108–14.

Izquierdo, C. 2001. Betwixt and Between: Seeking Cure and Meaning among the Matsigenka of the Peruvian Amazon. Ph.D. diss., University of California, Los Angeles.

Janzen, D. H. 1985. Plant Defenses against Animals in the Amazonian Rainforest. In G. T. Prance and T. E. Lovejoy, eds., *Amazonia*, pp. 207–17. Oxford: Pergamon Press.

Jelliffe, D. B. 1966. *The Assessment of the Nutritional Status of the Community*. Geneva: World Health Organization.

Johnson, A. W. 1971. *Sharecroppers of the Sertão: Economics and Dependence on a Brazilian Plantation*. Stanford, Calif.: Stanford University Press.

———. 1972. Individuality and Experimentation in Traditional Agriculture. *Human Ecology* 1: 149–60.

———. 1975. Time Allocation in a Machiguenga Community. *Ethnology* 14: 301–10.

———. 1978. *Quantification in Cultural Anthropology*. Stanford, Calif.: Stanford University Press.

———. 1981. Separation-Individuation of the Self in a Native Amazon Community. Paper presented at symposium Self and Person in Lowland South America. Annual meeting of the American Anthropological Association, Washington, D.C.

———. 1983. Machiguenga Gardens. In R. B. Hames and W. T. Vickers, eds., *Adaptive Responses of Native Amazonians*, pp. 29–63. New York: Academic Press.

———. 1987. The Death of Ethnography: Has Anthropology Betrayed Its Mission? *The Sciences* (March/April), pp. 24–31.

———. 1989. How the Machiguenga Manage Resources: Conservation or Exploitation of Nature? In D. A. Posey and W. Balee, eds., *Resource Management in Amazonia: Indigenous and Folk Strategies*, pp. 213–22. New York: New York Botanical Society.

———. 1995. Review of *All the Mothers Are One* by S. N. Kurtz. *Psychoanalytic Psychology* 12: 457–61.

———. 1996. Time Allocation. In D. Levinson and M. Ember, eds., *Encyclopedia of Cultural Anthropology*, pp. 1313–16. New York: Henry Holt.

———. 1998. Guttman Scaling: An Analysis of Matsigenka Men's Manufacturing Skills. In V. C. de Munck and E. J. Sobo, eds., *Using Methods in the Field*. Walnut Creek, Calif.: Altamira Press.

———. 1999a. Making a Living. URL: www.sscnet.ucla.edu/anthro/faculty/johnson/.

———. 1999b. The Political Unconscious: Stories and Politics in Two South

American Cultures. In S. Renshon and J. Duckitt, eds., *Cultural and Cross Cultural Political Psychology,* pp. 159–81. London: Macmillan.

Johnson, A. W., and M. Baksh. 1989. Ecological and Structural Influences on the Proportions of Wild Foods in the Diets of Two Machiguenga Communities. In M. Harris and E. B. Ross, eds., *Food and Evolution: Toward a Theory of Human Food Habits,* pp. 387–405. Philadelphia: Temple University Press.

Johnson, A. W., and C. Behrens. 1982. Nutritional Criteria in Machiguenga Food Production Decisions: A Linear Programming Analysis. *Human Ecology* 10: 167–89.

Johnson, A. W., and T. Earle. 2000. *The Evolution of Human Societies: From Foraging Group to Agrarian State.* 2d ed. Stanford, Calif.: Stanford University Press.

Johnson, A. W., and O. Johnson. 1988. *Time Allocation among the Machiguenga of Shimaa.* Cross-Cultural Studies in Time Allocation 1. New Haven, Conn.: Human Relations Area Files.

Johnson, A. W., O. Johnson, and M. Baksh. 1986. The Colors of Emotions in Machiguenga. *American Anthropologist* 88: 674–81.

Johnson, A. W., and D. Price-Williams. 1996. *Oedipus Ubiquitous: The Family Complex in World Folk Literature.* Stanford, Calif.: Stanford University Press.

Johnson, A. W., and R. Sackett. 1998. Direct Systematic Observation of Behavior. In H. R. Bernard, ed., *Handbook of Methods in Cultural Anthropology,* pp. 301–31. Walnut Creek, Calif.: Altamira Press.

Johnson, O. 1978. Interpersonal Relations and Domestic Authority among the Machiguenga of the Peruvian Amazon. Ph.D. diss., Columbia University.

———. 1980. The Social Context of Intimacy and Avoidance: A Videotape Study of Machiguenga Meals. *Ethnology* 14: 353–66.

———. 1981. The Socio-Economic Context of Child Abuse and Neglect in Native South America. In J. Korbin, ed., *Child Abuse and Neglect: Cross-Cultural Perspectives,* pp. 56–69. Berkeley: University of California Press.

Johnson, O., and A. W. Johnson. 1975. Male/Female Relations and the Organization of Work in a Machiguenga Community. *American Ethnologist* 2: 634–48.

Jordan, C. F., ed. 1989. *An Amazonian Rain Forest.* Paris: UNESCO.

Junk, W. J., and K. Furch. 1985. The Physical and Chemical Properties of Amazonian Waters and Their Relationships with the Biota. In G. T. Prance and T. E. Lovejoy, eds., *Amazonia,* pp. 3–17. Oxford: Pergamon Press.

Kaplan, L., T. F. Lynch, and C. E. Smith Jr. 1973. Early Cultivated Beans (Phaseolus vulgaris) from an Intermontane Peruvian Valley. *Science* 179: 76–77.

Kay, P. 1965. A Generalization of the Cross/Parallel Distinction. *American Anthropologist* 67: 30–43.

Kensinger, K. 1995. *How Real People Ought to Live: The Cashinahua of Eastern Peru.* Prospect Heights, Ill.: Waveland Press.

Kerr, R. A. 1996. Ice-Age Rainforest Found Moist, Cooler. *Science* 274: 35–36.

Kohut, H. 1977. *The Restoration of the Self.* New York: International Universities Press.

Krebs, W.A.W. 1960. *A Program for the Industrial and Regional Development of Peru.* Cambridge, Mass.: Arthur D. Little.

Kurtz, S. N. 1992. *All the Mothers Are One: Hindu India and the Cultural Reshaping of Psychoanalysis.* New York: Columbia University Press.

Kuwayama, T. 1989. The Japanese Conception of the Self: The Dynamics of Autonomy and Heteronomy. Ph.D. diss., University of California, Los Angeles.

Landon, J. R. 1984. *Booker Tropical Soil Manual.* New York: Longman.

Lanning, E. J. 1967. *Peru before the Incas.* Englewood Cliffs, N.J.: Prentice-Hall.

Lathrap, D. W. 1970. *The Upper Amazon.* London: Thames and Hudson.

———. 1981. La antigüedad e importancia de las relaciones de intercambio a larga distancia en los trópicos húmedos de Sudamérica pre-Colombina. *Amazonia Peruana* 4: 79–97.

———. 1987. The Introduction of Maize in Prehistoric Eastern North America: The View from Amazonia and the Santa Elena Peninsula. In W. F. Keegan, ed., *Emergent Horticultural Economies of the Eastern Woodlands,* pp. 345–71. Occasional Paper 2. Carbondale: Center for Archaeological Investigations, Southern Illinois University.

Lee, R. 1979. *The !Kung San.* Cambridge: Cambridge University Press.

Leon-Portilla, M. 1992. Men of Maize. In A. M. Josephy Jr., ed., *America in 1492,* pp. 147–75. New York: Knopf.

Lévi-Strauss, C. 1969. *Elementary Structures of Kinship.* Translated by J. H. Bell, J. R. von Sturmer, and R. Needham. Boston: Beacon Press.

Lévy-Bruhl, L. 1923. *Primitive Mentality.* New York: Macmillan.

Löffler, L. G., and G. Baer. 1978. Zur Verwandtschaftsterminologie der Matsigenka, Ost-Peru. *L'Uomo* 2: 53–70.

Long, A., and P. S. Martin. 1974. Death of American Ground Sloths. *Science* 186: 638–40.

Lynch, T. F. 1978. The South American Paleo-Indians. In J. D. Jennings, ed., *Ancient Native Americans,* pp. 455–89. San Francisco: Freeman.

Lyon, P. 1981. An Imaginary Frontier: Prehistoric Highland-Lowland Interchange in the Southern Peruvian Andes. In P. Francis, F. Kense, and P. G. Duke, eds., *Networks of the Past,* pp. 3–17. Proceedings of the 12th Annual Conference of the University of Calgary Archaeology Association, 1979.

MacBride, J. F. 1960. *Flora of Peru.* Botanical Series, vol. 13, pt. 1, no. 2. Chicago: Field Museum of Natural History.

MacQuarrie, K. A. 1991. Dissipative Energy Structures and Cultural Change among the Yora/Parque-Nahua (Yaminahua) Indians of Southeastern Peru. Master's thesis. California State University, Fullerton.

Mahler, M., F. Pine, and A. Bergman. 1975. *The Psychological Birth of the Human Infant: Symbiosis and Individuation.* New York: Basic Books.

Marcoy, P. 1872. *A Journey across South America from the Pacific Ocean to the Atlantic Ocean.* 2 vols. Glasgow: Blackie and Son.

Martinez, H. 1983. Los estudios acerca de la migración y ocupación selvatica Peruana. *Amazonia Peruana* 5: 7–21.

Maryanski, A., and J. Turner. 1992. *The Social Cage: Human Nature and the Evolution of Society.* Stanford, Calif.: Stanford University Press.

Matteson, E. 1954. *The Piro of the Urubamba*. Paper 10. Berkeley: Kroeber Anthropological Society, University of California.

———. 1972. Proto Arawakan. In E. Matteson, A. Wheeler, F. L. Jackson, N. E. Waltz, and I. R. Christian, eds., *Comparative Studies in Amerindian Languages*, pp. 160–242. The Hague: Mouton.

Matthiessen, P. 1961. *The Cloud Forest*. New York: Viking Press.

McIntyre, Loren. 1972. Amazon: The River Sea. *National Geographic* 142 (4): 445–95.

Meggers, B. J. 1971. *Amazonia: Man and Culture in a Counterfeit Paradise*. Chicago: Aldine.

Mertz, W. 1981. The Essential Trace Elements. *Science* 213: 1332–38.

Migliazza, E. C. 1982. Linguistic Prehistory and the Refuge Model in Amazonia. In G. T. Prance, ed., *Biological Diversification in the Tropics*, pp. 497–519. New York: Columbia University Press.

Montgomery, E. 1978. Towards Representative Energy Data: The Machiguenga Study. *Federation Proceedings* 37: 61–64. Lancaster, Pa.: Federation of American Societies for Experimental Biology.

Montgomery, E., and A. W. Johnson. 1973. The Energy and Time Costs of Technology: The Case of the Bow and Arrow. URL: www.sscnet.ucla.edu/anthro/faculty/johnson/.

Moran, E. F. 1995. Disaggregating Amazonia: A Strategy for Understanding Biological and Cultural Diversity. In L. E. Sponsel, ed., *Indigenous Peoples and the Future of Amazonia: An Ecological Anthropology of an Endangered World*, pp. 71–95. Tucson: University of Arizona Press.

Murdock, G. P. 1960. *Social Structure*. New York: Macmillan.

Murra, J. 1980. *The Economic Organization of the Inka State*. Greenwich, Conn.: JAI Press.

Myers, T. P. 1983. Redes de intercambio tempranas en la Hoya Amazónica. *Amazonia Peruana* 4 (8): 61–73.

Nichols, J., and D. A. Peterson. 1996. The Amerind Personal Pronouns. *Language* 72: 336–71.

Noble, G. K. 1965. Proto-Arawakan and Its Descendants. *International Journal of American Linguistics* 31 (3), pt. 2.

Ohno, T., and M. S. Erich. 1990. Effect of Wood Ash Application on Soil pH and Soil Test Nutrient Levels. *Agriculture, Ecosystems and Environment* 32: 223–29.

Parsons, J. R., and C. M. Hastings. 1988. The Late Intermediate Period. In R. W. Keatinge, ed., *Peruvian Prehistory*, pp. 190–229. Cambridge: Cambridge University Press.

Pereira, D. 1970. Machiguenga Beliefs (collected by Patricia Davis). Yarina Cocha, Peru. Manuscript.

Pereira, F. 1942. Leyendas Machiguengas. *Revista del Museo Nacional* (Lima) 11: 240–44.

———. 1944. Chaingavane: El Pongo del Mainiqui y los petroglifos. *Revista del Museo Nacional* (Lima) 13: 84–88.

———. 1952. Leyendas y costumbres Machiguengas. Pangoa, Peru. Manuscript.

Pericot Y Garcia, L. 1936. *America indígena*. Barcelona: Salvat.

Peru, Government of, Organization of American States, United Nations Environment Programme. 1987. *Minimum Conflict: Guidelines for Planning the Use of American Humid Tropical Environments*. Washington, D.C.: Department of Regional Development, Executive Secretariat for Economic and Social Affairs.

Pires, J. M., and G. T. Prance. 1985. The Vegetation Types of the Brazilian Amazon. In G. T. Prance and T. E. Lovejoy, eds., *Amazonia*, pp. 109–45. Oxford: Pergamon Press.

Pope, S. T. [1923] 1974. *Bows and Arrows*. Berkeley: University of California Press.

Radin, P. 1956. *The Trickster*. New York: Schocken Books.

Raymond, J. S. 1988. A View from the Tropical Forest. In R. W. Keatinge, ed., *Peruvian Prehistory*, pp. 279–300. Cambridge: Cambridge University Press.

Reynard-Casevitz, F.-M. 1984. Fragmento de una lección de Daniel, shamán Matsiguenga. *Amazonia Indígena* 4 (8): 4–6.

Reynard-Casevitz, F.-M., and T. Saignes. 1988. *Al este de los Andes*. Vol. 1. Lima: Instituto Frances de Estudios Andinos.

Richards, P. W. 1952. *The Tropical Rain Forest*. Cambridge: Cambridge University Press.

Roe, Peter G. 1982. *The Cosmic Zygote*. New Brunswick, N.J.: Rutgers University Press.

Roosevelt, A. C. 1980. *Parmana: Prehistoric Maize and Manioc Subsistence along the Amazon and Orinoco*. New York: Academic Press.

Roosevelt, A. C., R. A. Housley, M. Imacio da Silveira, S. Maranca, and R. Johnson. 1991. Eighth Millennium Pottery from a Prehistoric Shell Midden in the Brazilian Amazon. *Science* 254: 1621–24.

Roosevelt, A. C., M. Kima da Costa, C. Lopes Machado, M. Michab, N. Mercier, H. Valladas, J. Feathers., W. Barnett, M. Imacio da Silveira, A. Henderson, J. Sliva, B. Chernoff, D. S. Reese, J. A. Holman, N. Toth, and K. Schick. 1996. Paleoindian Cave Dwellers in the Amazon: The Peopling of the Americas. *Science* 272: 373–84.

Rosengren, D. 1983. Proximity and Interaction: The Case of the Matsigenka of the Upper Urubamba, Southeastern Peru. In *Annual Report for 1981/82*, pp. 48–63. Gothenburg, Sweden: Ethnographical Museum.

———. 1987a. *In the Eyes of the Beholder: Leadership and the Social Construction of Power and Dominance among the Matsigenka of the Peruvian Amazon*. Etnologiska Studier 39. Göteborg: Göteborgs Etnografiska Museum.

———. 1987b. Matsigenka Social Organization as Expressed in Their Settlement Pattern. In H. O. Skar and F. Salomon, eds., *Natives and Neighbors in South America*. Etnologiska Studier 38. Göteborg: Göteborgs Etnografiska Museum.

Ross, E. 1947. Tales of Mercedes Pereira, Pangoa 1947. Yarina Cocha, Peru. Manuscript.

Roush, W. 1997. Squash Seeds Yield New View of Early American Farming. *Science* 276: 894–95.

Rowe, A. 1977. *Warp-Patterned Weaves of the Andes*. Washington, D.C.: Textile Museum.

Rutter, R. A. 1990. *Catalogo de plantas utiles de la Amazonia Peruana*. Yarinacocha, Peru: Instituto Lingüístico de Verano.

Sadr, K. 1997. Kalahari Archaeology and the Bushman Debate. *Current Anthropology* 38: 104–12.

Sahlins, M. 1972. *Stone Age Economics*. Chicago: Aldine.

Sanchez, P. A., D. E. Bandy, J. H. Villachica, J. J. Nicholaides. 1982. Amazon Basin Soils: Management for Continuous Crop Production. *Science* 216: 821–27.

Savoy, G. 1970. *Antisuyo: The Search for the Lost Cities of the Amazon*. New York: Simon & Schuster.

Schauensee, R. M. de. 1970. *A Guide to the Birds of South America*. Wynnewood, Pa.: Livingston.

Schwerin, K. H. 1972. Arawak, Carib, Ge, Tupi: Cultural Adaptation and Culture History in the Tropical Forest, South America. *Actas y Memorias del XXXIX Congreso Internacional de Americanistas* 4: 39–57.

Service, E. 1962. *Primitive Social Organization*. New York: Random House.

Shepard, G. H. 1989. Kashibokani: A Matsigenka Myth of Creation and De-evolution. Department of Anthropology, University of California, Berkeley. Manuscript.

———. 1990. Health and Healing Plants of the Matsigenka in Manu, Southeastern Peru. Department of Anthropology, University of California, Berkeley. Manuscript.

———. 1991. Kepigari: The Concept of Medicines as Poisons among the Matsigenka of Peru. Paper presented at the Kroeber Anthropological Society Conference, April 13. Department of Anthropology, University of California, Berkeley.

———. 1995. Noun Classification in Machiguenga, an Arawakan Language of the Peruvian Amazon. University of California, Berkeley. Manuscript.

———. 1997. Monkey Hunting with the Machiguenga: Medicine, Magic, Ecology and Mythology. Paper Presented at the American Anthropological Association Meetings, November.

———. 1998. Psychoactive Plants and Ethnopsychiatric Medicines of the Matsigenka. *Journal of Psychoactive Drugs* 30: 321–32.

———. 1999. Pharmacognosy and the Senses in Two Amazonian Societies. Ph.D. diss., University of California, Berkeley.

———. 2002. Three Days for Weeping: Dreams, Emotions and Death in the Peruvian Amazon. *Medical Anthropology Quarterly* 16 (2): 1–30.

Smith, B. D. 1997. The Initial Domestication of *Cucurbita pepo* in the Americas 10,000 Years Ago. *Science* 276: 932–34.

Smith, E. C. 1950. *The Story of Our Names*. New York: Harper.

Snell, B. 1973. *Report on the Formation of the Comunidad de Monte Carmelo*. Yarina Cocha, Peru: Summer Institute of Linguistics.

———. 1998. *Pequeño diccionario Machiguenga-Castellano*. Yarina Cocha, Peru: Instituto Lingüístico de Verano.

Snell, W. 1964. Kinship Relations in Machiguenga. Master's thesis, Hartford Seminary, Hartford, Conn.

Speth, J. D. 1990. Seasonality, Resource Stress, and Food Sharing among So-Called "Egalitarian" Foraging Societies. *Journal of Anthropological Archaeology* 9: 148–88.

Spiro, M. 1987. Collective Representations and Mental Representations in Religious Symbol Systems. In B. Kilbourne and L. L. Langness, eds., *Culture and Human Nature: Theoretical Papers of Melford E. Spiro,* pp. 161–84. Chicago: University of Chicago Press.

Stearman, A. M. 1989. Yuquí Foragers in the Bolivian Amazon: Subsistence Strategies, Prestige, and Leadership in an Acculturating Society. *Journal of Anthropological Research* 45: 219–44.

Steward, J. 1938. *Basin-Plateau Aboriginal Sociopolitical Groups.* Washington, D.C.: Bureau of American Ethnology.

————. 1955. *Theory of Culture Change.* Urbana: University of Illinois Press.

Steward, J., and A. Metraux. 1949. Tribes of the Peruvian and Ecuadorian Montaña. In J. H. Steward, ed., *Handbook of South American Indians,* vol. 3, pp. 535–656. Washington, D.C.: Smithsonian Institution.

Stocks, A. 1987. Tropical Forest Development in Peru. *Development Anthropology Network* 5 (2): 1–8.

Strauss, C. 1992. Models and Motives. In R. G. D'Andrade and C. Strauss, eds., *Human Motives and Cultural Models,* pp. 1–20. Cambridge: Cambridge University Press.

Taylor, T.M.C. 1983. *The Sedge Family (Cyperaceae).* Victoria: British Columbia Provincial Museum.

Thomas, D. H. 1983. On Steward's Models of Shoshonean Sociopolitical Organization: A Great Bias in the Basin. In E. Tooker, ed., *The Development of Political Organization in North America,* pp. 59–68. Washington, D.C.: American Ethnological Society.

Urban, G. 1992. A história Brasileira segundo as línguas nativas. In M. Carneiro da Cunha, ed., *História dos índios no Brasil,* pp. 82–102. São Paulo: Fundação de Amparo a Pesquisa do Estado de São Paulo.

Varese, S. 1972. Inter-ethnic Relations in the Selva of Peru. In W. Dostal, ed., *The Situation of the Indian in South America,* pp. 115–43. Geneva: World Council of Churches.

————. 1973. *La sal de los cerros.* Lima: Retablo de Papel.

von Hassel, J. M. 1907. *Ultimas exploraciones ordenadas por la junta de vias fluviales a los Ríos Ucayali, Madre de Dios, Paucartambo y Urubamba.* Lima: La Opinion Nacional.

Webb, S. D. 1995. Biological Implications of the Middle Miocene Amazon Seaway. *Science* 269: 361–62.

Weisner, T. 1996. The 5 to 7 Transition as an Ecocultural Project. In A. Sameroff and M. Haith, eds., *Reason and Responsibility: The Passage through Childhood,* pp. 295–326. Chicago: Unversity of Chicago Press.

Weisner, T., C. C. Matheson, and L. P. Bernheimer. 1996. American Cultural

Models of Early Influence and Parent Recognition of Developmental Delays: Is Earlier Always Better Than Later? In S. Harkness and C. M. Super, eds., *Parents' Cultural Belief Systems: Their Origins, Expressions, and Consequences,* pp. 496–531. New York: Guilford Press.

Weiss, Gerald. 1975. Campa Cosmology: The World of a Forest Tribe in South America. *Anthropological Papers* (American Museum of Natural History, New York) 52: 219–588.

Wieseke, N. M. 1965. *A Medical Survey of Two Machiguenga Villages.* Beni, Bolivia: Summer Institute of Linguistics.

Wilbert, J. 1973. Magico-Religious Use of Tobacco among South American Indians. In V. Rubin, ed., *Cannabis and Culture,* pp. 439–61. The Hague: Mouton.

Wilbert, W. 1992. Bush-Spirit Encounters in Warao Life and Lore. *Antropologica* 77: 63–92.

Willey, G. R. 1971. *An Introduction to American Archaeology.* Vol. 2, *South America.* Englewood Cliffs, N.J.: Prentice-Hall.

Wilshusen, R. H., and G. D. Stone. 1990. An Ethnoarchaeological Perspective on Soils. *World Archaeology* 22: 104–14.

Winnicott, D. W. 1965. The Theory of the Parent-Infant Relationship. In *The Maturational Processes and the Facilitating Environment.* New York: International Universities Press.

Wise, M. R. 1986. Grammatical Characteristics of Preandine Arawakan Languages of Peru. In D. C. Derbyshire and G. K. Pullum, eds., *Pullum Handbook of Amazonian Languages,* pp. 567–642. Berlin: Mouton de Gruyter.

Young, A. 1976. *Tropical Soils and Soil Survey.* Cambridge: Cambridge University Press.

Index

Text:	10/13 Galliard
Display:	Galliard
Cartographer:	Bill Nelson
Compositor:	G & S Typesetters, Inc.
Printer and Binder:	Thomson-Shore, Inc.